WORKERS LIKE ALL THE REST OF THEM

D0920127

Workers Like All the Rest of Them

Domestic Service and the Rights of Labor
in Twentieth-Century Chile

Elizabeth Quay Hutchison

DUKE UNIVERSITY PRESS

DURHAM AND LONDON

2021

© 2021 Duke University Press
All rights reserved

This work is licensed under a Creative Commons
Attribution-NonCommercial-NoDerivatives 4.0 International License.

Printed in the United States of America on acid-free paper ∞
Typeset in Garamond Premier Pro by PageMajik

Library of Congress Cataloging-in-Publication Data
Names: Hutchison, Elizabeth Q. (Elizabeth Quay), author.
Title: Workers like all the rest of them : domestic service and the rights of labor in
twentieth-century Chile / Elizabeth Quay Hutchison.
Other titles: Domestic service and the rights of labor in twentieth-century Chile.
Description: Durham : Duke University Press, 2022. |
Includes bibliographical references and index.
Identifiers: LCCN 2021025299 (print) | LCCN 2021025300 (ebook) |
ISBN 9781478013952 (hardcover) | ISBN 9781478014898 (paperback) |
ISBN 9781478022183 (ebook other)
Subjects: LCSH: Women household employees—Chile—History—20th century. |
Household employees—Chile—History—20th century. | BISAC: HISTORY /
Latin America / General | SOCIAL SCIENCE / Sociology / General
Classification: LCC HD6072.2.C5 H883 2022 (print) | LCC HD6072.2.C5 (ebook) |
DDC 331.40983—dc23
LC record available at https://lccn.loc.gov/2021025299
LC ebook record available at https://lccn.loc.gov/2021025300

Cover image: Chilean domestic workers marching with their broom float at the
Young Catholic Workers "Festival of the Worker" in 1956. "Festival: 12.000 Chilenos
mostraron unidad obrera," *La Voz* 3, no. 60 (October 28, 1956): 16.

*This title is freely available in an open access edition made possible in part by a generous
contribution from the Division for Equity and Inclusion, The University of New Mexico.*

S | H   **The Sustainable History Monograph Pilot**
M | P   Opening Up the Past, Publishing for the Future

This book is published as part of the Sustainable History Monograph Pilot. With the generous support of the Andrew W. Mellon Foundation, the Pilot uses cutting-edge publishing technology to produce open access digital editions of high-quality, peer-reviewed monographs from leading university presses. Free digital editions can be downloaded from: Books at JSTOR, EBSCO, Internet Archive, OAPEN, Project MUSE, and many other open repositories.

While the digital edition is free to download, read, and share, the book is under copyright and covered by the following Creative Commons License: BY-NC-ND 4.0. Please consult www.creativecommons.org if you have questions about your rights to reuse the material in this book.

When you cite the book, please include the following URL for its Digital Object Identifier (DOI): https://doi.org/10.1215/9781478022183

We are eager to learn more about how you discovered this title and how you are using it. We hope you will spend a few minutes answering a couple of questions at this URL: **https://www.longleafservices.org/shmp-survey/**

More information about the Sustainable History Monograph Pilot can be found at https://www.longleafservices.org.

In Memory of Aída Moreno Valenzuela, 1939–2021

For Regina, Dante, Pasqual, and Tita

CONTENTS

ILLUSTRATIONS

ABBREVIATIONS

AAS	Archivo del Arzobispado de Santiago
ANECAP	Asociación Nacional de Empleadas de Casa Particular
ARNAD	Archivo Nacional de la Administración
CEM	Centro de Estudios de la Mujer
CSO	Caja de Seguridad Obligatorio
CNCD	Congreso Nacional, Cámara de Diputados
CNCS	Congreso Nacional, Cámara de Senadores
CONSTRACAP	Comisión Nacional de Sindicatos de Trabajadoras de Casa Particular
ILO	International Labor Organization
JOC	Juventud Obrera Católica
MEMCH	Movimiento Pro-Emancipación de la Mujer Chilena
PDC	Partido Demócrata Cristiano
RITHAL	Red de Investigaciones sobre el Trabajo del Hogar en América Latina
SINTRACAP	Sindicato de Trabajadoras de Casa Particular
UP	Unidad Popular

ACKNOWLEDGMENTS

If this book is by now old enough to be a teenager, the original idea for it is ready to get a teaching job. Thirty years ago, during one of many meetings with the Chilean feminist and historian Alicia Frohmann to discuss my dissertation research, Alicia asked me: "Why focus on women industrial workers, when it's the *empleadas* (domestic workers) who are the real key to understanding Chile's history?" Shaken by Alicia's challenge, I have never forgotten it, and now—after more than thirty years of investigation, presentation, consultation, and publication—that question has led me to this book. Along the way, I have accumulated more than a few debts, and it is well past time that I acknowledge the many people and institutions that have helped me complete this book.

World events of 2020—particularly the COVID-19 pandemic—have turned the world upside down, so I will do my part to set it upright by reversing the usual order of things. Rather than thanking friends and family last (who decided that?), I will thank them first, since it is really the case that nothing is possible without their love and support. My partner, Regina, and our sons, Dante and Pasqual, along with our *comadre* Betsy (Tita), make up our noisy, nurturing pod, and Hutchisons and Manocchios spread far and wide celebrate our successes: Victor, I hope you enjoy this book, too! But without Betsy's Martha, and Ezra Jude, the precious third brother in our Albuquerque family, we are forever changed. I am grateful to my family for their steadfast support.

Since challenges like writing a book are best faced in teams, I have to thank my closest, bestest friends for spurring me on and catching me when I fall: Kymm Gauderman, co-conspirator in all struggles; Linda Garber, guardian of my younger soul; Margy Hutchison, such a good friend I forget you are my sister; Amy Levi, administrative mentor extraordinaire; Soledad Zárate, fellow survivor of the Chilean gender wars; María Angélica Rojas Flores, *hermana*; and Miguel Kaiser, *hermano imprescindible y solidario para toda una vida*. Along this often dark road we call the academic life, I have been fortunate to encounter fellow travelers with flashlights: Eileen Boris, Heidi Tinsman, Nara Milanich, Jolie Olcott, Sam Truett, Jason Scott Smith, Ericka Verba, Krystyna von Henneberg, and the amazing Ann Blum, gone too soon. Margaret Randall, whose oral histories with women and Christians first drew me to Latin America, has offered inspirational friendship as our lives converged in Albuquerque. Books may be shelved and forgotten, but the patience and kindness of friends and family will never be.

I thank the many colleagues who have supported this work by buying me coffee, hosting me in their homes and offices, collaborating on panels and publications, and inviting me to share my work with their students and colleagues. My career has been indelibly marked by the sisterhood of Latin Americanist gender historians, including (but not limited to) Heidi Tinsman, Nara Milanich, Jolie Olcott, Ann Blum, Rebekah Pite, Brenda Elsey, Ricardo López, Tom Klubock, Jadwiga Pieper, and Lara Putnam. I am also deeply indebted to those Latin American scholars who have regularly encouraged my work, including Thelma Gálvez and the Chilean historians María Soledad Zárate Campos, Alicia Frohmann, Iván Jakšić, Sol Serrano, Julio Pinto, and Jorge Rojas; in Buenos Aires, Silvia Hirsch, Isabella Cosse, Lila Caimari, Mariano Plotkin, and Graciela Quierolo have received me with unfailing generosity. Inés Pérez and Joan Casanovas, who arranged for Fulbright to carry me all the way to Mar del Plata and Tarragona, respectively, deserve special mention for their warm hospitality, intellectual generosity, and more than a few lively meals. It has been my great honor to work with students of gender and history in the Universitat Romiro I Virgili and the Universidad de Granada in Spain, as well as the Instituto de Desarollo Económico y Social (IDES), Universidad Nacional de Mar del Plata, and the Universidad Nacional del Centro de la Provincia de Buenos Aires in Argentina, who always gave as good as they got. The recent surge in interdisciplinary research on domestic work has also fostered a new community of committed scholar-activists, the Red de Investigación sobre Trabajo del Hogar en América Latina (RITHAL), led by the indefatigable Erynn Masi de Casanova. The University of New Mexico, my institutional home for over twenty years, is much more than the place I work: there I treasure History and Latin Americanist colleagues, the many students I have been privileged to teach, brave leaders in faculty governance and administration, the UNM staff who challenge us to be better, my colleagues in Faculty SAFE UNM, and the good trouble team in the Division for Equity and Inclusion. It is truly a privilege to call these folks—from Albuquerque to Mar del Plata and Berkeley to Barcelona—my beloved community.

Turning now to those who quite literally made it possible for me to write this book, I must start again with *las imprescindibles*: the domestic worker activists, past and present, whose struggles have marked Chile's twentieth century and continue in the twenty-first. Among the many leaders who received me in their offices, told their stories and showed me their archives, I am most grateful to Aída Moreno and Elba Bravo. Fathers Bernardino Piñera and Mauricio Hourton were generous with their time and boundless in their enthusiasm for this history. Also indispensable for their help with archival research, transcription, and processing were the assistants who have gone on to greater things: Carolyn Watson, Fernanda Caloiro, María Soledad Zárate Campos, Scott Crago, Carson Morris, and Lucrecia Enríquez. The historian and translator Jacqueline Garreaud has never failed to render my English into even better Spanish, helping me contribute to Latin American debates on gender and history.

I am also grateful to the many institutions that have funded this research over the past two decades. At the University of New Mexico, I have received generous support from the Department of History; the Feminist Research Institute; the Faculty Senate's Research Allocation Committee; the College of Arts & Sciences; the Latin American and Iberian Institute; and the Division for Equity and Inclusion. My writing has been supported at critical junctures by a National Endowment for the Humanities Summer Stipend; a Fulbright Senior Scholar Award for work at the Instituto de Desarollo Económico y Social (IDES) in Buenos Aires; and a residential fellowship at the Women's International Study Center in Santa Fe, New Mexico. Invitations from colleagues around the world have allowed me to discuss my ongoing research, parts of which I have presented in Chile at the Universidad Alberto Hurtado and the Universidad Nacional Andrés Bello, and in Argentina at the Universidad Nacional de La Plata, the Universidad Nacional de San Martín, and the Universidad de San Andrés. I have also received valuable feedback from colleagues at the Newberry Conference on Labor History, the Duke University Latin American Labor History Conference, the Berkshire Conference on the History of Women, the Latin American Studies Association, the Jornadas Nacionales de la Historia de las Mujeres (Argentina), the National Women Studies Conference, and the International Conference of Labour History (Austria). These associations gave me access to a broad range of critical perspectives and relevant scholarship, without which this would have been a very different book.

Finally, I am grateful to Duke editorial director Gisela Fosado, who—like the indomitable Valerie Milholland before her—believed in this project and encouraged my scholarly life beyond *The Chile Reader*. Alejandra Mejia and Ihsan Taylor shepherded the manuscript's transformation to a book with care, and Dylan Maynard helped me create the index for it. My anonymous readers provided many excellent suggestions for revision, and I am (again) deeply indebted to Nara Milanich, who told me, with great precision and kindness, how to make this a better book. Parts of this work have been previously published in *Labor, Hispanic American Research Review, Nuevo Mundo/Mundos nuevos,* and two edited collections, *Mujeres* (LOM) and *Towards a Global History of Domestic Workers and Caregiving Workers* (Brill).

After a harrowing year of pandemic, which has again exposed the inequality and precarity that shapes domestic workers' lives, it seems fitting to dedicate this work to the memory of Aída Moreno Valenzuela, who passed away at age eighty-one in June of 2021. Doña Aída's unfailing energy and leadership spurred the extraordinary mobilization for domestic workers' rights in Chile, and her written history of this movement—painstakingly researched in newspapers and national archives and distributed in grainy mimeographed copies during the dictatorship—inspired this project. Aída's spirit, as well as the domestic workers' movements she helped foster, live on in this book.

INTRODUCTION

Empleadas Lost and Found

M Y RESEARCH INTO THE history of domestic service in Chile started in 2000 with the archives; or rather, the archives started with me. On several trips through the gray streets of downtown Santiago, as the sun barely broke through the layers of the afternoon's winter smog, domestic worker activists guided me to the leaning, floor-to-ceiling bookshelves that housed archives of many decades' work from Chile's two most important organizations for domestic workers: the union SINTRACAP (which dates, through several organizations, back to 1926) and the Catholic association ANECAP (which emerged from groups formed in 1947). Eager to delve into any uncatalogued records of this long history of the domestic workers' movement in Chile,[1] I soon realized that it was the living archive—members and retired leadership of these organizations—who could help me tell this story. *Workers Like All the Rest of Them* maps out stories culled from workers' life histories—filtered through memories of half a century and the realities of Chile in the twenty-first—within domestic workers' century-long struggle for dignity and rights.

Unfailingly generous in the midst of the many challenges of organizing work, these leaders made sure I got in touch with veteran activists of their movement. In meetings at the headquarters of the Asociación Nacional de Empleadas de Casa Particular (ANECAP or the National Association of Household Employees), some of the activists present at the group's founding over five decades prior huddled near paraffin stoves in the group's main office, a small room with a bookshelf stuffed with albums and pamphlets on one wall, and file cabinets holding decades' worth of material on the other.[2] It was in this room, lit almost entirely by dim light edging through a wall of windows, that I sipped the first of many black teas with Elba Bravo, one of the domestic workers who helped to found, recruit for, and lead the original Federación Nacional de Empleadas (National Federation of Empleadas) in the 1950s. Already in her early seventies, hunched over photo albums and clothed in the empleada's blue starched cotton uniform, Doña Elba's eyes sparkled and her hands leapt about her face as she

FIGURE I.1. Doña Elba Bravo, September 2004, ANECAP, photo by author

described her early days building the empleadas' movement in the 1950s and '60s. As the struggle to maintain the organization intensified in the early 2000s, Doña Elba was always eager to meet, happy to share her stories of other, equally challenging but clearly invigorating times, many decades before.

Even at her advanced age, Doña Elba did not limit her storytelling to any office, or even the historic buildings on Tocornal Street, built in the 1950s with domestic workers' own funds to shelter and educate domestic workers. In our very first meeting, Doña Elba looked up from the albums and documents spread out on the room's large table with a suggestion that was at once a command: "To learn about this movement, you must meet Don Bernardino." So off we went, following Doña Elba's swift pace through narrow side streets in the deepening dusk and cold, smoggy air, to arrive at a side door of the Iglesia San Francisco, one of Chile's oldest churches, which sits high on Santiago's main avenue, the Alameda. Rushing down long corridors and up grand staircases to the vast, chilly, dimly lit living quarters of the former convent, Doña Elba eagerly clasped Don Bernadino's hands in both of hers and urged him to tell me, a historian from the North, the story of how, as a young Catholic priest in the 1940s, he worked with a handful of domestic workers to establish one of the most enduring and

FIGURE I.2. Don Bernardino Piñera, circa 2010, from *Mensaje* (July 31, 2020)

influential Catholic associations of empleadas in the Americas. Don Bernadino, by then white-haired and moving stiffly in his eighties, was more than happy to oblige, on this and many other occasions, always stressing how he valued his work with empleadas over all else: more than his religious career as bishop of several Chilean cities; public opposition to the military regime's human rights abuses; or membership in one of Chile's most distinguished families (his nephew, Sebastián Piñera, would in 2010 begin his first of two presidential terms). In meetings arranged at first in Church offices and cafes, and much later at a residence for retired priests, Don Bernardino proudly offered up his stories about the origins, challenges, and evolution of the domestic workers' movement over the last half century.

In those days I also interviewed the enduring leader of Chilean domestic workers' movements, Aída Moreno Valenzuela, whose warmth, sharp wit, and love of history has made her one of the most sought-after spokespersons for the Chilean domestic workers' union movement since the 1970s. Younger by ten years than her colleague Doña Elba, Aída, too, got her start in the Federación de Empleadas in the 1950s, but from the start she also participated in the Sindicato de Trabajadoras de Casa Particular (SINTRACAP or Household Workers' Union), rising to leadership positions at the national and international levels in the 1960s. Active in elected positions in the 1980s, Aída Moreno nurtured the movement's alliance with Chilean feminists in the struggle against the military dictatorship, a network that would later sustain her participation in regional and international domestic workers' movements and inspire her businesses that sold cleaning products and services to the public. Moreno's close friendship with

FIGURE I.3. Doña Aída Moreno, 2004, Barrio Santa Rosa, photo by author

the US anthropologist Elsa Chaney, and the international travel and activism through which it was nurtured, also elevated Aída Moreno's historical research on Chilean domestic workers to an international and academic audience. Moreno's long engagement in domestic worker politics, along with her skills as an amateur historian, broadened the horizons of this study, beyond the realm of Catholic mobilization in the 1950s, to the world of domestic worker activism under socialism and dictatorship.

Meetings with lifelong activists and their allies, along with my research in the organizations, ministries, and courts that recorded the lives and activism of domestic workers across the twentieth century, has inspired and shaped the conceptualization of this book. Like the long struggle for visibility by domestic workers' movements themselves, *Workers Like All the Rest of Them* pushes back against the continued *invisibility* of a certain kind of "women's work"—paid domestic labor—that has been as ubiquitous as it was necessary in Chilean households throughout the twentieth century. As elsewhere in Latin America, much of the dominant discourse about "la empleada" portrays her as a fixture of Chilean family life, the living legacy of a long tradition of service that confounded and crossed class boundaries through affective relations, as women from rural or working-class origins cared for the homes and children of wealthier families.[3]

Domestic worker activists and their political allies, however, began to seriously confront and disrupt this traditional view by promoting labor legislation and feminist analysis of domestic service in the 1970s and '80s.[4] In recent years, the Chilean government has gone on to grant empleadas critical labor rights, devoted Cabinet-level programs to addressing their concerns, and begun to implement the requirements of the 2011 International Labor Organization's Convention 189 on domestic workers, ratified in Chile in 2016.[5] Despite these changes, many Chileans continue to insist on the power of more traditional representations of empleadas, revealing how history, culture, and trenchant inequality continue to shape employers' expectations, even as the legal and political context for paid household labor has continued to change.

What we already knew about the history of domestic service in Chile has long been embedded in a trenchant nationalist narrative of *Chile tradicional*, a saga of rural paternalism, national integration, and economic modernization that remains a source of powerful, if conservative, social norms in Chile today. This affection for an idealized rural past, as well as specific gender and racial hierarchies that sustained it, has been reinforced time and again by the representation of servants and servitude in Chilean arts and popular culture. Chile's high literary canon includes iconic "servant" figures, from the subservient but indispensable characters of Blest Gana's *Martin Rivas* (1862) to those that populate the declining noble households preserved in José Donoso's *Coronación* (1957). The *criollista* tradition in Chilean arts is rife with examples of these static "historical" portrayals of social hierarchies expressed and affirmed through master-servant relations. Stereotypical and melodramatic representations also informed popular poetry and song, which invariably showed female domestic workers as passive agents, exploited both physically and sexually by their masters.[6] Subsequently, as Chilean society confronted the challenges of development, political instability, and social change by mid-century, empleadas appearing as characters in radio, film, and television dramas illustrated the change and uncertainty in Chilean social relations across class, racial, and gender lines. In iconic characters from radio and stage to television and movies, representations of domestic workers have been critical to Chilean struggles over national identity and progress in the twentieth century.

This investigation began, then, as a study of the *hidden history* of domestic service that lies beneath those divergent perspectives, a history that documents not only workers' agency but also how class, race/ethnicity, and gender were constructed through domestic service relations across time. Although the vast majority of the Chilean women employed in domestic service never participated in a labor union or encountered a state inspector, for example, their choices about where and for whom they would work shaped modernization, class formation, and political development in Chile as fundamentally as labor history's more celebrated copper and nitrate workers. Although countless Chilean scholars warned me that the historical sources for such a study simply do not exist, by starting with the activists' own accounts of migration, work, and activism I was able to identify a wide range of relevant archival sources, including newspaper accounts, law and social work theses, archives of domestic workers' associations, and the many songs, plays, and scripts that have portrayed domestic workers in popular culture.

These abundant oral and archival sources demonstrate that the purported "invisibility" of domestic workers is, like so many stories people tell about the past, a kind of myth that can be used to justify their continued exclusion from labor rights and from history itself. In addition to restoring domestic workers to the histories of Chilean labor and politics, this book explores the historical constructions of *labor* and *gender* that allowed the Chilean state to systematically deny labor rights to so many women (and some men), further rendering them hidden from history. In the process, I show how the efforts of priests and feminists, inspectors and legislators, state and international officials—and, most significantly, domestic workers themselves—made Chilean empleadas visible as "workers like all the rest of them" over the course of the twentieth century.[7] From the earliest associations for domestic workers formed in the 1920s, through the expansion of those unions and the creation of Catholic associations after World War II, to the diverse non-governmental and international organizations that exist today, for more than one hundred years Chilean domestic workers have collectively and simultaneously defended both the labor rights and dignity of workers in their profession.

Workers Like All the Rest of Them recounts this long struggle for domestic workers' recognition and rights, a history familiar to domestic worker activists in contemporary Chile but one that has remained largely ancillary to scholarly histories of labor in Chile and beyond. On the one hand, this history has been obscured by categories of labor and citizenship that relegate domestic service to the private realm, where it is ostensibly sheltered from the gaze of both the state and organized labor. But domestic workers were *not* hidden from history: on the contrary, they were everywhere, shaping among other things the organization of families, rural-urban migration, and state welfare policy throughout the twentieth century. Moreover, the fact that domestic workers mobilized earlier and more extensively in Chile than in other parts of Latin America has left an important record of their experience and agency, a record that challenges their exclusion from Chilean history and reveals how and under what conditions domestic workers were able to mobilize for change.

At the heart of this continuing movement has been, in Chile as elsewhere, the struggle by some domestic workers and their allies to name their employment as "work," and those who perform it as "workers." Although women's historians in particular have long examined domestic service as a key site for women's labor, domestic workers and their allies have continued to struggle for their formal recognition as workers deserving of labor rights.[8] Why, and how does this matter? Why would cleaning, childcare, cooking—activities that, when they take place anywhere else besides a private home, are simply "work"—ever be considered something else? Why does the location of work, or the private arrangement between employer and domestic worker, result in the exclusion of so many women workers from protective legislation, union mobilization, and the history of labor?[9] And why has it taken so long for an inter-governmental body like the International Labor Organization, which has intervened in so many different labor relations since the early twentieth century, only recently created an international convention on domestic work?[10] This book approaches these questions from a local and historical perspective: the case of twentieth-century Chile, where a small union movement grew into a vibrant and visible movement for domestic workers' rights at midcentury.[11]

In that country, as in other places throughout the Americas, families and individuals have relied on the work of "servants" to organize the work of the household, who perform a wide range of duties from cooking and cleaning to childcare. Once a phenomenon limited to wealthier families, in the twentieth century domestic service proved crucial for the operation and well-being of middle-class households, among other things providing the reproductive labor that allowed middle-class professional women (and men!) to work outside the home.[12] In Chile throughout the twentieth century, women's domestic service labor remained critical to both the reproductive work of Chilean households and the economic survival of poor families, particularly in the rural sector. According to the Chilean population census, roughly 40 percent of economically active women were employed in domestic service (higher than the regional average), and women in turn comprised over four fifths of that occupation.[13] Despite employers' frequent assertions that domestic workers are "part of the family" because they perform caring work, the persistence of poor treatment and low wages tells a different story. It shows the erstwhile "kin" speaking out, organizing, and seeking recognition in their struggle for change, often in ways that reflect the same ideological diversity, strategic differences, and political ties evident in the political struggles of workers in other sectors.

On the workers' side, of course, the significance of domestic service as a source of income, and sometimes dignity and financial security, is also undeniable. Women and men, young and old, rural migrants and urban residents have worked to sustain themselves and their families through paid domestic service, often traveling far and sacrificing attention to their own families to do so. In Chile, their story has been told elsewhere, and in multiple ways—literature, song, film, testimonials, news reports—but to date no one other than the activist Aída Moreno has told this story of the Chilean empleadas' struggle for recognition and protection as workers.[14] For Chilean activists, this global struggle is grounded in a local history of domestic activism and alliances, where workers continue to confront social prejudice and racial and gender discrimination in their quest for labor rights.

AS IN MUCH OF Latin America, throughout the twentieth century women's domestic service labor remained critical to both the reproductive work of Chilean households and the economic survival of poor families, particularly in the rural sector. But by the 1980s, women domestic workers remained as marginal to formal labor organization as they were essential to Chilean social relations, family economic organization, and childhood education. Particularly when compared to today's domestic service sector—dominated not only by day laborers but also characterized by women of diverse education, rural/urban origins, and nationalities[15]—most paid household labor in Chile's earlier decades was performed by poorly educated women who migrated as teenagers from southern communities to find live-in work in urban households.[16]

The personal stories of many empleadas form part of a larger story of Chile's rural sector, a story rife of extreme poverty, unstable employment, cultural and economic domination, and political exclusion.[17] But there is certainly more to this story: instead of dichotomous renderings of pastoral family life versus urban labor exploitation, domestic workers pursued survival and independence through domestic service work. Particularly in light of the range of representations of empleadas that dominated public discourse in this period—from criminal elements to suffering victims and everything in between—it is vital that we appreciate the kinds of experiences, choices, and limitations faced by so many empleadas, then as well as now. *Workers Like All the Rest of Them* begins by centering the stories I collected in interviews between 2002 and 2005 with over a dozen Chileans who were involved in Catholic associations and the secular union in the 1950s through the 1980s. Their memories of migration, city life, sociability, religion, employment, and sometimes romantic and family life,

FIGURE I.4. Young empleadas, Rancagua, 1929, photographer unknown.
Photograph provided by María Angélica Rojas Flores from a family collection.

inform the central narrative of this book, which begins—as they did—with the deepening poverty that drove so many young women to leave their families in the countryside to seek better wages and situations in Chile's growing postwar cities.[18] In what follows below, we learn about these transformations through the experience of Elba Bravo, whose personal narrative of rural poverty and migration, household employment, urban opportunities and dangers, as well as her path to religious and labor militancy, reflect a common pathway traversed by women who became leading activists in Chile's domestic workers' movements.

Dating back to the early years of the Republic, Chilean systems of landholding and agricultural labor have remained central to the country's economic growth and social organization, evolving in the decades after independence to an enduring system of large private estates that relied on the *inquilinaje* system—in which rural men and some women were paid, mostly in kind and access to land on the edges of large estates—and progressively thereafter to one that by the 1950s depended mostly on the waged, temporary labor of a migrant male labor force. Even though women participated in rural labor systems—as workers as well as landowners—attention to rural labor by the Catholic Church, Chilean state, and political parties typically privileged the subject of the exploited migrant male workers whose political participation was at first repressed, then recruited, especially as populist and revolutionary parties shifted their attention to the countryside in the 1950s and '60s. However, women's role in the rural sector, from their participation in *inquilinaje* to their labor in male-headed households, reveals characteristics that help explain how and why so many young women chose to migrate to urban areas for domestic work, and did so with increasing frequency by the 1930s.

Although women had often engaged in rural labor—usually through milking and care of animals—by the 1930s the mechanization of the dairy industry and the increasing monetarization of wages meant that most rural employment and land contracts were made by men, and that more and more of the available waged labor in the rural sector was performed by men, relegating women to unpaid work for their families or, where family income could not sustain them, migration to urban areas in search of work. But there was an intermediate step that young, unmarried women in the *campo* frequently passed through before migration: a contract to perform domestic service in the home of their family's rural *patrón*, through which some women became attached to families that later relocated to the capital.

Empleadas attached to specific families were often forced—if they wanted to keep their jobs—to move from rural estate to city homes and even foreign destinations, a reality that presented difficulties for some and opportunities for others. In other cases, it was the poverty of the *inquilino* arrangement itself that pushed young women to seek work as domestics in distant cities. Elba Bravo recounted how, rather than help out with her father's labor obligations, she decided to seek work in Santiago at age fourteen, leaving the rural community of Graneros, several hours south of Santiago by train: "we had enough to eat and nothing more and so I said I'll talk to the *señora* who did laundry for the rich folks on the estate and ask her 'isn't there work in Santiago?'—Santiago, which in that year 1948 was like going to another country, there was only the train—and she said 'sure, I'll see if they need a nanny.'"[19] Even though Bravo's relatives warned her father that she would "come back a mother or a prostitute," her parents allowed her to move to Santiago to work as a cook in the household associated with the estate on which her father worked, telling her to come back home if her employers abused her.[20] Families and employers alike were preoccupied with protecting empleadas' virtue, for example prohibiting the young Elba Bravo from leaving her employers' home, even to attend parish events.

Although cities were considered dangerous for migrant empleadas, so were employers' homes. The sexual predations of male employers and family members were widely known, and Church teachings frequently warned empleadas to guard their sexual virtue. Despite the frequency of sexual abuse in the household, as in so many other workplaces these dynamics were rarely acknowledged, even in interviews conducted many decades after the fact. Doña Elba was one exception, reporting that she had once been threatened with sexual assault by her employer's nephew. When she reported the encounter to her *patrona*, her employers asked for her forgiveness and banned the offending youth from the household. Most empleadas, Bravo reported, were not so lucky, guarding silence about the abuse or getting fired when employers did not believe them: "the empleada's credibility is worth nothing to the employers: it's like we can never have the truth or be right, because they are always right."[21]

Bravo was quick to point out, however, that what she experienced as an empleada was an improvement overall from what girls like her faced back at home, where they were also vulnerable to sexual threats and abuse of male family members, including that of husbands. As she argued to the laundress she begged to find her work in Santiago, "It's just that, mamita, there's nothing for me here. What girls my age do is get pregnant, then they get hit, they change partners, they marry, the husband hits them, and so on for the rest of their lives."[22] For some, migration also meant greater freedom from family supervision. For Bravo and others, their stories of migration for work were not about victimization, but rather (and in retrospect) were presented as evidence of their early maturity and commitment to making better lives for themselves: in these personal narratives, they conveyed their pride in deciding to leave home for the big city.[23]

Once installed in their new "homes," the new empleadas relied on older employees to teach them their trade, which depending on circumstance could provide a sense of belonging in the household or alienation from it. In their reflections as well as in contemporary popular culture, empleadas recounted with humor their own stories or those of the "new girl" whose lack of familiarity with her new environment led to mistakes and confusion: Bravo recounts with shame that on her first day as a cook she burned the family's rice. These new circumstances could also provoke overwork and a sense of isolation, as Bravo recounted, complaining at length to her parish priest: "I told him that I was suffering all by myself, and that the people we served were older . . . they were all housewives who did their work, took naps, and I finished in the kitchen, did the mopping, did everything and then kept ironing: I was the first up in the morning and the last to go to bed at night. . . . it's just that some people put up with all this, but I couldn't tolerate it, it was something that no, no, no!"[24] Young women like Doña Elba faced many challenges in the transition from *campo* to *ciudad*; from family to the employers' homes; and in learning the skills and discipline associated with their new jobs. Whereas earlier generations of servants—particularly young women—had found employment on the estates to which their families were already attached through inquilinaje, by the 1930s and '40s the economic conditions of the rural sector were pressing greater numbers of women to migrate to urban centers in search of domestic employment.[25]

The interviews with aging empleadas provided ample evidence of the range of treatment they received at the hands of employers, from long-term employment that resembled the much-vaunted "family" in which the young servant was "like a daughter," to the many cases of mistreatment (lack of food and clothing, unhealthy living conditions, and abusive treatment by employers and other family members). Elba Bravo recounted the story of Eugenia—so different from her own experience—in which her friend who worked in the same parish decided to leave her employer because they provided so little food, controlling portions of bread and potatoes given to the workers. When Eugenia announced her intention to leave, she was prevented from doing so and accused of stealing a fountain pen that had been lost by one of the family's children. Inspired by Father Piñera's instruction that empleadas should share in the food they prepared for employers, Bravo encouraged Eugenia to leave, and found herself excluded from parish events and scolded by her employer (mother of Eugenia's employer) as a result. Through stories of her outreach to suffering colleagues, Bravo illustrated the spirit of solidarity and justice that motivated her work, even before she began working with the Catholic empleadas' association.

In the absence of clear regulations governing domestic service relations, moreover, empleadas sought to improve their labor situations by seeking better-paid employment. In a case that speaks to the ways that employers might have been influenced by peer pressure, Elba Bravo recounted how her patrona reacted when she announced her desire to leave her position after six years. At first, the patrona queried Bravo about her prospective job, then argued that as patrona she would be obligated instead to return Bravo to her parents' household in the summer months. Bravo then went and obtained her mother's permission to change jobs, arguing to her mistress (*misia*) that her new position would be less work for more pay, and ultimately securing her patrona's blessing.[26]

Curiously—but not surprisingly—the aging leaders of the domestic workers' movement I interviewed reported excellent relations with their long-term employers, including many episodes not only of good treatment but also of disagreement, in which the activists reported having spoken up to their employers with complaints and requests. This is in many ways not surprising, since this cohort included empleadas whose employers allowed them time off for religious, and later associational, activities, and women who went on to become public figures and activists in their own right. Again, for Elba Bravo, her strong relations with her employers allowed her to endure disagreements (such as Eugenia's exit) and keep her job, and in the end, she was able to work *puertas afuera* (by the hour/day) for the same family. But her departure to work full time in domestic workers' associations sparked conflict and negotiation with her patrona: her employer objected, but Bravo insisted: "I won't stay in any case, for any amount of money, because I felt humiliated—I'm telling you the truth, Señora Yaya . . . I was humiliated by Señora María, her daughter." After much back and forth with her employers, they made her an offer: that she work half days puertas afuera for the salary she already received, and they would keep a room open for her should she wish to occasionally spend the night.[27] Such accommodations might have been common among some activist leaders, but it was surely exceptional among the many more stories that ended in loss of employment.

Stories of good treatment notwithstanding, and despite these memories of mutual affection between patrona and empleada, none of the activists interviewed reported that they had become "part of the family" in the households where they worked. In fact, when it came to making choices about their job and living situations, they reported disagreements with employers in which they ultimately made their own choices. The disjuncture between their accounts and the narrative of domestic workers as "part of the family" reveal a great deal about the construction of labor as such, even in the intimate quarters of household employment in twentieth century Chile.

For these "successful" empleadas—those who were fortunate to encounter benevolent employers, send money home to their families, work with the parish priests and other activists in support of their trade, and perhaps purchase their own homes for retirement—the contrast between their rural lives with family and their new and more independent lives in Santiago is striking. Among her many fond memories of good employers and even better work as an activist, Elba Bravo treasured her memories of her yearly visits home, when she brought presents for her parents and siblings, helped pay for parties, and was praised by family and friends for her success in the city. Although her brothers teased her mercilessly for her supposed "airs" of a city girl—wearing nice dresses, and later, owning a home—she tells of how proud her parents were of her achievements. Her father, she reported, was moved to tears at the sight of the small house she bought through the Housing Cooperative, while "my mother was crying with happiness, saying 'after so much suffering, who would believe this change, so much change, her work has done her so much good.'"[28]

The stories of aging empleada activists—filtered through memory, nostalgia for home, youth, and their work in specific households—are important because they provide a different, albeit selective, view of domestic service in mid-twentieth-century Chile. Significantly, from interviewees selected because of their decades-long struggle for empleadas' associations and rights, we gain some insight into the complex emotions and conditions that structured their lives as migrants, workers, and activists. From rural homes where poverty, violence, and limitations were prevalent, to the urban homes where empleadas labored under kind as well as cruel regimes of isolation and hard work, we gain a fuller picture of the limits and choices faced by empleadas as they made their way in the world.

IN THIS INTRODUCTION, as in the rest of the book, workers' memories provide an important touchstone for the enduring cultural representations and public controversies over their labor that also shaped that history. Together with archival materials and popular representations, interviews provide a sense of the *ubiquity* of domestic workers in Chilean society: it is only a slight exaggeration to point out that in Chile, everyone has a nanny, listens to La Desideria,[29] and knows that empleadas are some of the most exploited workers in Chilean society. In the early decades of this longer history—by now inaccessible to oral historians—public debates about the plight, shortcomings, and demands of domestic workers brought debates about domestic service fully into Chilean public discourse by the 1920s, when serious debate on the need for protective legislation was first inaugurated. Widely known as the era of "the social question" in Chile, these early decades of the twentieth century were marked by increasing preoccupation with workers' rights, resulting in legislation concerned primarily with industrial male workers. With the codification of corresponding labor laws, however, the attention of legislators, religious leaders, and even state officials turned increasingly to Chile's numerous domestic workers, challenging their exclusion and fueling a small but vocal domestic workers' movement. It is to these actors and their interventions on behalf of domestic workers in the 1920s that we now turn.

CHAPTER I

From Servants to Workers in Chile

The petition we are sending to Congress shows you, our brothers and sisters in work and suffering, that we are not alone in our aspirations, and this is how our Society for the Future of Household Employees will become the largest in Santiago, and without exaggeration we can say the most powerful in all of Chile, because everywhere in the country there are domestic workers, called "domestic servants" (*sirvientes domésticos*) by our bosses. This is why, brothers and sisters, we should have no fear in asking for our most legitimate rights as citizens; it is our own brothers who invite us, without hatred for anyone, to join this Society.

—Society for the Future of Household Employees, November 1923

Girls: we have to decide whether or not we are workers like all the rest of them, because we work with our hands. . . . If we do not take this step [of joining the national union confederation], our Union has no reason to exist, because we will not free ourselves on our own.

—Ivania Silva, April 1972

IN A LETTER DIRECTED to the many thousands of domestic workers laboring in Chilean households in 1923, a handful of Santiago union activists issued their call for mobilization, drawing readers' attention to the contrast between the employment of massive numbers of men and women in domestic service and their lack of rights, as workers and citizens, in Chile's emerging labor relations system.[1] In the heady days of expanding urban and industrial growth, increasing worker mobilization, and legislative debate on "the social question," the 1920s provided an auspicious moment for Chilean domestic workers—from gardeners and cooks to cleaners and nannies—to petition and agitate for increased government oversight of their working conditions, salaries, and benefits. The starting point for a domestic workers' union that has lasted more than a century, The Society for the Future of Household Employees laid the foundation for activist *empleados'* recurring demand for labor rights and full citizenship, spawning labor activism that would spread to Catholic associations in the 1950s, to political parties in the 1960s, and to women's movements by the 1980s.

Half a century after domestic worker activists first published these complaints, and in the throes of Salvador Allende's socialist experiment, Ivania Silva urged her colleagues in domestic service to recognize that empleadas were "workers like all the rest of them," entitled to what had long been recognized in Chile as workers' legal right to contracts, hour limits, minimum wage, severance pay, accident protection, and the right to strike.[2] The violent military coup of the following year abruptly ended not only civilian democratic rule, but also debates on proposed legislation to grant domestic workers those same rights. Only after the transition to civilian democracy in 1990 would domestic workers' demands be partially ratified, through laws that protected domestic workers' maternity leave, severance pay, and vacations. Having already established a powerful presence in the women's movements that protested the Pinochet dictatorship, domestic workers reaped some benefits from the return to democracy, even as the political transition itself was constrained by the neoliberal economy and authoritarian enclaves that remained a partial legacy of the military regime.[3]

How exactly did domestic workers move from "servants"—a highly visible but informal occupation, subjected to multiple forms of paternalistic control—to "workers"—a mobilized and vocal labor sector that could effectively lobby the state for recognition of their basic labor rights? This chapter starts to answer that question by exploring domestic workers' legal status in the nineteenth century and evolving political role in the early twentieth, as employers and union organizers struggled to define the terms and conditions of service work in Chile's rapidly changing urban centers. In a manner entirely consistent with the representation of other non-industrial workers in this period, the men and women employed in domestic service were treated as non-workers, viewed with fear by employers and sympathy by organized labor in the larger struggle over workers' rights and the role of the state. As domestic workers began to mobilize in their own associations in the 1920s, however, legal and social norms regulating their work and rights began to shift. It was in these early decades of the twentieth century, therefore, that we find the first evidence of domestic workers demanding their rights—to dignity and protection—"like all the rest of them."

From Servants to Workers in Chile

Domestic service relations during the colonial *Reino de Chile* and the early Republic were shaped by patterns of indigenous slavery, rural migration, child circulation and domestic economies that varied tremendously over time and with respect to region and administrative authority (both Spanish and national).[4] The founding of the Chilean republic had codified the legal exclusion of *criados* (or servants, as they were then still known) from the country's earliest legal codes and practices: Chile's first Constitution, for example, explicitly denied suffrage to servants, an exclusion reaffirmed in the Civil Code of 1857. Without exception, in Chile as elsewhere in Latin America, in the late nineteenth century statesmen established rights of liberal citizenship through legal codes that both enshrined and constrained individual rights, usually in service to the requirements for labor and capitalization demanded by the expanding raw export economies of the late nineteenth century. Early nation-building in Spanish America relied by the 1870s on a series of anti-vagrancy laws that served not only to maintain social and racial hierarchies, but also to address labor shortages in both household labor and local industrial production. In places as distinct as the Argentine interior and the Guatemalan highlands, for example, by the 1860s national laws were introduced to surveil the movement and economic activity of both male and female "vagrants," whose inability to show legitimate, stable employment led to their arrest and forced domestic and industrial labor with local employers.[5] For states that had only recently abolished African slavery following independence, or ones like Chile still engaged in "Indian wars," individuals' lack of documented employment facilitated the provision of coerced and often unpaid labor in economies driven by rapid expansion in both commercial agriculture and extractive export industries.[6] In similar fashion, the growing cities of late-nineteenth-century Latin America were busy sites for the forced redirection of female and child labor to elite households, a process upheld by city police and the religious organizations that housed orphans and prostitutes, training them for placement in elite homes.[7]

As they consolidated political and administrative control in the late nineteenth century, therefore, republican regimes of Spanish America consolidated export-led economic growth and codified emerging social hierarchies, excluding domestic workers from the rights of citizenship and codifying their status as dependents within employers' households. Labor relations, including the right to written contracts, were duly enshrined in these same civil codes, but explicitly excluded both domestic servants and rural *peones* or day laborers.[8] As documents marking the transition from common to rationalist law, the civil codes of Latin America and Iberia drew an intractable distinction between domestic and other forms of salaried labor. Significantly, this distinction formalized the subordination of domestic workers not on the basis of gender or racial identity, and not because the private space of the home was sacrosanct, but in the interest of public order in new and disorderly nation-states.[9] In a period when domestic service was performed by men as well as women, and more often than not embedded in complex family structures that subordinated family members along with *allegados* (kin from other households), illegitimate children, and other workers under the rule of a male patriarch, the status of those engaged in reproductive labor for other families was structured through law as well as multiple registers of social inequality such as age, race, gender, and rural, family, and/or national origin.[10]

By the late nineteenth century, surging industrial employment in predominantly male industries of mining, transportation, and manufacturing led to workers' increasing participation in political organizations visibly impacted by global labor movements. Increasing numbers of strikes and the violent repression of organized labor provoked urgent reform efforts in the first decades of the twentieth century, during which legislators and political leaders from a range of ideological perches proposed new mechanisms to study, regulate, and control workers and their organizations.[11] With very few exceptions, *empleados domésticos* (along with rural day laborers) continued to be excluded from these legal reforms, which did not consider them workers in a formal sense, subject to state protection. Even the most liberal legislative proposals, such as President Alessandri's 1921 Project for Labor and Social Welfare Codes, which at least addressed women workers' need for maternity leave and the regulation of industrial homework, nevertheless excluded domestic workers from labor contracts, accident protection, and other rights provided for other workers. This exclusion was made more evident in the 1931 Labor Code, which included a separate article on *empleados* but provided few benefits for a narrow category of domestic workers, those who worked full time for a single employer. By contrast, when in the 1930s Chile consolidated its extensive social welfare system—a diverse set of institutions that guided social security, health services, and other social welfare efforts—the state included domestic workers as contributors to and beneficiaries of the state's welfare largesse. So, while the legal status of *empleados* shifted significantly in the 1930s—recognizing their status as *workers* in both labor law and social welfare policy—the Chilean state continued to treat domestic and rural labor as distinct categories of work, ones regulated more by aspirational paternalism than state intervention.

Although domestic workers' legal exclusion was explicit in emerging labor rights granted other workers, so, too, was the struggle against it. By the 1920s domestic worker activists could rely on the support of multiple allies in their struggle for rights—labor inspectors, journalists, Catholic priests, socialists, feminists—who protested the inadequacy of the state's domestic service provisions. In particular, the participation of lawyers and social workers in the expanding welfare state by the late 1930s generated extensive data and analysis about domestic workers' health, income, and sexual abuse. The focus of reformers on *women* domestic workers only intensified in the postwar period, as the service occupations performed largely by men—drivers, cooks, gardeners—were redefined and "domestic service" performed almost exclusively by women. The feminization of domestic service in the 1940s—and a corresponding increase in female leadership of the union—proved fertile ground for Catholic mobilization of domestic workers in the 1950s, a movement that provided religious services, primary education, and social services to increasing numbers of empleadas in cities across Chile. Catholic organizing among domestic workers in this period proved extraordinarily effective, an effort that began in Santiago's parishes and grew into a movement that offered basic services and advocacy for tens of thousands of empleadas across Chile in the 1960s. The tide of political reform and revolution that swept through Cold War Chile also shaped domestic worker mobilization, in which leaders of the Catholic association turned increasingly to union activism, and launched under the Allende government a sustained effort to transform their trade through new labor legislation and union participation. Domestic workers who organized and promoted such legislative proposals in the late sixties and early seventies came closer than any other regional movement to claiming their full status of workers, an effort truncated by the same military intervention of 1973 that brought the Chilean road to socialism to a violent end.

Notwithstanding the systematic violence and political repression instituted by the military government after 1973, Chile's domestic workers' movement continued, relying on their continued invisibility as "workers" and association with the Catholic Church to provide support and solidarity to domestic workers throughout the country. Forming new alliances with labor and feminist movements mobilized to unseat Augusto Pinochet in the 1980s, domestic worker activists highlighted their occupational exploitation to challenge both state and domestic patriarchy. Domestic workers and middle-class feminists worked closely together in the 1980s, producing new studies of domestic service, migration, and class relations that shaped both movements and strategies of women's struggle against the dictatorship. These collaborations in turn directly impacted the social policies of the civilian democratic governments after the 1990s, which moved quickly to address the most egregious and damaging exclusions of domestic workers from labor law.[12]

For most of the twentieth century, then, important changes in the discursive construction of paid domestic work and workers in Chile was linked to organized domestic workers' access to new political allies, their grassroots activism, and the sensitivities of successive political movements and regimes. On the one hand, the political mobilization (and consequent polarization) that characterized reformist and revolutionary projects for social change in the 1960s and early '70s strengthened the syndicalist and political content of domestic workers' mobilization, justifying their incorporation into the Workers' United Central trade federation (*Central Unitaria de Trabajadores* or CUT) and inaugurating important legislation to strengthen domestic workers' labor rights. The political repression and economic conditions of the military period, on the other hand, forced domestic worker activists to take up new strategies of self-defense and solidarity, encouraging new alliances with both domestic women's movements and international funding agencies. *Workers Like All the Rest of Them* traces these shifting solidarities, in order to better understand how the mobilization and visibility of domestic workers has contributed the steady transformation of legal and political discourse in Chile around paid domestic labor, a transformation reflected in the semantic journey from "servants" to "workers."

What's in a Name?

At the center of the ubiquitous representations of domestic workers in twentieth-century Chilean sources—in which they appear as everything from victims of bourgeois consumption and male sexual prerogative to the affective center of family life and Chilean culture—lies a persistent struggle over the appropriate terminology to apply to those women engaged in paid domestic work. The politics of domestic service in Chile have been marked by this struggle over terminology, and by the transformation—in fits and starts, without much broader consensus—of *las sirvientas* (servants) into first *empleadas domésticas* (domestic employees) and later (briefly) *asesoras de hogar* (home managers), *empleadas de casa particular* (household employees) and, finally, *trabajadoras de casa particular* (workers in private homes).[13] Most of the twentieth-century archives and interviews used for this study employ the shorthand dominant in Chile at least through the 1960s and common even today: la empleada or "employee," which in this context is shorthand for empleada doméstica or "domestic employee." The empleada/o doméstica/o, literally "domestic employee," originally referred to men and women paid to provide household services, whereas obrera/o described those employed in manufacturing jobs; since the 1940s, empleada commonly refers to a female domestic worker, and should not be confused with the empleado or empleada/o particular, a white-collar worker entitled to greater social status and rights in the workplace.[14]

Leaving behind the nomenclature of "traditional Chile"—in which they had most commonly been called "criados" and "chinas"—twentieth-century activists asserted their preference for "empleados domésticos," invoking the respectability associated with public and private-sector "empleados" (employees) and distinguishing their trade from the morally suspect "woman worker" employed in industry. As early as the 1920s, however, some activists had begun to substitute "de casa particular" (of private homes) for "doméstica," a term that provoked repeated complaints for the subordination suggested by the word "domesticated." Although in the 1960s some politicians began referring to domestic workers as "asesoras de hogar" (home managers), such terminology was never widely adopted, giving way instead to the continuing use of "empleada de casa particular." Finally, due to a strange convergence between domestic worker activists, the feminist movement, and military reforms to the labor code, the terminology for domestic workers still employed today in Chile was legalized in 1978 as "trabajadora de casa particular" (worker in a private home), a phrase that continues to compete with its popular equivalent—la empleada—and the revival of older terms, such as *la nana* (the nanny) in recent decades. The importance of these struggles over naming cannot be overstated, since in the past as well as today, traditional terms such as "la nana" and "sirviente" are regularly and strategically deployed in public discourse, suggesting the continuing vulnerability of domestic workers to extra-legal arrangements and pressures.

The importance of this terminology as a site of historical struggle is further illustrated by the reflections of a Father Bernardino Piñera, who in a 1997 interview observed that:

In the 1940s, there was nothing degrading about being an "empleada de casa particular," who later was known as a "trabajadora de casa particular," which complicated things for employers, who suspected that the workers had been organized by the CUT. Later they were called "asesores de hogar," which seemed silly to me, since the only thing the empleadas don't do is "manage [the household]" . . . she is the one who works. . . . The changing terms imply that there is something about the profession that doesn't function: before they were "the servants," then "the domestics," "the underlings (criadas), . . . "the chinas" (which was derogatory). And so the "empleada de casa particular" was an appealing term because it sounded a little like the "empleado publico" and "empleado particular." . . . In the end, I don't know what term works best.[15]

Workers Like All the Rest of Them relies upon but modifies the terminology of choice of contemporary Chilean legal and political discourse—trabajadoras de casa particular, or workers in private homes—adjusting this term further to assimilate the English-language terminology common in US and international workers' movements: domestic workers.[16] Where sources uniformly referred to domestic workers as empleadas—rather than empleadas domésticas—I have likewise adopted the shortened term.

Domestic Service in Historical and Comparative Perspective

Despite the relative scarcity of studies that have examined the significance of domestic service in Latin America from a historical perspective, domestic workers' central role in mediating a wide range of social relations would seem self-evident.[17] The field's first wave of scholarly research in the 1980s reflected the urgency of raising critical questions about servants' "place" in their employers' households: leading titles included "Myth of 'Being Like a Daughter,'" *Muchachas No More*, "She Has Served Others in More Intimate Ways," and *Precarious Dependencies*.[18] These titles reflected feminist scholars' dominant concern with the ways that domestic service confounds and conflates familiar conceptual categories: between family and work, intimacy and struggle, and productive and reproductive labor. While this scholarship successfully identified the discrepancies between employers' and domestic workers' understanding of paid domestic work, this literature examined only female service workers and treated them as victims of economic exploitation, urban anomie, and patriarchy, paradigms that have since received more careful scrutiny.[19] But at the time, Elsa Chaney and Mary Garcia Castro defined the state of the field through *Muchachas No More*, an edited collection of historical and ethnographic case studies on Latin American domestic service, including several activist essays and primary visual materials for use in the study of contemporary movements.[20] The emerging legitimacy of domestic workers as subjects for study was further confirmed by two monographic works that integrated the study of domestic workers into broader social and political histories. According to Sandra Lauderdale Graham's classic study of domestic service in late-nineteenth-century Rio de Janeiro, the social and economic relations evident in the institution of domestic service owe their apparent inflexibility in large part to the legitimizing function of tradition, in which employer and servant are bound by unspoken laws of patronage and fictive kinship, as well as to the racial and sexual hierarchies that ensure the continuing availability of servants for hire.[21] However, as Lesley Gill has shown in the case of twentieth-century Bolivia, the diversification of the female labor market, employers' changing expectations and requirements, and the impact of revolutionary political movements have undermined both the social legitimacy and structural conditions for "traditional" domestic service, providing female domestic workers with greater opportunities for autonomy.[22] The study of continuity and change in the social relations of domestic service has proven to be an important avenue for investigating broader issues of race, class, and gender relations in Latin America from both historical and social science perspectives.[23]

The pioneering work of Chaney and Castro spurred a new generation of social science research on Latin American domestic workers in the 1990s, producing a wave of studies and scholarly activism on subjects as diverse as labor legislation, political identity, cultural representation, race/ethnicity and class relations, women's movements, and transnational migration.[24] As research studies of gender and sexuality, informal labor, and global care chains expanded in the early 2000s, so too did investigations and linked activism on domestic workers and "care work" in Latin America and across the globe.[25] In the current moment, led by US and Latin American scholars primarily in the fields of sociology, anthropology, and political science—but with the continuing participation of early pioneers such as María García Castro and Mary Goldsmith—researchers in this field have established the RITHAL research network (Red de Investigaciones sobre el Trabajo del Hogar en América Latina or Network of Research on Domestic Work in Latin America). RITHAL's growing scholarly network, publication archives, and conference activities testify to the relevance of the domestic and care work research agenda for scientific inquiry as well as feminist scholarly activism in contemporary society.[26]

Existing scholarship on *Chilean* domestic service, by comparison, has been both temporally and conceptually limited until fairly recently. As elsewhere in Latin America, information about Chilean domestic service burst into public spaces because of the commitments and labor of both activists and middle-class feminists, producing a range of ethnographic, testimonial, and economic publications about domestic service conditions in the 1980s. These studies condemned domestic service as a manifestation of sexual, ethnic, and class subordination. While this left us with a rich and diverse record of working conditions and mobilization of domestic workers in that period, the research tended to assume a static view of the occupation—and solely of the women employed in it—across time. As advocacy, this scholarship served its purpose, sustaining feminist scholars' emerging solidarities with domestic workers' associations, but was more limited in advancing our understanding the central role domestic workers have played in Chilean society. Since the 1990s, Chilean social scientists have returned to the study of women's labor with a sustained focus on Andean and Caribbean immigrants employed in the domestic service sector.[27]

Studies of domestic service in Latin America, a subject that became increasingly relevant in the expansion of feminist history and social science literature of the 1980s, have argued that service occupations are the most important sectors of female economic activity in the modern period, making it a quintessential form of "women's work," and one that sustains a gendered division of labor even as modern economies incorporate other women into other forms of industrial and service labor. To a greater degree than other service and industrial occupations, scholars argued, domestic service has been ruled more by social custom than by the labor relations constructed throughout the region in the early twentieth century. More recently, the burgeoning social science literature on global migration and domestic service has exploded national boundaries and emphasized the importance of migration—both internal and international—in the domestic service employment sector. Focusing largely on cases of massive flows of female migrants from underdeveloped to developed economies in the late twentieth century (such as the Philippines to Italy, or Ecuador to Spain), Rhacel Parreñas and others have effectively refocused and reenergized the comparative study of domestic service, positing the framework of "global care work" to emphasize the interdependence of global economies through the cleaning, cooking, babysitting, and other care work performed by migrant women.[28] Along with recent studies of protective legislation debated in Latin American polities as well as international nongovernment bodies, these studies also explore the contested definition of domestic workers' labor, socioeconomic status, and political rights.[29] *Workers Like All the Rest of Them* builds on this interdisciplinary, activist, social science scholarship, taking a century-long and national-level approach to similar questions regarding the construction of domestic workers as legal and political subjects.

Arguments about Domestic Workers in Chile

Workers Like All the Rest of Them not only restores domestic workers and their agency to the history of Chile: it also makes a series of arguments that should change how we think about the origins of social inequality, the nature of reproductive labor, the role of the Catholic Church, and women's political participation in twentieth-century Chile. One of the most exciting results of the historical approach I take in this book is that it forces us to rethink common assumptions about domestic service in Latin America. As I discussed in the introduction, domestic workers—past and present—have regularly been deployed in service of traditionalist narratives to normalize and justify persistent racial and ethnic hierarchies. Likewise, self-styled advocates for domestic workers rely on a variety of rhetorical strategies—legislative, political, and religious—to press for changes intended to uplift and protect domestic workers from unscrupulous employers. What both these approaches have in common is their reliance on distorted and teleological notions of the past, in which domestic service—portrayed as yet another symptom of European conquest of the Americas and the fixed racial and gender orders it imposed—persists despite the rise of liberal nation-states as a persistent legacy of colonialism and social inequality. However appealing this underlying narrative, *Workers Like All the Rest of Them* shows that these workers, as well as the measures they promoted to defend their work and their trade, encountered obstacles that were *not* colonial in origin, nor were they structured through fixed and ahistorical categories of personhood. Rather than inhabiting a timeless and oppressed social category, domestic workers chose jobs and employers under historically changing conditions, and did so from subject positions that included male and female, rural and urban origins, indigenous and mestizo identities. Their stories, including the abuses and barriers they faced and the victories they won, challenge dominant narratives about Chilean domestic service as a timeless form of women's work and subjugation.

The second major finding of this study is that, when we restore domestic workers to Chilean history, we also challenge their legal and political erasure from the history of workers' rights, recognizing empleados' agency and participation in the political struggles of their day. As in much of Latin America, throughout the twentieth century women's domestic service labor remained critical to both the reproductive work of Chilean households and the economic survival of poor families, particularly in the rural sector. By placing this service sector, indispensable for the operation of Chilean households as well as the economic survival of working-class families, at the center of Chile's national history, this work pushes the conceptual boundaries of both women's and labor history, and offers a critical rereading of Chilean labor relations and political discourse from the point of view of those historically left out of national narratives. This reading challenges the much-vaunted history of Chilean modernization—and implied exceptionalism—that was effectuated through this and other exclusions (of rural workers, for example) from state oversight and welfare benefits. Chilean discourse on the status of domestic workers—evident in legislative debates, social work studies, union demands, and priestly declarations—illustrates the androcentric and class boundaries of democratic citizenship, demarcating class, ethnic, and gender identities that provided a steady supply of cheap reproductive labor—and working-class "care"—to more affluent households in Chile throughout the twentieth century. The unlikely mobilization of domestic workers in this same period, particularly in alliance with the Catholic Church, challenges liberal and Marxist historiography alike. Centering domestic workers in the history of Chilean labor disrupts the orthodox binaries of public-private, skilled-unskilled, and productive-reproductive labor that have for too long dominated histories of organized labor and obscured the role of service workers in the history of Chilean class relations.

Despite this worker-centered approach, *Workers Like All the Rest of Them* also tells a third story—about the nature of the state in modern Chile—informed by recent histories of social welfare, middle classes, and professions in Latin America. In their struggles for social and legal recognition, domestic worker activists made a series of strategic alliances with key social and political groups, which earned them material, ideological, and political benefits. Responsive to these demands, as well as independent motivations rooted in socialism, social Catholicism, and transnational professional norms, Chile's doctors, labor inspectors, and social workers—many of them employed in the expanding services of the Chilean welfare state—rendered domestic workers *visible* through studies that assiduously documented their working conditions and challenges. Mobilized domestic workers in turn lobbied these state allies, demanding labor protections and social services, a journey that began in the 1920s with persistent outreach to state officials and the executive, continued through the extraordinary activism and outreach sponsored by the Catholic Church in the 1950s, and culminated in campaigns for new labor legislation under the socialist coalition government of Popular Unity in the 1970s. The subsequent reversals in public and government support for domestic workers' labor rights under the military regime were hardly specific to this occupational sector, but they did reinvigorate traditional representations of servant-employer relations, perhaps strengthening the post-transition demand for subservient, informal domestic labor from non-Chileans in the 1990s. Thus workers in this trade came full circle over the course of the twentieth century, first struggling openly against informality in the 1920s, only to return in the 1990s to a struggle to maintain labor rights finally recognized in the early 1990s for all "workers in private homes."

A fourth set of conclusions arrived at in this study are centrally concerned with the ways that gender and sexuality shaped both the working conditions and the workforce of empleados over time. Although in recent decades domestic service has become a global women's occupation, it has not always been so. As the history of early domestic workers' associations reveals, men's withdrawal from "domestic service" tells a critical story of how—as male labor of all kinds was codified, protected, and politicized—domestic service persisted as a cheap and docile labor force ("domesticated"), because by the 1940s, rural indigenous and mestiza women became its most important demographic. The long view of Chilean domestic service movements therefore also reveals the importance of both men and women domestic workers as subjects, and examines of their connection to a variety of service occupations performed both within and outside of domestic spaces. In the broader literature on global domestic service, male domestic labor has been studied in the many specific cases where men and boys have dominated particular occupations, such as Chinese immigrant workers in nineteenth-century California or African houseboys in colonial Tanzania,[30] but too rarely have scholars examined male and female domestic service together and across time, subjecting the changing sexual division of labor in this trade to historical scrutiny. Domestic service was also a significant employer of Chilean men in the early decades of the twentieth century—almost 19,000 were employed in 1907 as gardeners, chauffeurs, and valets—but by the 1940s most men in these service jobs were no longer considered empleados domésticos, but rather independent contractors with their own rights and unions. In spite of their fewer numbers, Chile's male domestic workers dominated associations in their trade until the 1940s, at which point servants' associations were increasingly defined as all-female, a transformation evident in the all-female composition of domestic workers' associations by the 1950s. To accept the classification of domestic service as "women's work" is to erase conceptually, and thus historically, the participation of men in an arena that has so crucially structured class and ethnic relations in Chile. Chapters 2 and 3 examine the shifting gender composition of domestics' associations in the 1940s and '50s, emphasizing the role of the Catholic Church in affirming the feminine and subservient nature of the occupation.

"The Servant Crisis" and Domestic Worker Mobilization

When we turn to the question of the struggle for domestic workers' rights as such, a goal that would take almost a century to obtain in any form, we can trace the origins of domestic workers' movements to the tumultuous first two decades of the twentieth century. At that juncture a variety of short-and long-term changes in Chilean economic and political organization converged to disrupt many of the basic terms of "traditional" Chilean class, ethnic, and gender relations. From the late nineteenth century, which saw the end of military struggle with indigenous forces on the nation's southern border as well as a brief civil war sparked by irreconcilable political conflict between conservative and liberal forces of the Chilean elite, Chile entered the new century in the midst of significant economic and demographic changes, spurring rural-urban migration and urbanization, expansion and consolidation of labor organizations, a shift of Catholic Church leadership toward greater pastoral and social Catholic activities, and an increasing rhythm of legislative proposals designed to address the "social question." Chile's 1910 *centenario* was marked by increasing levels of change, conflict, and possibility, particularly for the nation's rural and working-class citizens. In the midst of these changes, of course, was *la sirvienta*, at once providing crucial caring labor for the reproduction of elite families, and symbolizing the traditional aristocratic households that would become less prevalent as the century progressed. By looking at how a variety of social actors—from elite employers to Catholic observers and labor activists—weighed in on "the servant crisis" and "the social question" in that period, we can better understand the origins of ideological formations and social movements that would endure and evolve over the course of the century.[31]

In the years following the turn of the century, and like their counterparts in Europe and the United States, employers found a ready forum for their discontent about their servants, airing their concerns about the "servant crisis" and servant misbehavior in Santiago newspapers.[32] Complaints ranged from bad attitude to theft, and frequently described an idyllic past in which an abundance of servants had worked with loyalty and energy without complaint. In an advice column to young housekeepers, one contributor to *El Porvenir* lamented the "general breakdown of the servant class, which is a calamity for the home"; in days gone by, she wrote, servants earned just three (rather than the current twenty) pesos per month and "there were some great empleadas, the kind who last forever and end up as members of the family."[33] Several contributors complained about their servants' preference for the term empleada or *joven* (young woman) over sirviente, leading one patrona to admonish: "In my humble opinion, I don't see any way to make these good people understand that it is not degrading to be a servant. If it's degrading to serve, well, we all serve *someone*."[34] Another employer blamed the growth of industry for the shrinking number of servants and their "exaggerated demands": "The factories, and workshops of all kinds have been consuming, slowly but in large numbers, the working hands (*brazos*) who were employed in managing brooms and operating stoves."[35]

In short, employer complaints abounded, prompting some Catholic ladies to engage in efforts to organize and (re)train women for domestic service. One of the first mentions of any form of collective organization for domestic workers, in fact, appeared in the popular press in 1914, which reported with some sarcasm on the existence of a society of domestic servants founded in 1907 by a group of elite women, whose over 600 members "listen to moral lectures intended to make them love their [social] condition." According to this account, in addition to teaching domestic education and founding an asylum for aging servants ("Asilo de la Casa de Purisima"), the talks to empleadas focused on persuading the society's members that industrial jobs were even worse than the ones they held in private homes: "They are told about the real advantages of their situation over that of women working in the factories, exposed to illnesses and without secure positions, and they are prudently warned against the dangers that can face them if they work in bad homes."[36] One letter that appeared in another popular daily complained that domestic servants in Valparaíso were organizing a strike for higher salaries, an event that was recorded nowhere else: "Cooks, laundresses, wetnurses and nannies, etc. etc., are working actively to cause a general strike among the domestic workers, in order to obtain through bad methods the salaries they say they have not been able to get by just working hard."[37] Articles published in the early workers' press also articulated a kind of normative paternalism, entreating employers to voluntarily treat their workers better; in return, servants were responsible for respecting their employers, serving them well, and resisting the temptation to gossip about former employers.[38]

Some observers of the servant crisis focused their attention—both positive and negative—on the vocational schools for girls operating in Chile after the turn of the century. Established in the 1880s by industrialists and educators seeking to improve the female workforce and enhance honorable and domestic options, the Girls' Professional Schools (Escuelas Profesionales de Niñas) offered courses in sewing, clothing design, cooking, hat-making, and other industrial skills to thousands of Chilean working-class women.[39] Some argued that creating vocational schools specifically for servants would raise the prestige of the occupation

FIGURE I.I. Sasso Oil advertisement, Zig-Zag, 1913

and allow "the ladies of the people to feel a great and enviable calling for personal service as hand-servants, to scrub the cutlery and clean the soot from the stove pipe."[40] But another, particularly vitriolic contributor attributed the shortage of servants to the heightened social expectations created by female education, both academic and vocational. Some women who learned sewing (or any one of fifty useless trades) in an industrial school, wrote "X.," then believed themselves to be above domestic service, while those who learned other subjects became critical of their social condition: "instead of learning practical things and the habits of order and cleanliness, we teach them a little bit of history, another bit of political constitution, the basics of geography and science, and a collection of meaningless things that only serve to distract them from the truth about their social condition."[41] A later contributor on this theme agreed, arguing that there were plenty of Chileans willing and needing to work as servants, but "now it's time for the Republic to regenerate and moralize them, and they all prefer to be citizens and not servants. What's to be done?"[42] Not only did such education undermine the availability of domestic workers, it also threatened the very existence of Chilean cuisine: "We could even lose the recipe for homemade *charquicán*—which just like the traditional chicken soup is already a relic—but on the other hand even the *china* from Curacaví knows her second-grade equations and that it is illegal to assault a public official."[43] Another commentator responded to the suggestion that servants would be more abundant and better trained if the government were to create specific vocational schools for them, arguing that this was impractical, however, as one unintended result of improved industrial training had already been to raise clothing and hat prices in Santiago.[44]

Other voices calling for change, however, focused on the behavior of employers. Citing minimum wage and working conditions legislated in the United States, one article in the daily press argued that although "the problem of domestic service" was caused by socialism, which sowed class hatred between servants and their employers, the state should intervene to regulate the trade, and female employers should rescue girls from dangerous factory jobs and provide safe, dignified domestic service jobs that would train them to run working-class homes. Invoking a paternalistic approach, this writer called on patronas to humanize the servant-employer relationship: "The young servants are at great risk. Their masters (*amos*) have to be not only their counsellors, but also their protectors. . . . The fact is that there are many masters who think they've done well when they pay exactly the right salary to their criados. The mistaken idea persists: that a servant is a machine for serving, and the boss is a machine for paying."[45] The same author, writing for a different newspaper, went on to clarify the role of the state: "The State should take good care of this social class, investigating their complaints with care and finding the solution to their problems" through labor laws and regulation of employment agencies.[46] But in both cases the author stressed that the responsibility for reversing the servant crisis—and rescuing women from factory work—lay with the proper conduct of the patrona, whose maternal oversight should ensure the good morals and proper education of the criada. It was not unusual for some, presumably male, writers on the servant crisis to call on patronas or their daughters to take up some of the housework and childcare created by the lack of available servants, and like their counterparts in the US and France, simply make do with less servant help overall.[47]

One of the most visible arenas where the servant crisis played out was in the Catholic, private, and state employment agencies that proliferated in early twentieth-century Santiago.[48] In June 1925, for example, the employment agency run by the Catholic Women's Unions (Sindicatos Católicos Femininos) detailed the agency's activity from January to May in three placement areas: sales and office workers, domestic servants, and industrial workers. Noting that commercial and office labor was at that point not regulated by the Labor Office, and that placement rates for *obreras* had been very low, the report shows the most activity in their work with "the servant class" (*la servidumbre*), where hundreds of monthly inscriptions resulted in modest placement of 52 to 128 women in domestic jobs each month. The agency matched women with prospective employers as cooks, personal servants, dining servants, washerwomen, errand girls, cleaners, servers, wet nurses, and nannies, and reported great success placing cooks and servers.[49] From this report we see that the agency was used more by women seeking work than by employers (308–470 worker registrations versus 79–199 requests for workers), and that women seeking work as general housemaids were less likely to find work than their more specialized counterparts. Significantly, in later decades (and as state regulation of private agencies increased) the Labor Office ran its own placement agency in Santiago, advertising in local papers the need for cooks, personal servants, and serving and specialized empleadas.[50]

Plenty of conversations about employment agencies, however, focused on their criminal activities: agents provided employers with false references and then tipped off thieves who were planning their next robbery. In a news article complaining about the "false servant class," P.P.H. described empleadas' strategy for deceiving unsuspecting employers: "Even in cases where they provide useful and valuable information, as when the household has valuable objects, the empleada who started by gaining the trust and respect of her bosses is quickly transformed into a diseased, unruly, and crude person, until she is fired and starts all over again, making new inquiries on behalf of the individual or gang that she serves." Further, the author argued, police and city officials had failed to regulate the agencies: "From the aristocratic Ladies' Club to the modest group of San Pablo, there are hundreds of agencies who earn 200–300 pesos every day, operating without responsibility or any kind of sanction."[51] Much later, after domestic workers had begun to form their own associations, they too would protest the existence of employment agencies that served only to assist crime and besmirch empleados' honor: domestic workers' union minutes from 1939 record that: "It was agreed, next, that the group should declare publicly to the heads of households, in response to some reports about an empleada who did her work only to steal, that we are in a position to offer people trained for service, and to whose honor our institution—which has been a legal organization for thirteen years—will attest."[52]

Quite another story of the domestic servant "crisis" emerged in the workers' press at the turn of the twentieth century. Despite the exclusion of female domestic workers from women's earliest mutual aid associations in the 1880s, domestic workers did appear with some frequency in some of Chile's labor publications, where characterizations of domestic workers ranged from symbols of the embodied (and sexual) nature of capitalist exploitation to actual complaints brought forth by domestic servants. In the newspapers of the Democratic Party—Chile's first workers' party, founded in the 1880s—domestic workers were enjoined to form their own associations and struggle alongside other workers in order to achieve their basic rights. Significantly, these accounts addressed both male and female domestic workers. In one particularly passionate argument in 1907, Francisco J. Zuñiga Reyes called for domestic workers to organize in the face of their evident, brutal enslavement. Citing a recent example of an employer beating in public the nanny who had who had served him for nineteen years, Zuñiga cited the example of an Argentine domestic workers' association and wrote that "it is long past time that we should pay attention to our colleagues, disgraced like us, to establish a resistance society, if possible, and make these high-class 'heroes' of the golden spoon understand that they are not masters of any servants, but rather employers of their workers."[53] Responding to an *Ilustrado* article on "rotos y chinos"—derogatory terms for working class men and women—a writer for another democratic paper urged male domestic workers to shed the old ways of compliant servitude in Chilean society, and to struggle for their rights as men: "you slackers, fight against your status as vassals, because you are men, men who may have more rights than we editors to live and subsist, because with your sweat you earn those rights for yourselves, you drones!"[54] In the labor press of the era, male domestic workers appeared as symbols of capitalist exploitation and icons of worker struggle, a pattern that would continue to mark mixed-sex unionization in the 1920s and '30s in Chile.

The virility of male domestic workers was also evident in other articles that protested men's low salaries in the domestic service sector. In June 1907, one Democratic Party newspaper reported the low salaries of domestic workers employed by the State Rail Company: "The comrade we're talking about, who has been in his position for sixteen years, now earns the miserable salary of twenty-four pesos per month." Asking the government to reduce the high salaries of railway managers, the newspaper asked for "a little more compassion from the gentlemen managers toward those poor slaves . . . and pay them—even if it's just to overcome hunger—what the domestic workers of the State Railways should earn for their work." This demand for a man's rightful wages was bolstered by the fact that the individual in question worked not in a private home but alongside other men, manual laborers in the railway system.[55]

For the socialist and even the daily press, the plight of the wet nurse also served to illustrate in graphic terms the exploitation of the proletariat. Starting with the figure of the bad bourgeoise mother, who "seeks for her 'blue blood' child, of 'aristocratic blood,' the services of a wet nurse with worker's blood, plebeian blood," the proletarian wet nurse was forced to deprive her own children not only of her milk but also of her love and attention. Bourgeois children, a socialist writer asserted, who are raised on wet nurse's milk are conditioned from this early age to live off the lifeblood of poor people: "The bourgeois gentlemen are born and need milk to survive, workers' blood; they grow up, and to keep on living, they suck, exploiting them, the blood of the workers."[56] Other stories in the labor press repeated this refrain, describing the dire consequences of the death of a wet nurse's child at the hands of the "third mother," the relative or neighbor who cared for empleada's children while she labored.[57] Through stories of extreme physical and emotional exploitation of wet nurses and nannies, labor journalists dramatized the effects of capitalist exploitation. Like contemporaneous accounts directed at women workers and prostitutes, the anarchist press also analyzed domestic service as a site of female sexual exploitation, extending the mantle of radical solidarity to this group of non-workers (the mothers and sisters of the "real workers").[58]

In another example, on May Day 1921, *Acción Directa* published a "Manifesto for our domestic service comrades," listing the many evils of servant-master relations: wet nurses sacrificing the milk meant for their own babies, older servants thrown out on the street, and the haughty condescension of masters (especially women) that included punishing servants for small mistakes, verbal abuse, and withholding servants' pay. Characteristically, compared to labor movement texts about women industrial workers in this period, this "manifiesto" also emphasized servants' sexual exploitation: "The woman's love in your heart does not even belong to you: you have to settle, many of you, for sometimes serving as mere instruments of lust and at other times, brothel slaves subject to the whims of the '*señorito*.' You have to suffer all of it!" The article ends with a call for domestic workers' organization, emphasizing the support offered by working-class men:

Comrades (*compañeras*): lift your heads, bare your breasts, dignify your sex. We men will be at your side, we who struggle to destroy the evil castle of so much tyranny. We are your brothers and we want you to be free, honorable comrades of men, since you are loving mothers, wives, daughters, girlfriends. . . . Get together, comrades, in one big family, to defend yourselves from the feline claws of your mistresses.[59]

In another call for female domestic workers to organize, a 1922 article told the story of Carmen Vargas, a real-life recent rural migrant who found work in a boardinghouse in downtown Santiago. After suffering the employer's verbal and physical abuse, and her sister having failed to gain her release from the house, Carmen escaped to a neighbor's house via the roof: "This true story is the story of almost all the empleadas. And as long as they don't change their attitudes they will suffer the same treatment. The only thing that can save them is forming an association."[60]

Despite the widely disparate diagnoses of the "servant problem" in early twentieth-century Chile—differences hewed along lines of class as well as ideology and religion—what these views collectively demonstrate is that the "servant," male and female alike, had become a controversial public figure. In ways consistent with contemporaneous views on "the social question," Chilean observers of domestic service subjected workers to instructions (be more compliant/rebellious), warnings (your manhood/maternity are in danger), disrespect (your occupation is criminal/passive), and encouragement (find good employers/throw off your chains). These discussions also presaged the competing assessments of domestic workers in the context of Chile's twentieth-century welfare state, labor movements, and political parties, predicting with a high degree of accuracy how these workers would be addressed, cultivated, and cajoled in a variety of social roles.

CHAPTER 2

Fighting Exclusion

Domestic Workers and Their Allies Demand Labor Legislation, 1923–1945

In 1924 we asked the honorable Congress . . . to grant and recognize suffrage for our trade: but the legislators of that time did not concern themselves with a petition brought by the same empleados who kept their houses clean, watched over their property, and sometimes risked our lives to defend them. We needed a savior, a revolutionary movement that would argue our just cause to end the constitutional ban on our suffrage, which was a stigma, a disgrace that humiliated our trade, considering the level of education, culture and progress that we are fortunate to possess.

—Domestic Workers Union President Lucas Salas,
1930 interview

How much more can I take, I ask myself? How long will I let them 'sploit (*que me speloten*) and exploit me? They don't make my social security payments or give me a day off, and they've even had the police after me.

—Ana González as "La Desideria," on Radiotanda's
Cinderella, circa 1940

ONE OF THE MOST persistent disputes over domestic work in Latin America over the course of the twentieth century concerned the status of paid domestic workers in national labor legislation. Chile was not unique in explicitly excluding workers in domestic service from early labor legislation, which was designed primarily to address the contentious relations between labor and capital in Chile's growing industrial sector.[1] Mired in the "traditional" and paternalistic relations of the home, domestic service was considered a private, quasi-familial relationship where the state should not intrude. The political transitions that marked Chile's early decades—from the Parliamentary Republic to military rule in 1924, and thereafter to civilian regimes driven by liberal, populist, and authoritarian agendas—reflect the political conditions that shaped labor relations and the emerging welfare state. Even as legislators reacted primarily to the "labor problem" they associated with the political mobilization of male industrial workers, however, empleados domésticos continuously lobbied for greater regulation of their work, demanding changes that would fully incorporate them into Chile's "family of labor." Whether it was Lucas Salas, rationally justifying the demands of domestic workers to a journalist in 1930,[2] or the radio personality "La Desideria," laughing with her audience about her employers' utter disregard for her right to social security,[3] the state's failure to protect and provide for Chile's most ubiquitous and vulnerable workers was a consistent theme in public discourse in the early decades of the twentieth century.

Chile's first labor regimes categorically excluded domestic workers from the fundamental protections it extended to other workers in 1924, such as the right to make contracts, unionize, limit the workday, take maternity leave, and earn a minimum wage. Even the 1931 Labor Code, which addressed domestic service labor through a special article requiring employers to sign contracts with their domestic employees, largely failed to recognize and regulate domestic workers' rights in the workplace. But even as the state excluded empleados domésticos from Chilean labor law, they included them—in their status as salaried workers—in its nascent social welfare system: the 1924 Social Security Law included paid domestic workers, granting them access to the maternity and child health services of state-run health clinics. As Chilean law increasingly recognized and regulated domestic service over time, it also inaugurated the state's persistent tendency to address those workers through separate laws and regulations, rather than reversing their exclusion from existing law.

This chapter examines how state officials, employers, and domestic workers engaged in debates over whether and how domestic service should be subject to state regulation in early-to-mid-twentieth-century Chile. Regularly excluded from emerging workers' associations in the late nineteenth century, the men and women employed in paid domestic work had by the 1920s begun to organize collectively and protest their working conditions in newspaper articles and petitions to parliamentary representatives. Most of this activism stemmed from the Sindicato Autónomo de Empleados de Casas Particulares de Ambos Sexos

(Independent Union of Household Employees of Both Sexes), a small union founded in Santiago in 1926 to petition legislators, labor inspectors, state health officials and journalists for greater regulation of their trade. The union addressed petitions to parliament and the Ministry of Labor; sent representatives to workers' congresses; documented cases of employer abuse; donated funds for other striking workers; and pursued cultural and social activities to strengthen their association. Arguing that empleados domésticos should be treated like other workers and recognized in labor law, activists also emphasized the super-exploitation of women and children in their trade.

Another important characteristic of these early efforts was the attention paid to empleados domésticos by journalists and state officials, many of whom regularly protested the injustice of denying to domestic workers the benefits afforded other workers by the state. As early as 1918, a newspaper editorial commented on the 1907 Sunday Rest Law, then under renewed discussion in Congress because it severely restricted male workers' holiday rights, protesting the fact that "the law's prescriptions do not apply to domestic service."[4] Officials from the Ministries of Labor and Social Welfare, in particular, focused increasing attention on the unjust exclusion of both domestic workers and peasants from protective legislation, arguing that, as workers who paid into state welfare accounts, empleados domésticos and peasants should also be protected by the country's labor laws. Finally, domestic service activists—through associations led early in the twentieth century exclusively by men—fought their wholesale exclusion from labor law by stressing the nature of domestic labor as skilled, salaried work, portraying empleados domésticos as "workers like all the rest of them."

This chapter describes when and how domestic workers struggled for attention to their status, analyzing how and with what success activists and their allies sought to remedy their exclusion from labor laws. Their efforts led to extended debates in parliament on a number of specific remedies, ultimately shaping the 1925 decree-laws that still excluded domestic workers from labor regulations but granted them status as salaried workers covered by state health insurance. Complaining that the unregulated status of domestic service in the 1925 legislation exposed them to employer abuse, domestic worker activists organized their first labor union in 1926 and got to work lobbying the press, labor and welfare officials, and politicians from the legislative and executive branches. While this activism undoubtedly shaped the articles on domestic service included in the 1931 Labor Code, which granted domestic workers some of the rights enjoyed by other workers (such as contracts, rest periods, and vacation pay), the lack of regulatory legislation made the article essentially a dead letter, while a narrow legal definition of "domestic employee" restricted protections to live-in, full-time domestic workers. Even in success, therefore, domestic workers' activism in the first decades of the twentieth century were both predicated upon and limited by the sharp distinctions drawn between domestic and other forms of wage labor. Activists and legislators alike stressed the uniquely exploitative conditions that prevailed in domestic service—particularly for women—promoting greater legal protections with arguments referencing the need for human dignity, the vulnerability of domestic workers, and the rights of citizenship. While legislators were clearly motivated by the distinctively intimate nature of domestic service relations—broadly referenced as *convivencia*—their repeated construction of domestic service as a family affair fundamentally constrained their legislative proposals, resulting in the 1931 creation of a separate legal code for domestic service protections that would remain in place for over half a century.[5]

Challenging Legal Regimes of Exclusion

Rooted in the slave and free labor regimes of the early Republic, domestic workers and rural day laborers remained, almost by definition, outside of the bounds of liberal citizenship and labor relations. Whereas the late nineteenth and early twentieth centuries saw the emergence of new coalitions between organized labor (primarily in the transport, industrial, and export industries) with leaders of new associations and political parties dedicated to the rights of workers, some categories of work—and workers—were not legible as such within emerging regimes and discourses of wage labor. Legislators and labor leaders alike were, in Chile as elsewhere across the globe, preoccupied with the revolutionary potential of industrial labor, the motor of economic modernization as well as political transformation. Dominant conceptions of domestic and rural labor as subservient and degrading—even when it was performed for wages—contributed to the continuing marginalization of domestic workers and peasants from early-twentieth-century debates about social legislation. Even the most liberal legislative proposals, such as President Arturo Alessandri's 1921 Project for Labor and Social Welfare Codes, excluded empleados domésticos from labor contracts, accident protection, and other proposed laws for Chilean workers.[6]

Frustrated by this continued exclusion, Chilean domestic workers during the 1920s increasingly demanded that their trade be incorporated into labor law, bringing evidence of employer abuses to the attention of responsive members of the media, Labor Office, and political parties. Using language and strategies typical of organized labor in this period, domestic worker activists went on to

lobby Congress and shape the content of a series of important legislative proposals between 1923 and 1931.[7] The first evidence of this activism was a 1923 letter
presented to Congress by members of "The Society for the Future of Household
Employees" (La Sociedad el Porvenir de Empleados de Casas Particulares), in
which activists from this patriotic trade association petitioned legislators to extend suffrage rights to male empleados and regulate domestic service relations.[8]
Although the mixed-sex union was led by men, the petition foregrounded the
exploitation of female domestic workers, arguing that domestic service work
put wives and mothers in particularly grave physical and moral danger. In this
respect, the Society's petition mirrored trends evident in the trajectory of protective legislation in Chile at the time, when observers across the social and political spectrum argued that the state should protect women's reproductive and
moral well-being in the workplace rather than the rights of all workers.[9] From
the petition's very prologue, which argued that "Domestic service labor should
be dignified by our political leaders, as a way to avoid begging, prostitution rings,
etc.," the petitioners reasoned that women's reproductive capacities and family
responsibilities had already been compromised by the state's failure to curb the
exploitation of women through domestic service. They argued, for example, that
work that endangered women's reproductive health—such as cleaning stairs and
windows, or waxing floors—should be prohibited in order to protect motherhood and *la raza* (the Chilean race). Echoing arguments made about female industrial labor, the petition argued that women's work hours in domestic service
should be contractually limited, allowing women to care for their own children,
attend night school, and form their own families, "which would prevent prostitution and illegitimacy." In a rare reference to the prevalence of sexual abuse
of female domestic workers, the letter also demanded that women domestic
workers be allowed to investigate the paternity of their illegitimate children.
The petition closed with demands for severance pay indexed to years of service,
the creation of a unit within the Labor Office charged with implementing the
proposed reforms, and effective suffrage for domestic workers, "equal in condition to the rest of the citizens of the Republic."[10] Activists also emphasized that
they preferred the term "workers in private homes" (empleados de casas particulares) over "domestic workers" (empleados domésticos), and called on both men
and women to join their Society and "ask for our legitimate rights as citizens."[11]
Unsuccessful in their immediate efforts to provoke legislative reform, the Society's efforts were criticized by other labor organizers, who argued that domestic
workers' rights would not be achieved by petitioning the Congress but rather by
joining a broader revolutionary movement.[12]

Speaking to journalists in 1930, activists retrospectively blamed legislators for the failure of the 1923 petition, which caused empleados to turn instead to building alliances with other unions and throw their support to the military leaders of the 1924 and 1925 revolutions. Because legislators had refused to act on their behalf, union president Lucas Salas reported, empleados domésticos had gone on to build stronger alliances with other unions and threw their support to the military leaders of the 1924 and 1925 "revolutions." The military regime quickly decreed seven labor laws, including laws on contracts, strikes, unionization, accidents, minimum wages, and work hours. For women employed in industry and commerce, like their male counterparts, the military decree-laws represented a dramatic shift in the mechanisms of available assistance and redress, particularly if they organized in legal unions that were entitled to arbitration through the Labor Office. But domestic workers were again excluded, as were the specific social concerns of female empleadas: as union secretary Mercedes Céspedes explained, paternity investigations were still needed to protect single mothers "and prevent women from looking for ways to abort their children because of ignorant prejudices that exist today, or from being pushed into prostitution by rape and other factors."[13]

Rather than protective laws, the single most important change for domestic workers stemming from the 1924 military intervention came in the form of the military's Social Security Law (4054), which granted state subsidies for illness, maternity, disability, and old age for workers in all trades, including two months' paid maternity leave and other benefits for pregnant *industrial* workers. Excluded from the other provisions of the sweeping 1924 legislation (such as obligatory contracts and the eight-hour day), domestic workers were limited to receiving medical and social assistance through the Caja de Seguro Obligatorio (CSO or Obligatory Insurance Fund), support that pregnant empleadas would rely on heavily in subsequent decades. The CSO provided pregnant women with prenatal and postpartum care, including a stipend equivalent to 50 percent salary for three weeks following the birth of a child, and 25 percent subsidy until the child was weaned.[14] However, pregnant domestic workers did not enjoy the broader benefits granted by the 1924 Labor Code to women employed in industry and commerce, such as longer paid maternity leave, or breastfeeding and child-care provisions.[15]

Despite military leaders' failure to respond to domestic workers' concerns, one of the more important effects of the new social security system they imposed was the provision mandating employer contributions to workers' insurance. Although this law empowered the Labor Office to determine the amounts that all workers and employers should contribute, this process that posed specific challenges in an unregulated, private labor relation like domestic service. Because domestic workers often lived in employers' homes and received partial payment in the form of food and housing, these contributions were calculated on the basis of salary plus the cost of food and housing (*regalia*), the latter estimated by the Labor Office in accordance with local salaries and expenses. While data for the twenties and thirties are not available, in 1941 the social security contributions for domestic employees and their employers throughout Chile were set at 2 percent for employees and 5 percent for employers, except for the nitrate regions, where employees paid 3 percent and employers 6 percent.[16] CSO inspectors could charge employers who failed to make payments 20 pesos for the first infraction and 100 pesos for the second, but despite these fines, many domestic workers never demanded or received the insurance payments to which they were entitled by law.

According to newspaper accounts, oral histories, and ministerial records, the savings book (*libreta*) for recording these insurance payments became one of the principle sites of struggle between employers and their domestic workers, many of whom worked for decades without receiving social security. The 4054 law establishing social security was important enough, and employers' failure to pay it so commonplace, that it also appeared thereafter as a trope in Chilean dramatic renderings of domestic service relations. One of the most famous empleadas in Chilean popular culture was "La Desideria," a comedic personality popular on radio and television in the 1940s. A caricature of a feisty, assertive, unrefined working-class woman, La Desideria was known for her constant complaining about her employers' failure to pay her libreta. Ana González Olea (1915–2008), the national prize-winning actress who played La Desideria on radio and television for over fifty years, also repeatedly deployed her celebrity to speak out for domestic workers' rights.[17] In another example, Fernando Debesa's 1954 play *Mama Rosa,* which portrayed the life of several generations of an oligarchic Chilean family from 1906 to 1950, was driven by tensions over the meanings of domestic service in a rapidly changing world. In a scene between the adult daughter of the household, Leonor, and Mama Rosa, the aging servant declares that times have changed for domestic workers, invoking the recent Law 4054 as evidence that she will enjoy social security in her retirement. However, calling social security "so many buildings and people, just so you can get an aspirin or a bicarbonate of soda," Debesa's tragic figure clings fervently to old ways of life-long service, ending up a senile and penniless dependent on the family's private charity.[18] Significantly, although they employed very different media, González and Debesa each centered the empleada in their criticism of Chilean social relations, acknowledging the limitations of Law 4054 as they did so.

The exclusion of empleados domésticos from the labor laws of 1924 did not prevent empleados and their employers from asking state officials to intervene in labor disputes. Responding to dozens of complaints from domestic workers that they had been denied severance pay, for example, Labor Office officials either indicated their lack of jurisdiction, sent the complainants to civil court, or in rare cases compensated workers whose employers would not pay severance fees. In several cases, employers correctly argued that the law on labor contracts "specifically excludes domestic workers from coverage by its provisions."[19] Likewise, Labor Office officials used the same reasoning to show that they could not intervene, instructing their inspectors to refer these cases instead to lower and regional courts.[20] Significantly, in most cases where employers ultimately paid severance to their empleados domésticos, workers had served their employers in places other than private homes, such as hotels, tailor shops, and laundries. According to Labor Inspector Arancibia Muñoz, "As we've noted before, the criteria accepted by the Labor Office is that those who work in these kinds of establishments are workers and not empleados domésticos. Moreover, in practice it has been confusing, since the employers in these establishments have accepted without objection the Labor Office criteria in the above sense."[21] The "confusion" referenced by Arancibia Muñoz illustrates the discursive segregation of empleados domésticos according to their place of work: as legal definitions of domestic service and workers themselves would later make explicit, empleados domésticos working in public spaces were more easily incorporated into labor relations indexed to public, industrial, wage labor than their counterparts who labored in family settings.

The status of domestic workers in Chilean law was not settled in the 1920s, either in local or international circles. Chile's Labor Office officials were certainly aware that, by the late 1920s, the International Labor Organization (ILO) had devoted some attention to the plight of domestic workers and mandated new regulations, making recommendations that would eventually shape the drafting of Chile's 1931 Labor Code.[22] According to Arancibia Muñoz, after 1927 the ILO introduced, and by 1935 Chile approved, agreements to secure welfare coverage for illness and retirement among industrial, commercial, *and* domestic workers. Debates over the application of the 1924 laws to empleados domésticos also appeared on the "Empleados y Obreros" page of *La Nación*, which published workers' questions about their labor rights. In January 1930, for example, the paper's "experts" clarified that, although domestic workers enjoyed social security, the law on severance pay did not apply to them: "The person you have served for such a long time does not owe you any payment when your employment ends. But we can hope that he realizes his *moral obligation* to reward or compensate someone who has served him so well."[23] This sentiment was apparently shared by other government officials, who lobbied the Labor Office to incorporate domestic workers into contracts: "For my part, I would be most happy to support, when the time is right, the Labor Office's proposals to include domestic workers and rural workers in Article 1 of Law 4053 (Labor Contracts), so that these servants (*servidores*) can also reap the benefits of our social laws, which I think would be just."[24] The wave of severance complaints and public debates that characterized the 1920s reflects the ambiguous status of domestic employees in the emerging labor relations system, further demonstrating continuing disagreement about the status of domestic service as "work."

Perhaps because of continuing legislative inaction on the question of regulating domestic service in the 1920s, the domestic workers' union continued to press for increased state oversight throughout the decade. After submitting their unsuccessful petition in 1923, the leaders of the Sociedad Porvenir went on in 1926 to participate in founding a new union for male and female domestic workers, the Independent Union of Household Employees of Both Sexes. This union, which in its early years boasted a membership of about 240 workers, functioned regularly with just few brief interruptions between 1926 and 1945.[25] Renamed in 1936 the Sindicato Profesional de Empleados de Casas Particulares (Professional Union of Household Employees), the group also cultivated close relations with unions of hotel workers, chauffeurs, waiters, and bus drivers and conductors, at times holding their meetings in the union halls of the bus inspectors and theater workers. These alliances stemmed from the shared trades practiced by workers in a variety of occupations that were performed in both domestic and commercial service settings—such as cooking, driving, food service, cleaning, or landscaping—which reflected how men in particular could move both in and out of occupations performed in both public and private spaces. In similar fashion, the leaders of the Professional Union of Domestic Workers frequently participated in and even led commercial service workers' unions. For example, recognizing that empleados domésticos were also employed in hotels, the Hotel Employees' Union in 1930 lobbied the legislature in support of a bill mandating minimum wage and tips for all hotel workers.[26] Domestic workers' unions also affiliated nationally with the Workers' Social Congress and the Chilean Workers' Confederation, which provided opportunities for broader alliance with workers in other trades.

At the local level, the Santiago union's activities resembled those of other unionized workers in this period, including their participation in the local newspaper's yearly beauty pageants, holding dances and parties to raise funds, and offering some courses in domestic economy and primary education as well as temporary housing for recent migrants to the capital. The union also cultivated ties with journalists, legislators, and state officials, organizing campaigns that emphasized three key issues: domestic workers' dignity (protesting cases of abuse), citizenship (advocating participation in the political process), and labor rights (i.e., extension of protections granted to other workers). Union activists tied their activities closely to Labor and CSO officials, labor media outlets, other unions, labor federations, and political parties. In some cases, activists used these alliances to draw attention to the plight of domestic workers (in particular the absence of labor protections), and in others cases to recruit membership: in mid-1936, for example, the union directorate issued a petition to leftist politicians, asking them to encourage their own empleados domésticos to join the union.[27] Likewise, union officers appealed to fellow union activists (such as the chauffeurs' union) to spread the word about their union among domestic workers, and in the late 1930s and early '40s, the union cultivated a particularly strong relationship with the Hotel Workers' Union. For these domestic worker activists, at least according to their meeting minutes and press releases, there was nothing specific to their occupation that prevented them from mobilizing politically.

The emerging union took advantage of new opportunities for exerting political influence, publishing a new petition in the Santiago daily *El Mercurio* in March 1927, demanding protection from dangerous work, time to eat during the workday, and Sunday rest: "If employers expect decency, loyalty, respect, honor, good conduct, etc., it is only humane and just that that they recognize the nature of our work and the demands of daily life."[28] These were the kinds of demands that were taken up and investigated by the lawyers and social workers employed as inspectors by the Department of the Labor Office,[29] who in early 1928 submitted a lengthy report to the Minister of Welfare in order "to answer the queries we have received about organization among male and female empleados domésticos, as well as the demands they have made." The report offered support to some of the union's requests, agreeing that domestic workers should be granted two hours off per week, allowed to unionize, bring complaints before the labor courts, and receive severance pay if fired without cause. But the report also went on to recommend against the union's request for regulation of work hours, Sunday rest, and a minimum wage, citing "current circumstances" and "the very nature of domestic service" as obstacles to regulating the trade. In other words, while some employer abuses could and should be curbed, state officials considered other aspects of domestic service relations to remain outside of the state's jurisdiction.[30]

The most significant changes in the regulation of Chilean domestic service began only in 1928, when first the House of Deputies, then a commission on social legislation convened by President Carlos Ibañez, began to study the problem. Congressional debate began in earnest when Deputy Luís Ayala delivered a scathing critique of Chilean domestic service, which he claimed ruined Chile's status as a leader in progressive social laws.[31] Citing Swiss and Austrian protective legislation as a model, Ayala introduced an elaborate legislative project for regulating domestic service in Chile, proposing articles for written contracts, union rights, better housing and treatment, nine hours' daily rest, severance pay and procedures, and Labor Office oversight. Ayala's bill would have voided nine titles of the Civil Code, including the article affirming the legal standing of an employer's word over that of the empleado doméstico, as well as the article of decree-law 4053 that excluded domestic workers from the right to make contracts.[32] Although Ayala's bill on domestic workers did not pass, it was the first of several attempts to protect empleados domésticos, and his provisions were later included in Deputy Francisco Araya's proposal to establish a minimum wage for women employed in industry, commerce, home work, and domestic service. Significantly, Araya addressed women's low salaries across industrial and domestic sectors, stressing that domestic workers in particular "generally work from seven in the morning until ten or eleven at night, and only receive scarce wages for it." Proposing that women's minimum wage be set at six pesos per day, and limiting their work day to eight hours, Araya's proposal highlighted the unequal status of women working in both industry and domestic service, but his motion died for lack of a second.[33]

For its part, the executive branch drew attention to domestic service in its comprehensive overhaul of social legislation in late 1928. Beginning its work under the Ministry of Welfare in November 1928, President Ibañez's special commission to reform social legislation criticized existing legislation (particularly Law 4053 on contracts) for failing to protect both rural and domestic workers, as well as workers in small industries. "The commission has concluded that it is not reasonable or convenient to totally exclude these workers from the law," and went on to argue that, even if some aspects of the labor code could not be applied to these occupations, "that should not stop us from including articles to address how these trades differ." Significantly, the Commission also went on to propose a broad definition of domestic service as all those employed in "private homes, hotels, boarding houses, residences, schools, and other similar establishments," a definition that would later be narrowed to cover only those domestic workers employed in private homes.[34]

Prompted by the work of that commission, Labor Office officials also contributed to discussions about regulating domestic service, presenting a preliminary proposal for domestic service laws to the Sub-committee for Union Organization and Labor Contracts in 1929. Like the Ministry of Welfare report, and notwithstanding the frequent distinction made in practice between domestic service performed in private versus public spaces, the Labor Office defined domestic service labor as that occurring not only in private homes, but also in hotels and boardinghouses, including in this way any personal services rendered to an employer. The Labor Office proposal required employers and their empleados domésticos to agree on the type of work, salary, and length of contract, fixing a maximum of five years as a limit of a single contract. Article 71 of the project is also telling, insofar as it stipulated that "domésticos will not have the eight-hour day, but rather the time period stipulated in the written contract executed by the parties; this must provide, in any case, a minimum rest period of two hours over the course of a day." Some articles clearly affirmed the rights already demanded by domestic workers themselves—such as time off each week to practice religion—but others were less generous than those proposed previously by other deputies, stipulating just one week's vacation per year and requiring clean housing and moral protection only for domésticos who are "female or under eighteen." In short, the proposal for regulating domestic service that the Labor Office presented to parliament mandated legal contracts for a broad range of empleados domésticos, but failed to indicate a minimum wage and provided a mere two hours' daily rest.[35]

Once again, however, this proposal remained just that, and never became law: new protective legislation for domestic service was not accomplished by parliament, but rather by legislative fiat, when in 1931 President Ibañez, exercising special executive powers granted him in light of the upheavals provoked by worldwide depression, authorized the 1931 Labor Code, one of the most comprehensive and enduring pieces of labor legislation in Chile's history. Decree-laws, rather than the proposals painstakingly defended in the parliament, would come to define the legal rights of empleados domésticos in Depression-era Chile.

Definition and Regulation of Empleados Domésticos in the 1931 Labor Code

In May 1931, operating with extraordinary powers granted him by the legislature, President (and former general) Carlos Ibañez promulgated Executive Decree

178, the code that would govern labor relations in Chile for the next forty years. The new Labor Code ratified existing military decree-laws from 1924 with respect to contracts, work hours, and accident protection, constituting a sweeping transformation of Chilean labor relations that shaped labor regulation and political mobilization thereafter, until the military coup suspended the provisions of the code and replaced it entirely in 1978.[36]

Significantly, the 1931 Labor Code also included the country's first legislative article on domestic service. When he sent a draft of the Labor Code to Congress in June 1930, President Ibañez noted that the articles on domestic service "establish specific rules that correspond to the labor conditions of that trade" and urged the labor courts and inspectors to more energetically enforce existing laws.[37] The prelude to the eventual legislation noted that existing laws "exclude from their benefits a sizable part of the salaried classes, such as the home-workers and empleados domésticos and others, who rightly demand the legal protection appropriate to their needs and social condition."[38] The new Labor Code's article on domestic service was significant because it specified the terms by which domestic service work could be defined and regulated, just like any other form of salaried employment. Even as the new regulations remained virtually impossible to enforce, they nevertheless affirmed domestic workers' status as a category of *worker*, a meaningful distinction for empleado activists, health and labor officials, and legislators who supported increased state intervention in domestic service relations.

By signing this new legislation, Ibañez accomplished by decree what President Alessandri, and Senator Malaquías Concha before him, had not: addressing the previous exclusion of domestic workers from Chilean labor law. The union president Lucas Salas recalled President Alessandri's speech (in his last address to Congress) about domestic workers, quoting him as saying: "It is an irritating injustice that, even in the twentieth century, domestic workers are deprived of their right to vote."[39] As Salas later noted, Ibañez was "the first president who remembered that there are two great trades at the margins of the law (domestic workers and rural workers), and thanks to his initiative they were included in the Labor Code, a just act that speaks loudly for the people's great love for our great president."[40] According to other newspaper accounts, President Ibañez had for several years cultivated support with domestic workers through the Republican Confederation for Civic Action (Confederación Republicana de Acción Cívica or CRAC), a national labor union in which domestic worker union delegates Manuel Rojas and Lucas Salas Suárez were active participants.[41] Speaking in a 1930 CRAC assembly, for example, Rojas called on the organization to "dignify" empleados domésticos and *campesinos* by lobbying for new legislation.[42]

After the fall of the Ibañez government in August 1931, the empleados' union suspended its activities "until the political [leadership] of the country should change, since the vested interests and current prejudices will never allow the just and human goals of our trade to thrive."[43]

The Labor Code's articles on domestic service established, for the first time in Chilean law, the status of all empleados domésticos as workers, as well as the state's interest in regulating their work hours, vacation time, probationary hiring, and severance pay. One of the most significant elements of this law was the new article's stipulation that contracts were not just recommended but obligatory for both parties to a domestic service arrangement. Sample contracts later approved and distributed by the Labor Office required employers and workers to agree on specific terms of employment, including workers' responsibilities and hours (including nine hours daily rest), the employers' responsibility to provide clean housing and sufficient salary (including the cost of food, light, and fuel), and the circumstances under which contracts could be broken, by whom, and with what compensation: notably, employers were required to give advance notice and pay severance to workers, except in cases of abandonment, immorality, or poor behavior on the part of the domestic worker. Such contracts entered into force after two weeks' probation, and defined fixed time periods of service that could be renewed by consent of both parties.[44] The 1931 mandate for signed contracts, and the specific forms promulgated to secure them, reflected the greater incorporation of domestic workers into the norms and practices of labor regulation in Chile.

However, breaking with previous Ministry of Welfare and Labor Office reports, the law also excluded important categories of domestic workers when it defined as empleados domésticos only those who worked in private homes and for a single employer. This narrow definition excluded temporary workers, those who worked for more than one employer, as well as workers in hotels, schools, and businesses.[45] Also, because the law allowed for oral contracts, written contracts in domestic service remained rare, leading to poor enforcement and no specific sanctions for employers who failed to sign contracts or honor agreements, leaving domestic workers with a largely empty victory.[46] According to the jurist Arancibia Muñoz, "the contracts of empleados domésticos are not written but oral, and do not allow therefore the inclusion of these kinds of stipulations [on hours, responsibilities, and end of contract]."[47] More importantly, as Arancibia Muñoz also noted, the emphasis on written contracts negatively impacted workers' subsequent claims before labor tribunals: citing three cases addressed in Iquique in 1933 and '34, Arancibia Muñoz demonstrated that the absence of written contracts implied that petitioners were not, in fact, empleados domésticos, but were rather dependents of the household. The absence of written contracts in such cases verified employers' claims the plaintiffs were engaged in a family relationship, "a reflection of the patrona's humanitarian sentiments, in taking in and protecting another person, as the complainant herself recognizes were like the attentions of a real mother."[48]

Such norms for domestic service relations established in the 1931 Labor Code, however, did allow labor inspectors greater opportunity for supervision, which they pursued with special attention to workers' maternity care. Labor Office officials not only made regular visits to private homes, but also received complaints from union officials, intervened in specific (and sometimes dramatic) cases, and studied and disseminated their findings about recurring problems affecting domestic workers. Labor Office reports and decisions in the 1930s demonstrate that, despite Executive Decree 178's lack of regulatory teeth, labor inspectors recognized domestic service as falling within the scope of the Labor Office's jurisdiction, although it would require additional legislation to sufficiently protect the rights of workers in that sector.

In most respects, in this period Labor Office officials treated empleados domésticos as just another category of worker, whose employment was subject to the normal operations of the Labor Office. When it came to the regulation of private employment services, Labor Office rulings were unequivocal in treating empleados domésticos as workers like any others. In statistics regularly reported in the government publication *Revista de Trabajo*, empleados domésticos were treated as a significant category of employment. In national figures for 1933, for example, 99 percent of domestic workers seeking employment remained, like empleados particulares, unemployed each month (unlike obreros, who found employment at rates of 11 to 13 percent).[49] In a study of the Santiago Labor Office's employment services in December 1935 and January 1936, however, over 50 percent of empleados domésticos seeking work through the office were contracted, rates far superior to those of white-and blue-collar workers in the same period.[50] In their attempts to regulate employment agencies and prevent debt peonage of workers, labor officials issued a number of findings to clarify the status of empleados domésticos in the Labor Code, in one case finding that employment agencies founded exclusively for domestic service arrangements were prohibited, since those workers were included in by the article's definition of "obrero," whose employment could not, by law, involve third parties: "In our opinion, empleados domésticos are included within the category of 'worker' used in the law, in Article 87."[51] This ruling, just one more exchange in the long-standing battle over employment agencies, demonstrated just how easily Labor Office officials incorporated empleados domésticos into the category of worker.

Finally, publications of the Labor Office throughout this period regularly included domestic workers in their rulings on worker maternity, singling out empleadas as the most disadvantaged group of women workers because they were excluded from the extended paid maternity leave guaranteed to women working in other sectors. In a report prepared by Olga Maturana Santelices in 1933, for example, the women's labor inspector observed that "the empleada has to face the prenatal stage without being able to work in a normal way and without any direct help, beyond that granted her by the law 4054 (of social security). She can't work after the birth, either, because of the difficulties her employers pose to letting her work with her baby." In her quest to secure better protections for breastfeeding working mothers and their children, Maturana advocated the creation of "breastfeeding insurance" that would compliment both the Social Security provisions and those of factory *creches*, securing better support for nursing mothers (including empleadas).[52] Despite these concerns, however, labor inspectors repeatedly upheld empleadas' exclusion from Article 67 of the Labor Code, which stipulated that employers could not fire pregnant workers in commercial or industrial establishments: "There is no legal impediment to firing the empleada doméstica, if her contract does not have a fixed duration and if she does not enjoy maternity leave. I'm telling you that the empleada never enjoys the maternity leave that the law grants to pregnant workers (obreras)."[53]

Through the collection of statistics on domestic workers, as well as regular inspections of workers' homes and studies of the situation of pregnant empleadas, the Labor Office gave regular attention to domestic service relations. Although union leaders often protested that labor inspectors ignored their trade, a high proportion of the inspectors' activities in 1939–1940 were in fact dedicated to domestic service. According to Labor Inspector Arancibia Muñoz, "Labor Inspectors carry out periodic home visits, in order to collect data on compliance with the articles governing empleados domésticos, and in order to send out reports on these articles." In early 1939 alone, the provincial labor inspectors made 2,136 visits throughout Chile to assess enforcement of domestic service relations, fully 12.6 percent of all inspections (whereas industry received just 10.8 percent of inspections, and commerce 19.4 percent). Inspectors then reportedly made *return* inspections of 718 sites (a lower rate of second inspection than in either industry or commerce).[54]

In this respect, Labor Office officials proved to be progressive in their broad interpretation of empleados domésticos' status as "workers" in Chilean social legislation. By 1952, interactions between Labor Office officials and domestic workers in the province of Santiago remained frequent, resulting in 1,343 interventions in domestic worker complaints and 1,485 letters from employers. According to the social worker Pérez Monardes' review of these records, empleadas domésticas sought labor inspectors' extra-official support for claims of unpaid salary, severance, and social security payments, as well as twelve cases of denial of paid annual leave. For their part, a majority of employers' letters to the Labor Office concerned abandonment of employ; others just recorded end of contract. Significantly, a third of all interventions resulted in successful agreements between domestic workers and their employers, while another third were remanded to the labor courts, where most were never tried because these workers lacked funds to pursue litigation; another third of these cases were abandoned, rejected, or ongoing at the Labor Office. From subsequent legal and social work studies, we see that the 1931 article confirmed the identity of empleados domésticos as workers, and that Labor Office officials exerted oversight, even though its regulatory authority remained ambiguous.

Service to Servants: Social Workers and "La Nueva Empleada"

The narrow dispositions of existing social legislation also attracted the sympathetic gaze of officials employed in the state's social welfare bureaucracy, where an emerging corps of lawyers, doctors, and social workers became increasing critical of domestic service relations as a remnant of Chile's celebrated traditional society. Engaging with domestic workers in domestic and clinical settings, this emerging group of middle-class professionals focused on material, psychological, and health effects of domestic service, at once certifying their expertise and asserting the role of the state in a modernizing Chile.[55] In the early 1940s, medical and social work students and professionals focused squarely on the plight of empleadas, publishing over a dozen academic studies that relied on sweeping generalizations about the historic roots of Chilean "servitude," but also analyzing domestic and international legislation and conducting field research through clinics and domestic workers' associations. While these welfare professionals' studies offer a wide range of diagnoses of the critical state of Chilean domestic service relations at midcentury—from pathologizing rural migrants' cultural and racial deficiencies to harsh criticisms of employer abuse—these observers universally attributed the immediate cause of the problem to the lack of state regulation of this sector. In this manner, state professionals combined "modern" prescriptions for incorporating empleadas into existing labor law, while simultaneously asserting the public health obligations of the state in protecting their maternity and the health of the Chilean "race."

Like the Labor Office, the CSO was one of the state entities whose officials most regularly interacted with domestic workers. Following decree-law 4054, after 1924 the CSO operated medical clinics and paid pensions for scores of ill, injured, and pregnant empleadas. In the regional CSO Medical Center of the port of Valparaíso, for example, roughly 10 percent of women and 1 percent of the men attended by the CSO in the late 1920s and early 1930s worked in domestic service, and almost 47 percent of insured women treated at the clinic were empleadas. In 1942 Dr. José Vizcarra, head of Santiago's CSO, reported that domestic workers in Chile received services at a variety of clinics, including the Medical Center's children's office, anti-venereal campaign, pulmonary clinic, heart clinic, and the Valparaiso anti-venereal campaign.[56]

This increasing attention to the plight of domestic workers came about not only because of their participation in social security benefits but also due to the expansion and reorientation of professional social work in Chile in the same period. Professional education in social work expanded after 1940 (from one school founded in 1925 to three in 1940), and this rapidly growing cohort staffed the growing offices of the CSO administration: between 1934 and 1941, the CSO budget nearly tripled, and by 1945, its staff of social workers had increased from 25 to 115.[57] This rapid expansion of social work education stimulated and responded to the re-orientation of professional social work from Catholic, charitable models to an approach informed by the "social medicine" movement among leftist health professionals in the 1930s. As Karin Rosemblatt has shown, leftist professionals argued that "the expansion and modernization of the state would make it more sensitive to social determinants of health and disease, well-being and misery,"[58] the expansion of the CSO in the early 1940s was deeply shaped by officials' progressive orientation toward the "science" of modern welfare. Among the growing population of predominantly female professional social workers, this transformation was slower to take hold, in part because of the profession's enduring ties to elite women's charitable activities, as well as the marginal status of social workers' primary subjects, working-class women, within the Popular Front project. But ultimately the work of progressive female social workers was no less visible: in 1945, led by a cohort of Communist social workers, progressives formed the Social Studies Circle (Circulo de Estudios Sociales) to promote their profession's increased status as well as modernize and democratize it from within. Consequently, many social workers' interest in domestic service shifted to reflect more progressive approaches to "the problem of domestic service" in

Chile, including the focus on labor conditions and maternity specific to women workers.[59]

The deep roots of professional social work in women's charitable activities were evident in Juana Concha's "La empleada doméstica y sus problemas," was submitted at the "Elvira Matte de Cruchaga" School for Social Work in Santiago in 1940. Graduates of this school of the Catholic University were known for their charitable and traditional approach to the poor, and Juana Concha presents the 250 domestic workers she studied as fatalistic and childlike. Following a brief overview of the relevant sections of the 1931 Labor Code, Concha focused her attention on the moral dangers of domestic service, which she argued were triggered by contact between empleadas and male members of the employers' family, as well as the limitations of domestic workers themselves, who generally lacked primary and vocational training and were products of families characterized by disorganization, weak manners, economic misery, and ignorance. Warning that she could not determine "the exact cause of [the empleada's] personal weaknesses and defects," Concha went on to attribute the 20 percent rate of single motherhood among domestic workers to "the poor moral, religious, and intellectual training she got at home and at school."[60] Concha's final recommendations called for marriage and religious training for the unfortunate, mothering empleada, as well as greater charity and consideration on the part of employers. Although she faulted the Labor Code for its lack of maternity protections, minimum wages, religious and professional training, her thesis advisor Guillermo Gonzalez P. criticized the thesis for failing to analyze existing social legislation or mention existing domestic worker organizations, two topics that would figure prominently in other social work theses produced in the 1940s.

The charitable and moralizing orientation that characterized Concha's thesis was soon eclipsed by the emergence of social work professionals who employed what they considered more scientific and "modern" approaches to "the problem of domestic service." In several presentations on domestic service delivered to the Inter-American Conference of Social Welfare, held in Santiago in 1942, three top CSO officials presented evidence of the dismal work and health conditions common among three marginal groups of workers: rural, "independent," and domestic workers. Pointing to the "principal difficulties" obstructing the work of the CSO, officials decried "the very conditions of the environment in which the [rural and domestic workers] live and exercise their profession," including geography, the hacienda system, ethnicity, and poor health, housing, and nutrition.[61] The solution, they argued, was to increase state intervention, improving rural workers' access to CSO services and strengthening the enforcement of domestic

service articles in the 1931 Labor Code. Noting that the libreta system had facilitated domestic workers' access to CSO services, the presenters blamed the lack
of state regulation for domestic workers' poor health; they lived in misery "since
the legal codes do not establish [their right to] a minimum wage, clean housing,
and nutritional intake suitable to their duties."[62]

In his own presentation to the same conference, Dr. José Vizcarra, drawing on
data from CSO clinics in Valparaíso, focused exclusively on the plight of female
empleadas, arguing that the deep and continuing barriers to domestic workers'
well-being could be solved only through professional training and changes to
the Labor Code.[63] Framing the contemporary exploitation of domestic workers
through a historical narrative of the abolition of slavery and the creation of the
Chilean social welfare state, Vizcarra drew on published legal studies of the 1931
Labor Code to demonstrate the inadequacy of existing social legislation: "Do
people comply with current social legislation? Do the laws resolve or satisfy the
effects of labor-capital relations that we see daily? Have they turned the empleado
doméstico into a citizen who enjoys society's benefits? Have they even challenged
class relations, or do they uphold the social inequality of the Spanish and early
Republican periods?"[64] Vizcarra then answered his own questions by detailing
the terrible health statistics for domestic workers, which showed alarming rates of
infant mortality, fertility, venereal disease, tuberculosis, heart disease, mortality,
and abortion.[65] Significantly, when it came to listing the systematic disadvantages
that empleadas in particular were facing, Dr. Vizcarra argued that more than
half of the hospital abortions performed from 1926 to 1930 were performed on
domestic workers, adding that his own clinical experience confirmed high rates
of abortion, illegitimacy, and prostitution among this population.

> This data eloquently demonstrates that current labor legislation has been
> ineffective for this group of workers, because of the working conditions
> and bio-social deficits we associate with the empleada doméstica. . . .
> Unfortunately, we must recognize that the labor laws and social policies so
> wisely applied to other groups of workers have not had the same beneficial
> effects for domestic workers. . . . By looking at the problem in this way,
> the solutions become clear: improving the domestic employee's education,
> changing employers' consciousness about their obligations . . . and making
> basic changes to current labor legislation.

Vizcarra concluded by recommending a maximum sixty-hour work week;
broadening the definition of domestic worker to include part-time workers and
those who serve more than one employer; minimum wage, or salaries calibrated

to reflect years of service; an increase of weekly time off; Sanitary Office oversight of domestic worker living conditions; and biannual medical examinations
of domestic workers at the CSO clinics. These changes, Vizcarra argued, would
allow employers "to improve their relations with these *new domestic workers*
(nuevas empleadas domésticas), who will be educated, honest, efficient, and fully
protected by the law."[66]

Six years later, the CSO clinics were also a critical source of data for the social
worker Violeta Paez Boggioni, whose study, "The empleada and maternity," also
emphasized the need for stronger protective legislation. But Paez Boggioni went
beyond the reiteration of Vizcarra's alarming statistics to present over seventy bi-
ographies of pregnant domestic workers treated in the maternal-infant ward of
the CSO's Epidemiology and Social Services unit in 1946–1947. The empleadas
discussed in Paez Boggioni's study sought maternity care in the CSO Servicio
Materno-Infantil (postpartum clinic), but many also received a variety of other
services, including medical attention and child care from the Mother-Child Institute, birthing at the public hospital, and receiving testing and treatment for tuberculosis and other infectious diseases in the CSO Epidemiology Clinic. Seven-
ty-seven empleadas, contacted with some difficulty through that clinic, provided
Paez Boggioni with information about their working and housing conditions,
marital status and sexual activity, economic, living and family circumstances, and
psychological health.[67] In contrast to the employers who relied on these skilled and
trusted workers, Paez Boggioni argued, empleadas faced enormous disadvantages,
including lack of time to form relationships and families, sexual harassment from
men in the homes of their employers (often followed by pregnancy and unemployment), and high levels of marital separation and child vagrancy. Criticizing the
values that "allowed our society to form this idea of a 'servant class,' based on class
and cultural differences," Paez Boggioni faulted employers' families for treating
domestic workers as "things," unworthy even of proper names (but rather "india"
and "china") and regularly subjecting them to physical and psychological abuse.
This context, according to Paez Boggioni, usually converted the empleada "into a
servile being, incapable of valuing herself" or mustering the initiative and self-con-
fidence necessary to seek work other than domestic service and prostitution.[68]

In addition to the painful details that emerge about the lives of the empleadas surveyed by Paez Boggioni, her study illustrates the regular engagement of
pregnant domestic workers with CSO social workers, doctors, and institutions
in the 1940s. In one case study after another, her study shows how social workers
intervened in these pregnant women's lives, inspecting their homes and those of
their employers; instructing young mothers in breastfeeding and *puericultura*

(child-rearing); seeking to legitimize consensual unions; tracking down errant "progenitors"; finding domestic service positions for postpartum mothers; tending to domestic workers' abandoned or ill children; and, at times, pressing employers' families to recognize children born of sexual unions between empleadas and male members of employers' families. An extreme example of the level of social worker involvement from Paez Boggioni's study includes that of "Rita R.R.," a twenty-five year-old part-time empleada, separated from her first husband and living with the alcoholic father of her child-to-be in precarious conditions:

> Given what had happened and the scarce support he gives her, we convinced Rita to separate from her boyfriend. We found her work in a home that allows her to bring two of her children with her. The older child went to live with the mother-in-law, until her skin condition improves. The infant was left with her boyfriend's married daughter. We gave an antifungal cream to the client's oldest daughter. We collected the infant from the boyfriend's daughter's house and brought her to Rita's workplace. We taught her *puericultura*, health, and family education. We will continue monitoring the infant's care.[69]

In Paez Boggioni's analysis, the systematic economic and social marginalization of empleadas domésticas were primary causes of high infant mortality, abortion, and child abandonment rates that represented both a social and moral crisis in Chilean society. Among Paez Boggioni's most striking conclusions was her observation that—contrary to prevalent assumptions about the advantages of independent living—domestic workers who lived within and outside of their employers' homes lived in equal squalor, since those renting their own homes typically had too many family members per bed and per room in unhygienic *conventillos* with little privacy and services.[70] In her final recommendations, Paez Boggioni attributed the poor circumstances of empleadas—particularly in relation to maternity—to the failures of both employers (for poor treatment) and domestic workers (for poor education and training), and like Vizcarra recommended reform of the social security system, changes to the Labor Code, and new schools for domestic workers. Better services and laws would, according to Paez Boggioni, ensure employers' proper treatment of domestic workers, while the latter would create a "new class of empleada doméstica," a woman trained in specialized domestic skills who would exhibit "the habits of professional honor, responsibility, and efficiency in her work and morals."[71]

In yet another social work study of domestic service—this one conducted by Gladys Pérez Monardes in 1954—the question of the empleada-patrona relationship took center stage. Pérez Monardez combined data collected from 469 single-mother empleadas attended at the CSO's maternal-infant service with interviews conducted with fifty domestic workers (located through the CSO) and fifty employers (whose selection was not explained). In addition to corroborating the demographics, working conditions, educational and marital status, age, and working patterns evident in other studies, Pérez Monardes explored the attitudes empleadas domésticas and their employers held about one another, principally to analyze the possibility for improving those relations through social workers' involvement. Like her social work colleagues, Pérez Monardes grounded her discussion in a review of quantitative clinic and CSO data, which confirmed the low educational level and poor salaries of most empleadas; significantly, of those treated in the mother-child clinic, an 82 percent majority worked as general housekeepers (*para todo servicio*) and almost 50 percent still lived *puertas adentro*.[72]

Another innovative aspect of Pérez Monardes's 1954 study was her detailed analysis of 145 histories taken from domestic workers interned at the Casa Madre, an institution created in 1936 by the National Children's Defense Council to provide pre-and postnatal care to poor women, with a focus on breastfeeding support. Focusing her attention on single empleadas at the Casa who enjoyed social security benefits—almost three quarters of the workers—the social worker drew an alarming picture of their extreme plight: 75 percent had been dismissed from jobs because of pregnancy (and others from parents' or lovers' homes). The social worker then recounted her intervention in these 145 cases, seeking to reestablish relations with family members, secure information about paternity, shore up domestic workers' access to CSO benefits, register children's birth and CSO benefits, and facilitate domestic workers' exit from the Casa by setting them up with jobs and housing.[73] Pérez Monardes's study once again confirms the multiple venues for empleadas' interaction with state agencies, and the regularity with which social workers came into contact with them, particularly during pregnancy and childbirth. In order for domestic workers to overcome the cruelty of employers and the abuses of employment agencies, Pérez Monardes argued, domestic workers needed to build their associations, secure the state's oversight of their labor, and access educational and social services.[74]

Emergence of the Women's Household Workers Union

In addition to fundamentally altering the legal framework for state regulation of domestic service relations, the 1931 Labor Code also transformed the politics of domestic worker activism, inspiring new waves of participation among female domestic workers and encouraging the movement of male service workers into separate organizations. In 1936 domestic worker activists revived their union, which initially demonstrated significant continuity with the earlier union with respect to leadership,[75] but now reflected the trade as it had been redefined in Executive Decree 178: as a group of workers engaged in full-time employment in private homes, now constituted almost entirely of women members. The new union was renamed the Professional Union of Household Employees (Sindicato Profesional de Empleados de Casas Particulares), an adaptation to the language of the 1931 Labor Code, which advocated "professional unions" dedicated to "the study, development, and legitimate defense of the common interests of the associated persons."[76] The revived union also worked closely with Labor Inspector Escudero, demanding that he enforce applicable laws, such as overseeing employers' homes to enforce the labor contract, certifying that workers were getting yearly leave, and reviewing their libretas. Announcing plans for a new unionization drive, the group called for mandatory union membership and promised to visit Senator Malaquías Concha, "the long-time defender and friend of our trade, so that he knows we are back in the struggle."[77]

And return to the struggle they did, starting with a letter and a visit to the newspaper *Las Últimas Noticias* in order to protest a letter previously published by the newspaper that had portrayed domestic workers in a negative light. Union leaders showed up in the newspaper's offices, bearing a letter signed by Manuel Rojas L. (President) and Ramon Reyes (Secretary) that detailed the inaccuracies and prejudice of the article by Eduardo Barrios, "Against the Poor," which they called "a degrading diatribe against a trade [of domestic work] that is as deserving of consideration and respect as any other." The union leaders took particular umbrage at Barrios's opposition to the unionization of domestic workers: "Perhaps the writer does not know that our country has a law of unionization, to which we have the perfect right to ascribe to as a trade . . . ?" The activists went on to reassure their readers that "our Union is not an association for struggle, nor can it be a danger to anyone; by unionizing, we are obeying social laws; and for this reason we would like to see these laws obeyed, which unfortunately is not happening." The letter went on to describe how employers had failed to comply with their labor contracts, skimping on workers' two week's paid yearly vacation and social security payments. Finally, the unionists launched a personal attack, citing Barrios's mistreatment of his own empleados domésticos: "He leaves them hungry. Yes, he confesses to this without embarrassment and then complains about how eating is 'animalistic.'" The activists responded that "many of us, in

the course of our basic struggle for existence and with no need of his paternalistic and gratuitous advice, have acquired that valuable virtue of "service" that
you like to boast about."[78]

Although the story of unionization and legislative debate recounted in this
chapter reveals the important presence of male workers in domestic service trades
in the 1920s, over the next two decades the domestic service sector—and therefore the discursive construction of domestic service as a "problem" in Chile—
became predominantly female, a process shaped both by the legal and political
redefinition of men's paid reproductive labor as well as by the continuing influx
of girls and young women from poor rural families to Santiago and other urban
areas. The increasing presence of displaced rural girls working in urban homes
provided the foundation for a score of efforts, both by and for domestic workers,
to ameliorate or transform the circumstances of their work from the 1930s to the
1950s. The Chilean winter of 1936 marked the return of domestic worker activists to public life. By 1939, the reinvigorated union of more than 10,000 workers
was supporting work to advance domestic workers' rights, studying proposed
reforms to the 1931 Labor Code and continuing to protest individual employer
abuses, strengthening ties to labor inspectors, and pressing the CSO for funding
to open a "social center" for their members. These campaigns were discussed in
multiple meetings of the union membership, and publicized in a long manifesto
penned by the union president, Manuel Rojas. The speech—which addressed the
need for greater legal protections for domestic workers and better enforcement
of existing legislation—is not as impressive as the list of those invited to a dinner
served up on the union's second anniversary, complete with live entertainment
and an orchestra.[79] Other activities organized that year by the union included
an assembly attended by the union's doctor, lawyer, and accountant; that same
meeting was attended by an employer recognized for raising his workers' salaries,
Abraham Atala. The union went on to hold a dinner for journalists and labor
inspectors, "in recognition of the work that they do in support of the goals of
union organizations." By this time, the union had grown to over ten thousand
members and was planning to offer classes in domestic economy and fashion,
designed for workers who wished to become more independent.[80] Outreach to
other unions continued apace, as did correspondence with the domestic workers'
unions of Viña del Mar and Osorno.[81] Despite union leaders' success in lobbying
the highest levels of government, they were discouraged about the slow pace of
change. In meetings with President Pedro Aguirre Cerda, union leaders learned
that domestic workers' problems "cannot be resolved as one would like, as long
as [the Popular Front] does not have a majority in both houses."[82] Although

FIGURE 2.1. President Pedro Aguirre Cerda with empleadas, Conchalí estate, c. 1940

the statutes of the domestic workers' union—like other workers' associations granted legal status by the Labor Ministry—prohibited partisan activity, by the Popular Front period such politics in fact regularly disrupted the work of the union's directorate.

The story of this union's political conflicts also reflects the changing composition of its membership, since the shift to female leadership coincided with the ousting of the union's male Communist president Valentín Navarro in 1940.[83] While women had always participated in union assemblies and served on the directorate, in the early 1940s women's membership and leadership of the union increased dramatically. By mid-1939, a woman named Graciela Sánchez started to lead the union from the treasurer's position, where she promoted union membership among empleadas domésticas in Viña del Mar and Santiago's elite neighborhoods. Sánchez enjoined new members to read the Labor Code and the union statutes, particularly the "rule of style" that committed union members to decorous behavior. Citing the recent recruitment of eighty-two new members from October to December 1940, the directorate agreed to "tell those skeptics that if they don't like what the union does, they can just stop being members of it, and that we beg no one."[84] Sánchez gradually became the union's primary political representative, traveling to Viña del Mar to make contacts with the Hotel

Workers Union and serving as a delegate both to the Popular Front government
and the Chilean Workers' Confederation (Confederación de Trabajadores de
Chile or CTCh). When she was sworn in as union president in July 1940, Sánchez declared the union's priority as setting up a social center and obtaining a
minimum wage for domestic employees, benefits already granted to other unions
by the Ministry of Labor. During her first presidency, Sánchez formed work
commissions composed almost entirely of female union members in the areas
of hygiene, parties, accounting, work placement, member relations, unemployment, and propaganda.[85]

If one reason for the rise of female participation and leadership in the domestic workers' union was the narrow definition of service contained in the 1931
Labor Code, another was the exodus of male chauffeurs and other workers previously defined as "domestic" from the sector by the late 1930s. As early as October 1934, Deputy Alejandro Serani had sponsored a bill proposed by President
Alessandri that would have excluded chauffeurs from the category of empleado
doméstico, categorizing them instead as obreros: "The functions that this class
of salaried workers complete, even if they are done in service to a domestic, they
carry out outside of the home, of a relatively technical and independent character, which makes us consider their work as more similar to that done by a worker
in a factory or a workshop than to that carried out by an empleado doméstico
as such."[86] Debate on the status of chauffeurs extended through early 1937, and
included Malaquías Concha's attempt to extend workers' rights to bus drivers
and conductors. In the end, the legislature approved Law 6242 in September
1938, effectively re-categorizing chauffeurs as workers, not empleados domésticos. The leaders of the new chauffeur's union, however, along with those of the
hotel workers and waiters' unions, remained in close contact with the domestic
workers' union for at least the next decade.[87] Despite the legal and political separation achieved by male service workers in this period, male activists fostered
the continued alliance with domestic workers into the 1950s.[88]

In 1941, Sánchez also reported the union's new affiliation with an unnamed
"organization of women of the left," most likely the MEMCH, a women's political movement associated with the parties of the Popular Front coalition.[89]
Attention to the plight of domestic workers had been evident in the MEMCH as
early as 1935, when the first issue of the organization's newspaper, *La mujer nueva*
(The New Woman), reported that MEMCH had included both obreras and
empleadas in its statutes.[90] Eulogia Román provided the first report on the topic:
protesting the unlimited nature of empleadas' workday, and poor treatment at
the hands of employers, Román called for domestic workers to organize within

the MEMCH, making no mention of existing unions for empleadas in Chile.[91] The following year, journalist and leading feminist Delie Rouge protested the lack of labor protection for empleadas, calling on the Panamerican Labor Congress to approve a MEMCH proposal for such a law.[92] Later news stories—this one profiling the populations suffering from illegal abortion—would point to domestic workers' exclusion from the Labor Code, including the child care and breastfeeding protections granted other workers,[93] and offer reports on training courses on gender inequality that included domestic workers; incipient provincial domestic service unions; and the implementation of new domestic worker legislation in New York. This and other bits of evidence from MEMCH publications illustrate the fact that domestic service, if not the reinvigorated union later led by Sánchez, had registered its concerns with the leading women's group of the Popular Front era, whose attention to women's work and reproductive rights made it a unique expression within Chilean leftist feminism of the era.[94]

Under Graciela Sánchez's leadership, the union's directorate pursued two key strategies for advancing their interests: strengthening alliances with other unions and active representation of the union in the CTCh.[95] In her travel to nearby Viña del Mar in January 1940, for example, Sánchez met with members of a fledgling empleadas' union, urging them to join forces with those "workers who are similar to us in work and exploitation," the Hotel Workers' Union (Central de Trabajadores Hoteleros).[96] The directorate went on to protest state repression of that union in July 1940—"even under the Popular Front governments"—and to express solidarity in November of that year with the hotel workers in their dispute with the Waiters' Union.[97] Sánchez's own involvement in the intra-union disputes became clearer in March 1941, when the former domestic workers' union president Valentín Navarro complained to hotel workers that Sánchez was corrupt, whereupon the empleadas' union promptly banned Navarro and reaffirmed its solidarity with the Hotel Workers' Union.[98] These episodes demonstrate the ways in which some domestic worker activists participated in—and debated—the wider politics of organized labor.

Serving as the union's delegate to the CTCh from late 1939 through at least 1946, Sánchez also ensured that the union's demands were voiced in one of the most critical arenas of Popular Front-era union politics. Sánchez offered the directorate of the domestic workers' union regular reports on CTCh activities, which sparked repeated controversy about her reports of partisan infighting and provoked members to ask whether the domestic service union should even participate in the confederation. Sánchez's prominence in CTCh activities is reflected in political attacks leveled against her leadership, as well as by her contributions to *CTCh*, the news arm of the confederation. In June 1946, for example, Sánchez (by then a provincial representative to the CTCh) published an editorial calling women to action in defense of their labor rights, as well as a report on the union's demand for the creation of professional certificates for domestic workers. In that report, Sánchez wrote: "our laws for domestic service are very insufficient, and make it necessary for public authorities to resolve this problem, which becomes more acute with the current economic crisis, and for which the Professional Union of Domestic Employees presses to achieve, as soon as possible, the creation of professional certificates."[99] Through her participation in CTCh, Sánchez repeatedly placed the specific concerns of domestic workers on the broader agenda of the CTCh, clearly articulating her union's struggle for empleadas' rights as workers' rights.

The clearest evidence of Sánchez's success in bringing the specific concerns of the domestic workers' union to the CTCh was the publication, in January 1947, of "Concrete Agreements on General Demands," authored by the General Demands Committee of the CTCh. Following a list of eleven legislative projects the CTCh was pressing on legislators, the Committee listed "problems that are affecting the professional trades," including hotel workers, domestic workers, state employees, and industrial workers. Sánchez's hand in the list of demands is evident, as it included a call for professional certificates, restaurant-schools, family salaries, vocational schools, and day care for the children of domestic workers. Notably, the list also included the demand that the word "domestic" be removed from the Labor Code, "because it is a damaging term for a respectable part of our citizenry."[100] Given the general invisibility of domestic workers on the political agendas of national labor federations in this period, the inclusion of this list of demands offers powerful evidence of the impact of Sánchez's participation in the broader labor movement in the 1940s.

While the meetings of the union were marked by members' systematic engagement with union leaders, legislators, and state officials, they were also frequently the site of heated discussions about the abuses suffered by individual domestic workers. In many cases, union leaders moved quickly to redress these claims, contacting the press, health and labor inspectors, and individual politicians. In one remarkable case, the employer accused of mistreating the domestic worker in his employ was David Lama, a doctor employed in the CSO, who refused to allow her to return to his house to collect her clothes. The dispute was finally resolved through the intervention of a labor inspector, who accompanied the worker to collect her things, which had already been ripped up by her angry mistress. "This matter was so serious that we debated for a long time," union minutes record, whereupon the group decided to have several female leaders send a note to the CTCh "thanking them for the way they have intervened in this case, and asking that they intervene again until we find a way that Señor Lama gets what he deserves; we would like the CTCh to put new notices in the newspapers and ask for punishment, because something like this cannot and should not be done."[101] This dispute, and the union's quick response, speaks to the union's close relationship with the national labor federation, as well as with the inspectors of the Labor Office, who they felt they could summon to intervene in this type of conflict.

Because there is a gap in the domestic workers' union records that extends from 1945 to 1950, we cannot know exactly what transpired within the union while Sánchez continued her efforts as a provincial delegate of the CTCh. When the union reconvened in 1950 under new leadership, no mention of the union's links to other unions or the CTCh remained. Instead, the union leadership worked closely in this new era with a new actor: the *Hogar de la* Empleada (Empleadas' Home), an association founded by a group of domestic workers previously active in union affairs, in league with some progressive clergy of the Young Catholic Worker movement. Characteristic of this phase of organization was conflict with Communist-identified unions, one of which sought to organize a competing union for domestic workers. Under new leadership by 1954, the union finally returned to activities promoting new labor legislation for domestic workers, under the supervision of the CTCh subsecretary Luis Gálvez. Finally, in this third founding of the domestic workers' union, the fact of the profession's almost entirely female composition came to be recognized in the union's new name: The Union of Women Household Employees Number 2 (Sindicato de Empleadas de Casas Particulares No. 2). Further, the work of the union and attention from MEMCH in the 1940s inserted domestic workers in Chilean political life as women *workers*, consolidating a discourse of political citizenship and women's rights that would emerge with great force in Cold War Chile.

Conclusion

This chapter has demonstrated an important finding: domestic worker activism in Chile was not a late twentieth-century phenomenon, the product of feminist and neoliberal forces. Rather, the men and women of domestic service organized and were consistently recognized as workers by journalists, state officials, and some labor organizers from early in the twentieth century. From the earliest petitions penned by La Sociedad el Porvenir, through the wholesale inclusion of domestic workers in the social security system, to the inclusion of special articles on domestic service in the 1931 Labor Code, the logic of regulating domestic service *as work* made steady if halting progress. At the same time, the limits placed on the regulation of service inside private homes (or rather, the absence of strict regulations) and the Labor Code's treatment of domestic workers as *separate* from industrial and other workers installed workers in that trade in a legally secondary status in the 1930s. This continuing failure in state oversight over a significant number of workers, along with the fact that many activists had developed strong connections to state agencies and organized labor, made social legislation both a source of continuing marginalization and a site of struggle for domestic workers.

Despite these limitations, however, domestic workers registered significant legislative triumphs, as paid domestic labor moved from private paternalism to separate treatment in articles of the 1924 laws and incorporation into in the 1931 Labor Code. But as union complaints and labor office rulings demonstrated, the significant curtailment of these workers' rights and barriers to regulation persisted throughout the period. Though scores of workers brought their complaints to the Labor Office, or sought collective redress through union activism, employer abuses of domestic worker wages, hours, access to medical care, and firing (particularly for pregnancy) continued apace. While state professionals from Labor Office inspectors to the doctors and social workers of the CSO generated studies and responses to the "problem" of domestic work, the increasingly female-led domestic workers' union and their union, feminist, and party allies continued to press for legislative protection and oversight for this group of workers excluded from 1931 Labor Code. Significant in their own right because of how they document the emergence of social medicine and other progressive influences in the profession, social work studies of the '40s and '50s also reveal important details about domestic workers' experience, from working conditions and maternity to participation in Church and union associations. In this respect, the story of domestic service regulation and services in this period reflects the broader developments of Chile's Popular Front era, especially its gendered history of female professionals, family allowances, and female suffrage, and links the visibility of empleadas to the rise of middle-class women's professionalization and political activism.[102] In these critical years, domestic service became even more closely associated with the economic and sexual exploitation of poor women—variously diagnosed as a problem of social inequality and/or moral weakness—in a manner that would later facilitate Church campaigns directed toward them in the 1950s, campaigns that incorporated union demands for domestic workers' citizenship and labor rights within a Catholic framework of the struggle for dignity and moral rectitude.

Over the first four decades of the twentieth century, therefore, a variety of historical sources testify to the existence of comparatively early debate and activism in Chile concerning the equal labor rights of domestic workers, a reality often ignored in social science literature on late-twentieth-century domestic worker struggles and legislative successes. Despite the categorical exclusion of both male and female empleados domésticos from legislative proposals in the teens and '20s, workers themselves sought state oversight and intervention, identifying common ground with industrial labor with respect to working conditions, family, and political struggle. In this struggle, empleados domésticos counted regularly on alliances with political leaders, labor office officials, journalists, and legal and social work professionals, all of whom recognized the exploitative relations evident in domestic service arrangements and promoted a "modernizing" vision of domestic service as work, rather than patronage or kinship.

CHAPTER 3

Rites and Rights

Catholic Association by and for Domestic Workers, 1947–1964

B Y EXCLUDING DOMESTIC WORKERS from the labor rights granted
other salaried workers, the Labor Code of 1931 and the emergent Chilean
welfare state neglected the increasing numbers of predominantly female
domestic workers migrating to Chile's urban centers in the postwar period. Into
this vacuum of familial care and supervision stepped the Catholic Church: the
most effective mobilization of women employed in domestic service at midcentury was led not by unions but rather by Catholic clergy, who—inspired by the
teachings of social Catholicism—worked with empleadas to build a movement
by and *for* domestic workers. Unlike religious orders founded in the nineteenth
century to shelter and train destitute orphans and prostitutes for domestic service to wealthy families, a postwar generation of Catholic priests turned their
attention to the women already employed as full-time empleadas, women active
in the parishes of the elite Santiago neighborhoods where they lived and worked.
Through parishes both geographically and economically distant from those of
their families, young migrant women sought spiritual and personal support from
urban clergy, in turn educating priests about the hardships, loneliness, and abuse
empleadas often suffered in their employers' homes. Those priests' increasing
awareness coincided with the expansion of Chile's progressive, worker-oriented
lay movement, the Young Catholic Worker (Juventud Obrera Católica or JOC).
By the 1940s, the Chilean JOC had become the only Latin American branch that
had fully incorporated empleadas, and the JOC de las Empleadas provided access
to religious and social services designed to suit their specific needs. In 1950 the
JOC established the Federation of Empleadas, a lay association guided by clergy
that would build a foundation for the political mobilization of empleadas in postwar Chile and Latin America. Although Catholic efforts in Peru, Brazil, and
Colombia also traced their roots to Acción Católica, they never reached the scale
and activist orientation that characterized the Federation of Empleadas in Chile.[1]

Sometime after their first meeting in 1947 with Bernardino Piñera, a priest designated by the Church to work with the empleadas, domestic worker activists established a permanent base of operations in the *Hogar de la Empleada* ("Hogar" or Home of the Empleada), a set of buildings in downtown Santiago that housed the group's classrooms, day-care center, chapel, and offices. The Hogar provided meals and temporary housing for domestic workers and their children, as well as child care, employment, legal, educational, and financial services. Centrally located on Tocornal Street near the city center, the Hogar's small chapel offered regular Mass, baptismal, and communion services for empleadas, who also gathered there every November 21 to make a pilgrimage to the statue of the Virgin Mary perched atop the nearby San Cristóbal Hill. In the 1950s, the Hogar also became the locus of domestic workers' activism, drawing some 7,000 empleadas to become members of the JOC de las Empleadas, and reaching thousands more in Santiago and the provinces through the services, religious activities, and social life supported by the JOC. This place, and the cohort of activists that it nurtured, would sustain the most significant organization of domestic workers that Chile had ever seen, one that for a time overshadowed Santiago's secular union and served as a base for Catholic outreach to empleadas elsewhere in Latin America.

This chapter begins by examining the nature of some Catholic clergy's support for domestic workers, drawing on Church archives and oral histories to trace how and why Church leaders started to work with empleadas in the 1940s. Though these initiatives depended primarily on the leadership of a particular priest, Father Bernardino Piñera, they relied for their success on a broader base of Catholic sympathy and support, which provided not only the resources, legal services, and personnel necessary to acquire and operate the Hogar, but also a ready parish-level network that brought empleadas to the Hogar, often with the support of their Catholic employers. Through Catholic celebrations and pastoral letters directed to empleadas in the 1950s and '60s, the highest levels of the Chilean clergy also offered public support for the empleadas' association, reassuring employers about the benefits of empleadas' participation. This Catholic movement also increased domestic workers' visibility to state officials, through activities that encouraged payments to social security, invited labor inspectors to intervene in disputes, and eventually advocated for improved protective legislation for empleadas. Because of its strong Church backing and access to empleadas through parish networks, the JOC impacted thousands of domestic workers throughout the country, building a movement that would outpace secular union efforts and later withstand the challenge of military rule.

The second part of this chapter draws on institutional archives and extensive oral histories with long-time movement activists and priests to trace the expansion of Catholic activism among empleadas in the 1950s, examining how and why thousands of women came to join this lay movement, make use of its services, celebrate its rituals, and read its publications. In correspondence with state officials as well as Catholic press articles, domestic worker activists and their priestly allies drew with equal facility on arguments for workers' dignity and rights on the one hand, while on the other promoting workers' humility and loyalty through Catholic instruction and ritual. While this combination of labor and religious discourse was common throughout the Young Catholic Worker movement, among empleadas it proved to be an especially potent mix, particularly when the movement centered female religious figures such as the Virgin Mary and Santa Zita, the patron saint of domestic servants. By the late 1950s, Chile's apostolic movement among empleadas had spread to provincial capitals throughout the country and established strong ties to the international Young Catholic Worker movement.

The final section of the chapter is devoted to analyzing the politicization of the Catholic domestic workers' movement in the early 1960s, as Catholic leaders were increasingly drawn into liberation theology movements and engaged by the Christian Democratic Party's campaigns. Following the election of the Christian Democrat Eduardo Frei to the presidency in 1964, the Federation of Empleadas became increasingly divided by partisan struggle, prompting some activists to join Christian Democratic and other political parties, and others to opt out of political mobilization in favor of purely spiritual or charitable activities at the Hogar. These emerging divisions within the Federation reflected broader debates in Cold War Chile about Catholic engagement with the politics of reform and revolution, and among empleada activists about the core mission of the Catholic empleadas' movement, a tension evident in competing emphasis on rites versus rights in the domestic workers' movement.

The JOC de las Empleadas, 1947–1958

In many ways, considering the Catholic Church's major role in Chilean public life as well as the Church's longer history of service to and evangelization among the poor, the mobilization of empleadas under the aegis of the Catholic Church in the 1950s evidenced the continuing influence and focus of the Church in a changing world. Several congregations of female religious had since the nineteenth century provided services, training, and/or religious education to poor women, many of whom had been or would be employed as servants. In particular, the House of María (founded 1861) and the Daughters of the Immaculate María Religious Institute for Domestic Service and Children's General Protection (founded 1913) focused their efforts on housing poor girls and training them for a life of "honorable work," which usually meant domestic service. [2] The Catholic movement among empleadas that emerged in the 1950s also built upon decades of lay activism to stave off secular and Protestant challenges by increasing Catholic participation in the Church: Catholic Action, a global Catholic movement that in the 1920s fueled the participation of laypersons in religious teaching and outreach, increased the participation of elite women and students, broadening the range of services offered and stimulating the rise of Christian Democracy in the 1930s. Around the same time, another international Catholic movement took hold in Chile, extending lay activism directly into the neighborhoods and workplaces of Chile's working classes: the Young Catholic Worker, founded in Belgium in 1924 by Father Joseph Cardijn. In Europe, the Young Catholic Worker was conceived as a powerful instrument against the encroachments of both secularization and world communism, designed to draw workers away from radical unions and enlist the working-class faithful in the battle against Marxism. [3] By 1938, the Young Catholic Worker movement had expanded to Canada, the United States, and four Latin American countries, and in 1940, the Chilean Juventud Obrera Católica was born. [4] Under the instruction of Cardinal José María Caro, the Catholic Action director Bishop Manuel Larraín Errázuriz selected a handful of like-minded priests to serve as *asesores* or spiritual directors of the newly founded JOC associations for male workers, university students, peasants, and women. In the 1940s, both Catholic Action and the JOC began to sponsor activities directed at domestic workers, reinforced by Father Cardijn's 1946 and 1948 visits to Chile; Chilean empleadas, inspired by Cardijn's personal audiences with them, would later name their professional school after Cardijn's mother, herself a former empleada. In 1947, the Chilean JOC founded an additional branch among domestic workers, known variously as the JOC or Federación de las Empleadas.

The launch of a new movement among empleadas depended not only on the institutional and doctrinal support of the JOC but also on the leadership of a new generation of priests devoted to energizing laypeople in defense of the Church. By 1948, over eighty priests had been trained for the rapidly growing JOC movement, [5] and in 1947 Father Bernardino Piñera and the empleadas known as *las fundadoras* (the founders) began to recruit and organize domestic workers at the parish level. Father Piñera—born to a powerful oligarchic family, trained as a medical doctor, and only recently ordained—had just been appointed one of the spiritual directors of the JOC. Piñera later explained his initial interest to work with empleadas as a response to his upbringing in Paris (1915–1932), where his family lived "very simply" with two or three servants, but without the mistreatment and disrespect he felt characterized Chilean treatment of empleadas. Piñera had also traveled in Italy during his religious training, where a visit with an Italian priest whose work focused on migrant domestic workers convinced Piñera of the need to address the plight of Chile's empleadas. From the start, Piñera says that he understood the need to create a separate branch of the JOC to accommodate the empleadas:

> And so it fell to me, with this group of leaders, to examine this: "Can we build a JOC for the empleadas that's the same as the JOC of the obreros?" No, it can't be done. One has to respond to the needs of the empleadas, and this is something the empleada leaders understood very well.... So we had to create something different that would distinguish us a little from the JOC; it was a little difficult to accept this kind of hierarchy within the movement, but it went all right, and finally we overcame these difficulties.[6]

As chaplain of the Sindicato de Empleadas de Casa Particular No. 2, which in 1948 had recently been reinaugurated after several years' quiescence, Piñera convened what he called "the five Saritas" of the union, and with them laid plans for founding the new movement and securing its physical home, the Hogar de la Empleada. Even though his superior, Father Larraín, and the ladies of the women's JOC wanted him to closely supervise the new association, Piñera defended a vision of "doing something that was of the empleadas, for the empleadas, and by the empleadas,"leaving the empleadas to run their association "without nuns or bosses."[7] After his initial involvement in setting up the association, Piñera says, he limited his visits to once a week, leaving the administration of the movement to the ten or twelve domestic worker activists who ran the group in exchange for small stipends.

Piñera's partners in the campaign to carry the message of the JOC to this sector were themselves young women who had migrated in their teens to Santiago from rural areas to work as live-in cooks, cleaners, and nannies in the multi-servant households of Santiago's elite neighborhoods.[8] Like Elba Bravo, who recounted her experience in the Introduction, this transition was often facilitated by family or friends in rural areas who could refer the young women to prospective employers. This was the case, for example, for Aída Moreno's aunt, who at age fourteen separated from her family and started to work: "Someone told my

FIGURE 3.1. Father Piñera, circa 1950

aunt that the *gringos* who ran the estate needed someone to care for their two children. My young aunt, who was only a teenager, decided to go to work, with my grandmother's permission, to care for the children of this German family. Later on the family bought the 'Cabana' estate near Graneros, taking my aunt with them."[9] Other stories did not end so well: Moreno recounts that she was upset about her mother's decision to send her younger sister at age twelve to work with a couple who simply drove through their community in search of a new servant. Moreno went looking for her sister, and found her working as a nanny for a family in the port city of San Antonio: "She was very happy, but [my employer] Señora Julita told me not to leave her alone there, and that she would look for a job for my sister among her friends where she could be close by and I could watch over her; she was too young to live in a port city with lots of sailors coming through, where something could happen to her. Soon after that I brought her with me to Santiago."[10]

The transformation of empleadas from new urban arrivals into savvy activists most often began at the parish level. Parish priests, working in elite neighbor-hoods populated by live-in workers, began to identify empleadas as a lay sector requiring special attention and services, creating special classes in catechism and basic education exclusively for them. Parish activities could bring empleadas into contact with sympathetic priests—often called upon to mediate conflict between employers and empleadas—and in activist Elba Bravo's case, provided a productive environment in which to support her fellow empleadas:

> I think that my solitude at work made me ready to commit myself com-
> pletely to the Federation. It started for me in the parish, where I went
> around getting people together—we managed to get 120 empleadas from
> the parish—and we shared our stories, we chatted, and girls arrived who
> didn't even know how to read, and I helped them write letters to send to
> their parents, and the next week when they brought the letter they received
> we would read it to them. So here you have the way we built the movement,
> we read to them and we chatted, we sang together, we celebrated Christmas
> when it came and the priest supported us a lot, and in this respect—I'm
> talking about 1948, 1949, Father Piñera appeared.

At one of the parish meetings for empleadas that she attended with her friend (and fellow *fundador*) Ester Vargas, Bravo and about 100 other empleadas met with Father Piñera and learned about the JOC. In her telling of the story fifty years later, full of emotion with remembrance her youth, Bravo recounted her first meeting with Father Piñera and Father Alberto Hurtado. Father Hurtado directed the youth branch of the Acción Católica after 1941 and founded the Catholic union movement, the Christian Jesuit magazine *Mensaaje*, and the charitable home Hogar de Cristo (Home of Christ). In that meeting, Bravo recalled, Piñera said:

> "I invite you, I call on you in the name of God, in the name of all those who
> today suffer and work when they are sick, who have no opportunity to ask for
> permission and go see a doctor, of all those who have no work and are suffer-
> ing injustice and have to endure everything all shut up indoors; in the name
> of all those who cry for their families and can't go to see their mothers, and if
> their mothers come, there's nowhere for them to stay; in the name of all those
> who want to marry and start a family and can't do it—where would they have
> the marriage, where do they court, where can they learn more about this
> man?" And my head was going a thousand minutes per hour, spinning as he
> said "anyone who's ready come over here into the office loaned me by Father
> Daniel, the parish priest here, and have a private conversation with me." Six
> empleadas went in but I didn't . . . I stayed there, just thinking, I was just
> thinking about this whole world and what one could offer it, and I found it
> so difficult, like it was impossible that these things could ever come to pass.[11]

Piñera's language, here recalled through a lens of Bravo's lifelong devotion to her spiritual adviser, rings with the jocist rhetoric of personal and social liberation through communal struggle: see, judge, act. Although she was initially concerned that Piñera's work had something to do with unions—"I was terrified of that word, '*union*'"—Bravo went on to volunteer her time at the Hogar, become a member of the Federation of Empleadas, and join the governing board of the group (and its successor organization, ANECAP), where she served repeated terms as president from the early 1950s to the 1990s. Bravo distributed flyers in butcher shops and other businesses frequented by domestic workers, contributed her own scarce income to the campaign to purchase the Hogar, and rode her bicycle to parishes around Santiago in an effort to recruit empleadas to the movement.

Another activist who came to the Hogar via the parish system in the early 1950s was Elena Prado, a domestic worker who had left her home in Temuco after one of Chile's many earthquakes, worked for a time in Argentina and Los Angeles (Chile), before migrating to Santiago for work in 1954 at the age of forty-two. Prado learned of the association first through a flyer advertising vocational classes, then was encouraged by her parish priest, who assured her that the classes were not just for young empleadas. At the Hogar, Prado studied high school level courses, religion, and sewing, and soon was charged with developing theater activities for the association, including raising funds by putting on small performances in public plazas.[12] Before long, Prado was directing and acting in the plays and poetry readings organized by empleadas to raise funds and celebrate anniversaries. In similar fashion, having moved from Paine to Santiago at age fifteen to work alongside her aunt as an empleada, Rudy Urzúa was allowed to participate in her parish literacy activities (as an instructor, having finished fifth grade): "During that time because of this group I began working with the Hogar of the empleada, and a leader from there came to train us in the values of Christianity and the trade, and we started to attend visit some of the bigger meetings at the headquarters, ones attended by representatives of the different parishes." Like Bravo, Urzúa dedicated all her free time to the work of the Hogar, visiting parish groups and encouraging other empleadas to participate: "It was really nice and fun because it was fulfilling, it was satisfying to be with other compañeras and do something good for others." Like the other empleada activists of the JOC, Urzúa gave up her work as an empleada to live and serve on the directors' council for five years in 1961.[13]

The emerging empleadas' movement also received critical support from the JOC Femenina, which Piñera estimates drew on its membership of about 300

FIGURE 3.2. Fathers Piñera and Hourton with Federation leaders, circa 1953

young women to establish key services for empleadas in Santiago. These women volunteered as teachers for primary and vocational classes, and the Women's JOC itself provided a model for the new association: as an empleadas' movement publication later noted, the empleadas' Federation "is based on the plans for the women's JOC, having adapted them to the empleadas' problems, which are different from those of the women who work in factories, workshops, offices, etc."[14] Although the JOC Femenina proved to be an enduring resource for empleada activists—who relied on the JOC Femenina for additional training, sociability, and international experience—the JOC de las Empleadas emphasized services over religion. As Piñera would later observe, although the fundadoras were themselves religious people, they did not insist that empleadas associated with the JOC participate in Catholic rituals or religious training.[15]

After a few years, empleada activists began to realize Father Piñera's vision for an "Empleadas' Home," where workers could congregate, take primary and vocational education classes, and stay for short periods when they were unemployed.[16] The empleadas rented, then purchased the Santiago property of the Hogar from the Hogar de Cristo in April 1957 for 5.5 million pesos, through an arrangement between Fathers Piñera and Hurtado. The Archbishopric of Santiago agreed to secure the loan—in exchange for permanent title to the

FIGURE 3.3. Celebrating ten years of the Santiago Hogar, 1960

property—while members of the Hogar de Empleadas made scheduled payments, organized raffles, and collected donations to pay it off.[17]

The resulting Hogar de Empleadas not only housed popular services for empleadas, but also because of its central location it also became a space uniquely suited to domestic workers' religious, social, and political activity as the movement expanded. On Tocornal Street, the Hogar, Federation, and later savings and housing cooperatives regularly sponsored gatherings for religious purposes (celebration of first communions, marriages, spiritual retreats and pilgrimages, and saints' days), entertainment (theatrical and musical performances), and commemoration (celebrations of the Hogar's anniversary and teas to welcome new clergy). As Piñera had anticipated, the Hogar was one of the only spaces outside of employers' homes where domestic workers could congregate freely, without incurring employers' wrath or exposing themselves to the sexual dangers associated with public streets and plazas. Although the Chilean Church's involvement with domestic workers in the 1950s was hardly new, rather than drawing young women into religious institutions for training and placement in domestic service, Piñera and his "many Zitas" served women already employed as empleadas, recruiting them through parish outreach rather than bringing them to service through the convent. The resulting institutions extended the Church's

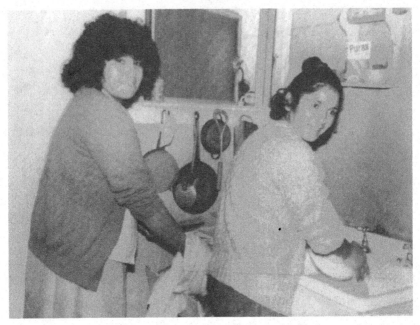

FIGURE 3.4. Empleadas in the Hogar kitchen

support to thousands of domestic workers in Santiago, and later throughout Chile's major urban centers: in 1959, the Hogar provided over 14,000 overnight stays and 56,000 meals to empleadas in Santiago alone, and over twenty Federation groups offered religious and social services to empleadas through Santiago parishes.[18] With the Hogar as its physical center, the JOC de las Empleadas was able to reach scores of otherwise isolated empleadas, disseminate its message of dignity and rights, and broaden its reach on the national stage, establishing the property at Tocornal and Marin as the enduring gathering place of the national empleadas' movement.

The domestic workers' movement of the 1950s prioritized the social and practical needs of live-in empleadas, many of them young, poorly educated rural migrants who depended entirely on their employers for food, shelter, and "family" in the capital city. In 1957, almost 90 percent of domestic workers still worked *puertas adentro,* living in their employers' homes and receiving some portion of their salaries in food and housing.[19] In any case, the JOC de las Empleadas—led primarily by recent migrants—privileged outreach to other migrant women employed as full-time empleadas, rightly assuming that their isolation in employers' households and distance from their families of origin made them particularly

FIGURE 3.5. JOC pamphlet cover, 1958

amenable to the religious instruction and professional services offered by the new Hogar de Empleadas. But Piñera's understanding also became—through Piñera's outreach to parish groups, publications in Catholic press, and shared understanding with the movement's original twelve militants—the functional definition of domestic workers and their plight. In Piñera's analysis, "the problem of the empleada" had three aspects: first, empleadas tended to be recent migrants from their rural families of origin; second, the women came from poor backgrounds to live in wealthier households, a kind of culture shock; and finally, empleadas were new to Santiago, and unaccustomed to "all the dangers of the city."[20] Piñera disseminated this characterization of the empleada as a rural migrant in many contemporary accounts as well as retrospective interviews, where he emphasized how out of place empleadas were in the city, their difference accentuated by the style of dress mandated by employers. According to Father Piñera, as recent migrants empleadas stood out in the residential districts where they worked: "I remember that before, everyone could tell who the empleada was . . . she looked different because of the way she dressed, the way she talked, for being a peasant, well, for the uniform or whatever it might be. These days, nobody knows if she's an empleada or a secretary, because she manages to erase any identifying marks, and before it was not like that."[21]

Contrary to Piñera's portrait of empleadas' plight, however, migration for work in the big(ger) city could also be a journey of personal discovery for these young women. So it was for Aída Moreno, who traveled with her aunt and stepfather to work in the household that already employed her aunt. Her new "home" was a far cry from her poor origins: "It was the first real dream that I was living; it was impossible to compare the poor rural home that I had left, with the beautiful house where I might live for a long time."[22] Moreno recounted her desire to live apart from her mother and earn her own money, saying "I did not want to keep living close to my mother or my sister, because she was always threatening to get me in trouble for flirting. Also, I dreamed of having dresses and shoes, of seeing new places, of helping my grandmother and my family."[23] On her visits home, Moreno felt the admiration of her cousins, who looked up to her "because I worked in Santiago." Eager to share her good fortune, Moreno arranged to bring her cousins with her on a trip to the big city, where they rode the streetcars, took a ride on the tram, and visited the zoo.[24] As these leaders became entrenched in an urban activist life, moreover, some of them also shifted to part-time work, or lived at the Hogar or in their own homes, successfully charting an independent life that rarely appears in Father Piñera's accounts of the early movement. Despite the quantitative importance of live-in domestic service in the 1950s, it is also likely that the JOC de las Empleadas failed to attract women who were less dependent on their employers for income and shelter, either because they worked for multiple employers or had homes of their own.

In another respect, the stories told by aging activists departed from Piñera's account: once employed in multi-servant households, empleadas developed close ties with fellow workers and sometimes even convinced employers to grant them greater independence. In what were multi-servant households, activist Rudy Urzúa remembered, a sense of "family" emerged mostly among the servants, as opposed to between the empleadas and their employers, because they worked and traveled as a group between their employers' city and rural estates.[25] In another example of employers' good treatment, Elena Prado reported that her long-term Hungarian employers allowed her to teach sewing to other empleadas, using the patrona's house for the classes and keeping the income she earned. In that house, she reported, she also saved money from vacation bonuses and tips she earned by tending to visitors' children.[26] Some empleadas reported leaving several jobs before finding one that paid enough, although it was not uncommon, as in Elena Prado's case, to work for several decades for the same family before retiring.[27]

Significantly, the JOC mobilized only female empleadas, even though men continued to engage in domestic service in this period. According to Piñera, however, male domestic workers had no interest in joining the JOC de las Empleadas, because they already enjoyed higher status:

> I never thought male and female empleados were similar. First of all because there were not very many empleados—butlers, gardeners, chauffeurs, etc. . . . and second, as in the case of the chauffeurs, they weren't interested in being seen as equal to the empleadas, because they had a different status. In general there was just one empleado for every hundred empleadas.[28]

Piñera also recounted the employers' reluctance to permit their empleadas to participate in the JOC, although the Church's oversight of the association offered some security:

> The employers never liked it that empleadas had a place to get help outside their homes, they didn't like it when they belonged to a group, whatever it was, just like they didn't like it if they dated some stranger. The fact that ANECAP was supported by the Church made the employers trust a little more, but not completely, because some said that the priests were stirring up the empleadas, and others said at least it was priests and not communists who were stirring them up. I got together with the [women] employers many times, and I think they had the wrong idea about the empleadas' organization.[29]

In later interviews, for example, Piñera delighted in telling stories about his interactions with the patronas, some of which took place at events he himself organized to draw them into conversations about their employees' participation in the JOC. In one of his favorite stories, Piñera describes a meeting with forty-odd patronas, in which they accused him of teaching empleadas to deceive their employers in order to attend JOC meetings, asking, "Do you think this is all right? That a priest teaches empleadas to disobey and rebel?"[30] Piñera countered that he did not foment empleadas' disobedience, and that patronas should not concern themselves with the empleadas' activities in defense of their rights, whether in JOC or through the union.

As Catholic successes among empleadas grew dramatically throughout the fifties, the Sindicato Profesional—the secular union—struggled to maintain an autonomous existence. The legal standing of the Sindicato Profesional as the official representative of domestic workers was never in doubt: the union maintained close relations with officials from the Ministries of Labor and Social Security, while the Ministry of Labor handed over the Libros de Actas from the first empleados' union for safekeeping and helped union officials fend off challenges from an (illegal) Communist union in 1953.[31] But repeated references in the union minutes from this period reveal that the relationship between the Sindicato and the Hogar remained ambiguous and sometimes conflicted throughout the fifties. Although secular unionists referred to a split with Piñera's group and called in 1952 for the organization of a second Hogar (presumably not under the Piñera's direction),[32] the Sindicato Profesional continued to store its furniture (including a statue of the Virgen del Carmen) in the Hogar at Tocornal 315, later lending some of that furniture for the Catholic center's activities, and made repeated plans to hold its monthly meetings at the Hogar.

The growing interdependence between these secular and Catholic organizations, however—as evidenced by the designation of the Hogar as the Sindicato Profesional's official meeting place in 1957—led to increasing friction over the leadership and activities of empleada unionism. President Raquel Riquelme of the Sindicato Profesional took advantage of the union's presence at Tocornal 315 to give regular recruiting talks to empleadas engaged in Hogar activities, but then complained that Hogar members regularly skipped union meetings in order to attend religious or jocist functions.[33] After repeated reminders and threats of fines to delinquent members, in late 1960 the Sindicato Profesional witnessed the rise in the directorate of new Hogar-oriented leaders, such as the former Hogar administrator Raquel Ortiz. At this point, although former union officers continued to participate, militants linked to the Hogar and the JOC became more visibly active in the Sindicato Profesional, effectively subsuming the union within the broader Catholic empleadas' movement. Subsequently, the Sindicato became increasingly active in recruiting more members through local parishes and urban JOC networks. These closer ties sustained the activities undertaken by the union in this period, such as the "proselytization" of new members through the parish structure, the establishment of an employment office, hiring a legal adviser for empleadas to consult when facing labor difficulties, and repeated roundtable discussions of labor legislation that were held at the Hogar.[34] At the same time, the activities of the Sindicato Profesional were eventually subsumed under the Asociación Nacional de Empleadas de Casa Particular (ANECAP), created in 1962 to direct the activities of the jocist Federación de Empleadas de Casas Particulares.[35] The founding of ANECAP—which became the principal force of ongoing unionization among empleadas in the 1960s—corresponded with the decreased visibility of autonomous and secular union organization among domestic empleadas in the same period.[36]

In addition to sharing some leaders and members, Piñera noted that when the Catholic movement was founded the union "joined us, putting some real muscle" into legal disputes between empleadas and patronas.[37] For a time in the 1950s, the union held its meetings at the Hogar, was granted free office and storage space when the union was without a site, and coordinated efforts with those of the JOC de las Empleadas. In those early years, Piñera urged the jocists to collaborate with union activists and, if possible, become members of both organizations: though careful to distinguish the Federation from the union, Piñera also encouraged Federation leaders to join that union and recruit other empleadas to it. But he recognized that the Hogar held much greater appeal to large numbers of empleadas, explaining in part the union's very small membership:

> For the empleada, "everything she needed was at the Hogar." The union offered "what she would need at a particular time." So one had to have a lot of communal spirit to join the union, whereas if the empleada paid her dues [in the Hogar] she benefited immediately. In the union, on the other hand, she would struggle on behalf of the whole trade of empleadas, but only got a direct benefit if she had a legal problem, and this didn't always happen.[38]

Despite his support for the empleadas' union, and repeated insistence on the importance of the union for the defense of labor rights, Piñera argued that only the JOC de las Empleadas could effectively intervene with employers on the empleadas' behalf, noting that "employers hated and mistrusted seeing the empleadas organize." These fears were often directly expressed to Piñera, who was approached by employers on more than one occasion and accused of fomenting rebellion among the empleadas, as well as by empleadas who, upon serving him on visits to their employers' homes, would lean in close and whisper "have more food, Father: I am from the Hogar."[39]

Over weekly afternoon teas, domestic workers like Bravo and Prado joined their spiritual adviser in launching a movement that would later offer multiple, vibrant institutions for female domestic workers, including the Hogar; housing and savings cooperatives; a school for primary and vocational education; a monthly magazine; and a lay association known variously as the Federation or JOC of Domestic Employees (Federación or JOC de las Empleadas de Casa Particular).[40] Inspired by jocist discourse, empleada activists and their clerical allies defended individual empleadas from the indignities of economic and

sexual exploitation, fueling a movement among thousands of empleadas nation-
wide through a discourse of human dignity and labor rights. Like the broader
JOC movement, the JOC of las Empleadas combined religious with material
objectives, seeking to "Christianize the trade, raising the moral, social, and economic level of the empleadas."[41] Retitled the Asociación Nacional de Empleadas
de Casa Particular (ANECAP), the group claimed more autonomy from the
Church but retained a spiritual adviser. Another distinctive stage in the history of Chilean domestic workers' activism, from 1950 to 1965 the JOC de las
Empleadas provided essential services to thousands of empleadas, channeling
Catholic advocacy for their trade and establishing a mass movement that would
later articulate, debate, and press forward legislation and political alliances to
improve the rights of domestic workers in Chile.

The Rights of Labor in the JOC de las Empleadas, 1950–1958

From its inception, the Federation worked to improve the status of domestic
workers in Chile, both individually and collectively, deploying a jocist discourse
that combined Catholic teachings on humility, dignity, and class harmony with
pointed criticism of the mistreatment and humiliation suffered by many empleadas, and at time included calls to defend the labor rights of the empleada.
Even as it represented a unique adaptation of progressive Catholicism in Latin
America, however, the JOC de las Empleadas shares with this broader history of
Catholic Action and the Young Catholic Worker movements a variety of fundamental characteristics: the apostolic mission shared by militants, their vigorous
recruitment of working-class followers, and its deeply anti-communist rhetoric.
But unlike the JOC activities directed at peasant, male worker, and other female populations, the JOC de las Empleadas addressed a distinctly marginal
occupation, one largely ignored by Marxist organizers, remaking the rules of
apostolic engagement and defense of labor as they did so. Empleada activists in
the JOC were particularly involved, for example, in the celebration of the *mes
de Maria*, a month devoted to the veneration of the Virgin Mary, practices that
had deep roots in the popular Catholicism empleadas brought with them to the
city, and that played out in diverse ways with respect to Mary's symbolic value as
a feminine figure. A majority of those active in the greater JOC of the 1950s were
rural migrants and recent additions to the industrial workforce, whose rural
origins combined with new worker identities to propel their affiliation with the
JOC.[42] By contrast, the empleadas recruited to the JOC de las Empleadas were
employed in occupations regularly and historically excluded from the family of

labor, privy to few viable rights and typically walled off from labor mobilization. Significantly, it was empleadas' systematic exclusion from formal labor rights—along with the clergy's access to empleadas via the parish structure—that allowed the JOC de las Empleadas to mobilize a large and sustained movement of domestic workers in Chile in the 1950s.

In addition to Federation activities that supported domestic workers' participation in the Church, activists and clergy argued for the social recognition of empleadas' human dignity, struggles framed within the radical Christianity of the JOC. As Father Piñera later recalled, "the thing we insisted upon most was the sense that the empleada had more dignity, that the best thing the empleada could do to improve her situation was to speak with dignity."[43] Piñera and other activists pursued "dignity" not only by educating employers about Christian treatment of their empleadas but also by providing legal advice and priestly intervention when empleadas were mistreated or accused of theft. According to Piñera, most complaints were handled on a case-by-case basis; the Federation helped workers to file complaints with the Labor Office or intervened on their behalf with employers.[44]

Leaders in the association also engaged systematically—and increasingly—in campaigns to honor and increase domestic workers' legal rights, regularly reminding Federation members (and their employers) of workers' rights to social security payments, weekly days off, yearly vacations, and severance pay. The Federation publicized in the Catholic press, for example, a 1955 Labor Office publication, "Domestic Employees: Rights and Obligations," which summarized domestic workers' rights and provided contact information for the Federation.[45] News about the Federation and Hogar published in the Catholic press in 1956 emphasized the Federation's "collective defense" of empleadas' rights—as well as the wealth of services offered through the Hogar—detailing the miseries faced by scores of rural women migrants "abandoned to strange hands" in the capital city.[46] Piñera's most passionate defense of the empleadas appeared in *La Voz* in 1957: in "The Domestic empleada and her professional problems," Piñera described for Catholic readers the hardship of migration; the disorientation and loneliness of young empleadas; their vulnerability to the economic crises of their employers; and the length and unpredictability of their workday. In closing, he sought to speak *for* the empleadas he had come to know, and to promote the "evolution" of domestic service:

> The empleada wants to aim higher. She understands that she has had insufficient education. She wants to finish her primary education, to acquire

technical knowledge of sewing and design. Not all of them want to be empleadas. Some try to work in another occupation, that of nurse or seamstress. Many would like to be obreras. But they are tripped up by the fact that they have no homes to come home to. It is just that the occupation of empleadas should evolve. The empleada's dignity derives from the fact that she serves the family and the home. This is an excellent occupation for the young woman who wishes to marry and have children. We must rid the occupation of its "servitude," which still characterizes it in part, and give the empleadas broad horizons.[47]

Under Piñera's direction, the first eight years of the Federation of Empleadas were concerned with practical, material realities as well as the spiritual and moral well-being of empleadas.

When it came to organizing domestic workers through the Church, however, Piñera discovered the limits of treating empleadas just like any other sector of the workforce. As participants and observers frequently noted, empleadas had little in common with the factory and office workers who made up the core constituency of the JOC Femenina, separated by very different experiences of employment, working-class community, and culture (particularly rural versus urban). According to Piñera, these differences were evident from the outset:

> The JOC (Young Catholic Worker), which was created for male and female workers, did not match up with what the empleadas did, first because the empleada is not an obrera (worker): she's a peasant, it's another mentality. Second, because the obrera lives in her own home, and the empleada doméstica in someone else's; and third, because the obrera lives in the workers' world and the empleada lives in the bourgeois world.[48]

In practice, Piñera soon discovered, these special characteristics made the usual models for JOC organizing—by which experienced militants would help organize new sectors—less than effective:

> There was a time when the JOC sent some women workers who were leaders to teach religion—I didn't ask for them. These two were good young women, but it created an unsustainable situation because they were rejected by the empleadas' group, who said that "why are these factory women getting involved?" . . . So after a while the two leaders came to be accepted, but they never had leadership positions in the Hogar, they just oversaw religious teaching. Pretty soon I had to ask them to leave, because their presence was like an irritating splinter.[49]

FIGURE 3.6. Empleadas marching at the JOC Festival of the Worker, 1956

According to the earliest activists in the JOC de las Empleadas, their activities and strategies were determined by the schedules, abuses, and needs specific to the empleadas who participated in the Hogar, and the leaders worked actively with Father Piñera to provide the services they needed.

These differences notwithstanding, empleadas who joined the JOC de las Empleadas enjoyed access to the resources and community of the larger JOC movement, including vacationing at the JOC retreat center in El Quisco, joining fellow empleadas on holiday trips to the countryside, and participating in citywide, regional, and national-level meetings of the movement's leadership.[50] These trips provided ample opportunity for Federation leaders to form more intimate bonds of friendship and deepen their involvement in jocismo more broadly. Nor did their differences keep empleadas away from the mass events organized by the JOC in the 1950s. In 1956 for example, members of the JOC de las Empleadas participated in the 1956 "Festival of the Worker," in which 12,000 workers and their families gathered to celebrate the JOC's ten-year anniversary at the Catholic University stadium, an event that also featured Monsignor Cardijin in his third visit to Chile. A news story about the event published in *La Voz* displayed photos of two of the event's parade floats: on the right, a half-dozen miners marched alongside a carriage featuring an oversized pickax, while on the left, the same number of empleadas (some sporting the traditional *delantal* or apron) accompanied a huge broom on a wheeled platform, described in the caption as an "allegoric float representing their daily work."[51] This juxtaposition illustrates the terms under which empleadas were present in Chilean jocismo: the giant broom affirmed empleadas' identity as workers whose labors entitled them to fair wages, labor regulation, and dignity, and their participation in the Festival signaled their solidarity with the family of labor. Although Catholic publications and correspondence of the 1950s often failed to mention the vibrant association of empleadas, Father Piñera worked tirelessly to draw attention to the movement, contributing numerous articles to Catholic publications and organizing high-profile celebrations of Federation anniversaries in the 1950s.

Empleada activists were also drawn into the international activities of the JOC, regularly participating in regional conferences and exchange opportunities, where they represented the only JOC de las Empleadas in the region. During the 1959 JOC Conference in Lima, for example, the Chilean empleada and Federation leader Ester Vargas was prominently featured in photos of JOC founder Cardijn's arrival at the Cerrillos airport.[52] According to published reports on that congress, jocists there enjoyed reports on the Chilean Federation of Empleadas, "about our problems and solutions; the Chilean Federation did this because we are the group with the most experience and greatest organization. . . . We already know that it depends on us; all the South American countries are waiting for Chile to lead where empleadas are concerned."[53] When Marta Pino, one of the founding members of the Chilean Federation of Empleadas, moved to Lima in August 1959 to be near her fiancé, she was greeted at the airport by a throng of jocists.[54] Movement publications also regularly published reports from Federation leaders residing in other countries and foreign JOC studies of domestic service, as well as correspondence received from foreign domestic workers' associations, all of which amplified the uniqueness of the Chilean JOC de las Empleadas.[55]

Ritual Marianismo in the Empleadas' Movement

As a Catholic lay movement, and notwithstanding the JOC's emphasis on class-based organizations, the JOC de las Empleadas consistently presented two key icons of female religiosity—the Virgin Mary and Santa Zita—as role models for Chilean empleadas. According to one movement publication, empleadas' reverence for the Virgin Mary played a central role in the all-female Catholic movement: the holy mother was portrayed as a model for empleadas because "Mary

FIGURE 3.7. Santa Zita, "Exemplary Lives" pamphlet cover, n.d.

was the first one to bring dignity to household chores.... More than anyone else, we are her daughters, since our entire lives we have been doing what she did in her little house in Nazareth!"[56] The "Empleadas' Prayer," a poem still recited at contemporary meetings of the association, emphasizes further the Virgin Mary's supposed domestic nature: "Virgin Mary, who like us worked your whole life in the noble and humble household chores."[57] While empleadas evidently attributed different meanings to the Virgin Mary—as personal savior, a model of proper motherhood, or emblem of female suffering—the marianismo expressed in frequent Masses and pilgrimages provided a locus of community for some members and allowed Federation militants to recruit others.[58]

Santa Zita, on the other hand, was promoted to Chilean empleadas an exact role model for their day-to-day behavior. In Chile, the story of Santa Zita was first circulated in pamphlet form in 1935, later appearing in Catholic publications and then in a later, undated ANECAP cartoon booklet.[59] In each rendition, "the empleada who rose to the altar" tells the story of a thirteenth-century girl from an impoverished Italian family who went to work as a servant at the nearby Fatinelli castle. Extremely devout, Zita performed all of her tasks to perfection, never joined her fellow servants in their revels, performed great acts of charity, and grew old in faithful servitude to the Fatinellis: "she obeyed masters and servants with exactly the same devotion and sweetness, no matter how rough and hard the task she was ordered to do."[60] In the didactic text of 1935, Zita had appeared as a model of penitence and observance with which employers could instruct their servants, a lesson that was reinforced in the Federation of Empleadas' public celebrations of individual, long-serving domestic workers. After her first five years of service, for example, Elba Bravo was awarded a certificate of appreciation by the Cardinal and embraced by President Gabriel Videla and his wife; after 48 years of service to the Donoso family, Margarita Cabrera Aceituno (of Santiago) received a silver medal from Cardinal Caro.[61]

Other lessons that empleadas drew from the life of Santa Zita, however, were slightly different, such as when jocists ascribed to her the characteristics of a JOC militant. As a 1961 *Surge* editorial argued, "Our trade desperately needs many Zitas, those who forget themselves for the good of their *compañeras*, who dedicate not just part of their life but rather completely dedicate themselves to the cause, ready to work with pure and clean soul, sanctifying their humble daily works."[62] The story of Santa Zita clearly illustrates the individual characteristics that have permeated marianist discourse in Latin America—humility, faith, service, charity, dignity, and purity—but also (in the hands of jocists) instructed domestic workers about the value of sacrifice in pursuit of collective organization.

By 1959, two massive annual events illustrated the wide reach of the movement, at least in Santiago, as well as its deep moorings in the Catholic Church: one (beginning at 4 a.m. each November 29) was a pilgrimage of thousands of empleadas from the Hogar to the statue of the Virgin Mary atop San Cristobal Hill, and a second celebrated the "national day of the empleada" each November 21. These events provided public Church sanction for the spiritual and vocational lives of empleadas, who defended their "right" to attend these outings before sometimes reluctant employers.[63] A third event, the anniversary celebrations of the Hogar, provided a platform for Church and state officials to demonstrate their gratitude to empleadas for their care work, and public commitment to the goals of the JOC de las Empleadas. On the Hogar's ninth anniversary, the Catholic press celebrated the Federation's successful outreach to empleadas far beyond its 3,500 members, lauding the activism of "these Chilean workers" (*estas trabajadoras chilenas*):

Alumnas del Instituto "Luisa Cardijn" hace un desfile, igualmente los Centros Culturales, mientras se va grabando una película.

FIGURE 3.8. National Day of the Domestic Worker, 1961

FIGURE 3.9. ANECAP folkloric dancers, 1965

In Santiago there are more than twenty cultural centers, which bring together about one thousand empleadas each week to study in a local center
that they have sought out. In this way, they are preparing to take control of
this numerous occupation, which has never been recognized for its importance, or for the value of its work on behalf of families.[64]

The tenth anniversary of the Hogar and Federation, reportedly attended by
over 500 empleadas, included a "spoken chorus," folkloric dances, and speeches.
According to Elena Prado, the empleada who directed and acted in these public
presentations, these events featured moving poetry recitations, as well as theater pieces written by the empleadas themselves. One of Prado's favorite plays,
the story of which she recounted with dramatic gestures and comments on the
public's enthusiastic reaction, told the story of an empleada who disobeys her
mistress by opening a cabinet of living toys when the mistress is out: it ends
badly, with the empleada's dismissal, but was intended as a comedy poking fun
at the empleadas' curiosity and independence. Another play Prado described re-
told the life of the Sargento Candelaria, based on the story of Candelaria Perez,
a Chilean empleada who reportedly joined the Chilean army and distinguished
herself in the Battle of Yungay in 1939, for which she was awarded the title "sargento." In the version presented theatrically by Prado and her fellow empleadas,
Sargento Candelaria appeared in a closing act (alongside Saints Peter and John
and the apostles) where "she arrived to celebrate the empleadas' day with them,
to celebrate the anniversary, the anniversary of the Hogar of the empleadas."[65]
According to some accounts, then, the anniversaries were times of unity and
celebration, a space for empleadas to express pride in their profession and the
association itself.

These celebrations also demonstrated some of the tensions among clergy and
public officials as to the primary goals of the association. Echoing the position of
priests involved with the movement since its inception, in 1962 newly appointed
Cardinal Silva Henríquez addressed the assembly with praise for the nobility of
domestic service, asserting that patronas "were learning better every day that an
empleada is not a slave, but rather a sister who collaborates in the beautification
of the home, and should thus be treated with dignity." But Ricardo Núñez G.,
then the spiritual adviser to the organization, called on empleadas at the meeting
to "value themselves more," adding that he believed in them "because you are
capable of suffering in the silence of your bedsheets and you give without tir-
ing."[66] Such appeals to Christian values of class comity, the dignity of work, and
suffering reveal tensions within the movement among diverse representations

of empleadas and their struggle: between the rhetoric of professional service (inherited from the Sindicatos 1 and 2 and amplified by the JOC) and Church instructions on the dignity of servitude, in which empleadas were exhorted to improve their performance of and attitudes about their work.

Movement Expansion and Politicization, 1958–1965

By the late 1950s, the success of the Federación de Empleadas was apparent not only to its activists but also to the Church hierarchy, which lamented Piñera's 1958 appointment as auxiliary Bishop of Talca as potentially disastrous for the entire JOC.[67] Shortly after Father Mauricio Hourton was named as the group's new *asesor,* JOC supervisors created a full-time position for the association's spiritual adviser, noting that the Federation's membership had grown to more than 3,000 empleadas:

> If Mauricio remains in the Parish by himself, we will have a permanent crisis in the whole Empleadas' movement, which beyond its numerical importance (in Santiago there are about 60,000 to 80,000 empleadas) is also delicate work: the "patronas" are very difficult and gossipy. With the appointment of Vega [to the Parish], Mauricio would get completely involved with the Federation of Empleadas of the JOC Femenina, where he has done magnificent work in such a short time.[68]

This endorsement from one of Hourton's spiritual advisers may reflect one of the most important changes brought by the priest's appointment in 1958: through an arrangement with the Catholic editorial house that published *Surco y Semilla,* Hourton expanded the Federation's bulletin from an irregular mimeo into a glossy, twenty-page monthly publication titled *Surge* ("Arise").[69]

Under Father Hourton's direction from 1958 to 1962, *Surge* became the movement's principal outlet for disseminating information about the Federation and the Hogar, offering Federation news, practical and romantic advice, and entertainment in equal measure. While several sheets of the eighteen-page magazine were regularly devoted to reports on local and national union activities, the remaining short stories, advice columns, editorials, and didactic material reiterated Church teachings on female virtue and honorable service. *Surge* offers convincing evidence of the multiple, sometimes internally contradictory strategies employed by Church and Federation leaders to increase domestic workers' involvement in the Federation. By examining closely the texts and

FIGURE 3.10. *Surge* cover, 1961

representations of the empleadas' magazine *Surge* in this period, we gain some insight into how the goals of worker dignity and moral uplift became linked and complementary elements of the Catholic empleadas' movement. As the official institutional organ of the Federacion, and subsequently of the Hogar's Luisa Cardijn Institute, *Surge* represents a limited view of the objectives and methods of the movement as dictated by the priest-director of the Hogar and the empleada militants involved in its production. At the same time, Federación membership rolls published in each issue confirm that the issues of the magazine were widely distributed throughout Chile (up to 4,089 members), and through the provincial hogares may have in fact reached a wider audience of empleadas. Most important, through *Surge* the fundamental lines of Church teaching for empleadas in that period come through loud and clear.

  Surge regularly instructed empleadas on the appropriate behavior and aspirations of JOC militants. "A Militant's Rainy Day," for example, recounted a day in the life of a Federation leader as she skipped Mass to feed a starving child, rushed to prepare lunch for her employers, and hurried across town to attend class. After this exhausting day, "Elsa" returned home, whistling a JOC tune as she went, and later wrote in her journal, "I, Elsa, Federation militant, have to be a saint: help me, Lord."[70] In another account, a Federation militant used *Surge* to spread news of the association, in this case to the household of a domineering Communist employer. The militant's intervention not only ensured that her ailing colleague could consult a priest, but also converted the employer to Catholicism: the militant concluded that "The empleadas must have the [strength of] character to be able to present their issues and make their rights respected."[71]

Father Hourton's leadership also coincided with the increasing emphasis in movement literature on paid household labor as *work*, a point driven home in the opening editorial of *Surge* in May 1960, possibly penned by Hourton himself:

> The young woman worker is worth more than all the gold in the world. You are one of these young women. Do you know what your work means? Have you ever valued your work? . . . What can we do so that we empleadas can be more content, more optimistic about our work? Don't you think that with greater achievement in education, professional training, we can make our work more valued and turn it into a profession?[72]

Even as Federation editorials in this period highlighted domestic service as an occupation, they drew attention to the peculiarities of paid household labor: "As Father Hurtado said: 'When the patrona pays the empleada her wage, she should thank her,' because the money she pays does not compensate for the energies used in her service."[73]

Another mechanism through which Catholic organizers sought to reach ever more empleadas was by recognizing and addressing their members' rural origins, something only rarely mentioned in the minutes of the secular Sindicatos. In addition to religious themes, *Surge* consistently provided romanticized illustrations of empleadas' rural origins. Perhaps for lack of alternatives—original photographs were apparently hard to come by—the celebrated full-color covers of the magazine often portrayed rural scenes that seemed to have little relation to the magazine's purpose. Even more puzzling, advertisers ran full-page ads for everything from fertilizers and tractors to offers of bank loans for empleadas working on rural estates, women who were otherwise never mentioned in the magazine's contents.

In stark contrast with these rural referents, the remaining text and illustrations that filled *Surge* addressed urban domestic workers' immediate surroundings, appealing to members' apparent thirst for romantic advice, recipes, clothing patterns, and movie reviews. The most consistent major advertiser in *Surge*—the Lucchetti pasta company—addressed the empleada as *the* key consumer in urban households: to make her charges happy, she was urged to prepare Lucchetti's pasta with their canned tomato sauce. Throughout the magazine, the most striking contrast that appears is that between union activities, accompanied by photographs of groups of Chilean empleadas in modest dress, and other representations of beauty drawn from the North American world of fashion and movies. Most often such images were appropriated without comment, much in the manner of other women's magazines of the era. But at times the textual interpretation itself illustrates the distance between the empleadas' reality and the available representation: the caption that accompanied one *Surge* cover—showing a portrait of an elegant brunette—read "This woman's face shows her exhaustion and weakness; so many of us find ourselves worn out by work." The magazine editors continued: "Let's change this on November 21. All together we will take a whole day off to rest."[74] The staff responsible for *Surge*—and perhaps their religious adviser—sought to produce a propaganda organ that would address empleadas' desire for the benefits of both association and entertainment. While it might be tempting to read *Surge* as a unitary expression of empleadas associated with the Hogar, the distance between these news reports and normative instructions in the magazine reveals the slippage between the magazine and the women it sought to represent.

At this point, the Federation also began to focus greater attention on the need for labor legislation for empleadas, juxtaposing stories about abusive señoras with demands for better legal protection. The opening editorial of the February-March 1960 issue of *Surge*, for example, featured a story about a señora who came to the Hogar in search of "a healthy empleada"; the editorial went on to explain how empleadas could not stay healthy under the typical work regimen of domestic service. "When will we get a law that regulates the hours of work and rest? ONLY THEN WILL HEALTHY EMPLEADAS BE AVAILABLE!"[75] According to *Surge*, "If we open up the Labor Code, we find there a huge gap, big holes in relation to the so-called 'domestic employee,' and the few times this is mentioned, it would almost be better if it were not addressed at all." The article went on to defend Catholic unionization, encourage the participation of Federation and Hogar members, and present suggestions for a preliminary legislative project on domestic service, including a work day limited to twelve to fourteen hours, guaranteed days off, prohibition of heavy labor, medical treatment for the sick, and retirement at age fifty-five.[76] This preliminary recommendation, reportedly the result of six Federation leaders' participation in a union workshop, anticipated several of the key demands that would surface in subsequent legislative proposals throughout the 1960s and '70s. The emerging focus on legislation in the Federation of the early '60s may reflect the fact that, in this period, more than a few Federation members were active participants in the union and its

efforts to bring forward a new legislative project.[77] The 1960s therefore inaugurated the Federation's greater attention to protective legislation; here, domestic
workers were encouraged not only to know and demand their existing rights,
but also to press for laws that would grant them fuller protections under the
Chilean labor code.

The early 1960s also saw the expansion of empleada activism into the organization of housing cooperatives, which were essential for empleadas who served
in employers' homes but wished someday to purchase homes of their own. JOC
activist Elba Bravo proudly recounted the lengths she went to in order to launch
new housing cooperatives in the early 1960s, which also led her to become active
in the Christian Democratic Party. According to Bravo, she became involved in
the co-ops because saw the need for organizers to address an important material
and emotional need of the empleadas:

> My understanding of the need for housing came later, it came after 1964,
> wanting to respond to the need that arose when the empleadas went out
> they had nowhere to go—maybe an aunt's house, maybe a cousin's—and
> when they got a house, maybe it was because they got married and the hus-
> band had parents with a house and so on: I saw all this. I mean, everything
> we did then was to answer the needs of the moment, and for me the coop-
> erative responded to the empleada's need to have her own house—married,
> single, or alone—that didn't matter, but what mattered is that she got legal
> ownership of the house.[78]

Building on the model of savings cooperatives previously organized by ANE-
CAP, activists like Elba Bravo helped to launch a dozen housing cooperatives for
domestic workers, a service that promised autonomy, privacy, and respectability
for domestic workers, especially those who wished to work puertas afuera, or
were single or retired.

Because ANECAP's spiritual director did not initially approve of the cooperatives project, Elba Bravo distanced herself for a time from ANECAP and
gradually became more involved with the Christian Democratic Party, which
she joined in 1964. Bravo's affiliation "opened up doors and windows" for her
activism on behalf of domestic workers, giving her office space for cooperative
meetings as well as letters of introduction to newly elected President Eduardo
Frei and Las Condes municipal councils that allowed her to ask for land grants
on which the cooperative could build. Bravo even met with President Frei and
secured his support for the cooperatives: "He said 'everything is possible for you
now: the agrarian reform is underway and if the agrarian reform succeeds, the

empleadas are also going to get land for their houses.'" Her connection with President Frei gave Bravo access to government offices that were closed to the public in the afternoons (when she was available), allowing her to set up first one co-op, then another. By her own account, Bravo did not shrink from conflict when the Las Condes municipal council offered the cooperative undesirable lands in western Santiago, suitable only for a shantytown:

> "And you listen here," I told them, "you people: who was it who first boiled, washed, and scrubbed your excrement from the diapers, who cleaned you up, who was beside those of you who are legislating today? The empleadas, the ones who made the soft food for you when you started to eat, who was it?" I said. "Bishops and cardinals today, who were the first ones there beside them changing their diapers and staying up all night because the patrones went out to eat and were watching the baby until late at night. When visitors came who was it who worked until one in the morning washing the dishes in the kitchen because the kids had a birthday, but now the empleada is out, she's old and she goes over there or to some old folks' home that's on Portugal Street, where there's a home that's so full it can't take more people." I said to them, "Go and see it, nobody else can fit in there now, and you people are telling me that we can't have this land here, we *can* do it," I said to them, "because it's not a gift, we are going to pay for it; we're young and we are going to work and we're going to pay for it, we're going to work shifts, not like slaves like it was when I started working. Yes, I'm telling you, maybe some of you will understand that no, we won't take the bad land."[79]

Reminding her elite listeners of their debt to domestic workers—and their complicity in the practice of discarding aged empleadas—Elba Bravo claimed victory in her campaign for domestic workers' housing, which resulted in the construction of seventy-eight houses for domestic workers in the Las Condes neighborhood "Población Santa Zita." Elba Bravo continued to organize housing cooperatives through 1984, and found it increasingly easy to secure the necessary bank loans and legal permission, even with the military government. One reason the co-ops for empleadas were approved, according to Bravo and others, was because women were considered more trustworthy, and less likely to misuse the loans granted for the purchase of new housing.[80]

The growth of the empleadas' housing cooperative movements, like the Association's increasing emphasis on labor rights and legislation, coincided with greater involvement of activists like Elba Bravo in the politics of Christian

Democracy in the early 1960s. For clerical and lay proponents of social Catholicism, by the mid-1960s Chile's political and ecclesiastical panorama offered both
challenges and opportunities. The increasingly vigorous grassroots organization
of the Christian Democratic Party drew heavily on Catholic apostolic movements—particularly those of Catholic Action—to expand numbers of party
activists, while a new generation of clergy rose to prominent positions in the
Church hierarchy.[81] Also in this period, pastoral letters expressed greater support
for structural change in agrarian and economic issues than in the past.[82] After
1962, however, Catholic Action entered a prolonged crisis, unable to sustain
the clerical or lay leadership necessary for the many associations, centers, and
movements it had generated outside the parish structure. The very success of
the Christian Democratic Party provoked internal crisis in Catholic Action, as
politicized militants left the movement and those who stayed resisted party attempts to instrumentalize the apostolic movements in support of new strategies
for grassroots action.[83]

Even as some activists left the Federation of Empleadas for more political
work, the Federation itself was renamed the Asociación Nacional de Empleadas
de Casa Particular (ANECAP or National Association of Household Employees), organized into regional and national directorates and still presided over by
a spiritual adviser. Significantly, the statutes of the association approved by the
Frei government in December 1965 inspired considerable controversy and legal
correspondence, as the new association's directorate insisted on the need to in-
sert language of "defending the fundamental rights of their trade" and including
all salaried workers (not just empleadas puertas adentro) in their association.[84]

The Federation of Empleadas experienced important changes in the early
1960s, gradually shifting under new leadership to a movement that was both
unionist in orientation and national in scope. Responding to pressures from its
own activists as well as the deepening political conflict, and extending its reach
by disseminating *Surge* to more readers in the provinces, Federation activists
prepared their membership for a greater emphasis on the campaigns for labor
rights that would soon follow.

Conclusion

The innovative nature of the Chilean Catholic domestic workers' movement
derived not from the evangelical and charitable aspects of the Church's outreach through the JOC de las Empleadas but from the enduring spirit of community and militancy these activities also promoted among empleadas; with a

membership of over 4,000 by the late '50s, the Federation constituted one of the largest sectors of lay Catholicism mobilized through the JOC.[85] In no small part, this success stemmed from the emergence of young jocist leadership in the 1950s, both lay and clerical. This apostolic movement's membership also far outstripped that of the Sindicato de Empleadas de Casa Particular No. 2 (SINTRACAP or Household Workers' Union), the secular union of several hundred empleadas active in Santiago since the 1920s. Although the Federation and SINTRACAP frequently collaborated and relied on shared membership and leaders, the much larger membership in the Catholic association demonstrates the ways that radical Christianity—with the Church's institutional and normative support— nurtured empleadas' sociability and trade militancy on a scale that its secular union counterpart did not. Although both movements shared fundamental concerns with empleadas' working conditions, only the Federation provided the diverse services and religious framework that would incite broader empleada participation.

Despite the Federation of Empleadas' impressive reach, the movement remained marginal to Chilean organized labor, both because of domestic workers' already marginal status in labor legislation as well as the JOC's competition with Chile's Marxist-led labor movement. Like the wider phenomenon of jocismo, empleada militancy in the Federation engaged only occasionally with organized labor and partisan politics; throughout the 1950s, activists sought to "dignify the empleada" by enhancing her religious experience as much as her labor rights, and rarely allied with trade unions or engaged in party politics.[86] Not until the rise of Christian Democracy through the Frei government, and the post-Vatican II ecclesiastical pronouncements that encouraged Catholic rapprochement with Marxists in the late '60s, would activists in the Catholic domestic workers' movements embrace more fully the syndicalism and party activism (both Christian Democrat and Christian Left) that had characterized the JOC in Western Europe in earlier decades.[87] In 1960s Chile, the consolidation of Catholic political forces around the Frei presidency, combined with increasing Catholic cooperation and assimilation with Marxism, critically shaped the Catholic domestic workers' movement, stimulating efforts to multiply domestic workers' unions throughout the country, advance legislative projects, and generate a revolutionary and religious discourse for the "liberation" of the empleada. Catholic liberationist discourse in Chile would have a profound impact on the domestic workers' organization, enhancing the importance of political, union rhetoric and transforming the legal and structural objectives of Catholic domestic workers' mobilization. In short, in the early 1960s the vision of empleada dignity and professionalism at the heart of the jocista campaign gave way to a stronger liberationist rhetoric of revolutionary transformation, not only of domestic workers' labor rights, but of the very structure of their occupation. As the next chapter will show, over the next decade the campaign for the empleada nueva—a worker cognizant of her rights and no longer isolated or subservient—was born.

CHAPTER 4

Domestic Workers' Movements in Reform
and Revolution, 1967–1973

The best time, if I'm really honest about it—I was not a fan of Salvador Allende, although I do have to recognize the good he did—but for the domestic worker, I would even say that this was the best time in history. Because, because, the employers suffered something that came upon them like a fright, like they realized "I have to treat her well."

—Elba Bravo, August 27, 2004

I N MANY WAYS, the politics of Cold War Chile aligned neatly with those throughout the region in the late 1960s: student, peasant, and union movements, sometimes in tandem with armed guerilla organizations, were empowered by a transformative momentum that launched both revolutionary and anti-communist agrarian reforms, as well as the rise of center and left parties seeking national power. Chile's well-known achievement in this period was the election to the presidency in 1970—over escalating fear campaigns fueled by US diplomatic and covert intervention—of the Socialist Salvador Allende Gossens, the first democratically elected Marxist head of state in the Americas. Allende's election, which ignited furious political clashes over the nationalization of industry, the structure of public education, and extensive land reform, represented the victory of an electoral coalition of left-wing parties over deeply anti-communist conservative and reformist Christian Democratic forces in the 1960s. With the inauguration of *el compañero presidente*, as Elba Bravo's testimony indicates, even his critics recognized the transformative impact of the new regime on social and economic relations in industry, agriculture, and service.[1]

What the numerous studies of Cold War Chile have not yet considered is how the political polarization and social mobilization that characterized the period, in combination with the apogee of liberation theology in Catholic circles, created new opportunities for the visibility and empowerment of domestic workers, empleadas who had long operated on the margins of formal politics. Were it not for the explosion of Catholic campaigns to institutionalize the "preferential option for the poor" by targeting empleadas for salvation (both material and spiritual), and the broadening of leftist coalitions to include previously unrecognized sectors of the lower classes—landless peasants, shantytown dwellers, and women—empleadas and their associations might have just stayed there on the margin. But something *did* shift, and forces both internal and external to domestic workers' organizations made empleadas newly visible as political actors, providing opportunities for expanded unionization and legislative action under reformist and revolutionary regimes.

As discussed in the previous chapter, by the mid-1960s the rise of Christian Democracy had begun to draw some domestic worker activists like Elba Bravo into politics; arguably, of course, SINTRACAP's members had been oriented toward legislative and political power since the first secular union was founded in the 1920s. But the last years of President Frei's government set the stage for the radicalization of empleadas' politics, first by exposing them to the currents and provocations of liberation theology dominant in the Chilean Catholic Church, and then through unionization strategies that encouraged partnerships between domestic workers and other unions. As Bravo noted, under Popular Unity the question for empleada activists was not whether domestic service would be regulated and their unions recognized at the national level: the question was when and how. Through intensive grassroots organization that mixed evangelization with unionization, and legislative proposals composed and vetted by empleadas themselves, the domestic worker movements were poised by 1972 to transform the structure and status of their occupation through a new law on domestic service proposed by Carmen Lazo, a Socialist elected to the House of Representatives in 1969 after serving more than a decade in the Social Security Administration. Had this bill become law before September 1973, when a bloody military coup ended Allende's socialist experiment and ushered in a seventeen-year dictatorship, Chile's domestic workers might well have become the first in the region to enjoy a wide variety of labor rights that were already well-established for workers in other trades.

Given the emphasis on recent studies of global care movements that have (understandably) focused on contemporary factors—increased migration, the rise of global care workers' movements, and the politics of the ILO—we might ask: how were Chile's early efforts to regulate domestic service even possible?

That the Church's liberationist discourse and associated pastoral plans, like the ill-fated legislation of Carmen Lazo, came to a dead stop in the short term is less surprising than the fact that these arguments about domestic service were made in the first place. In these efforts, we can see the distinctive institutional and partisan interest that made advocacy for domestic workers' rights possible: for the Catholic Church, embracing a politics of the poor (and of poor women) was both a religious and institutional priority, making the Church more relevant in a time of greater competition with evangelical and Marxist challenges for Chilean "souls."[2] For the Left—primarily the female leadership in the Socialist Party—cooperation with empleadas' unions positioned the Popular Unity government to incorporate new voters into the revolutionary project, adapting the language of class exploitation (as had socialists before them) to the specific conditions and demands of domestic workers. By deftly cultivating these alliances, empleadas gained ground in their quest for dignity and protection, just as the Church and the Left gained greater access, respectively, to capturing their souls and votes.

ANECAP and the Theology of Liberation

In the history of Catholic domestic workers' organization in Chile, the period 1967–1973 stands out for ANECAP's increasing pace of organization and a noticeable increase in labor rights discourse among its activists. ANECAP's increasing focus on unionization and legislative change was not just a response to the ascendant strength of Chilean unions in this period. The increasing radicalization of domestic workers' movements was fostered—and vigorously, emphatically so—by the upper reaches of the Catholic hierarchy, already identified as leaders in the region's movement for liberation theology in the 1960s, which in this period explicitly promoted unionization and labor legislation for empleadas. In fact, following two National Bishops' Conference meetings held in 1967 that were deeply marked by liberation theology, Cardinal Silva Henríquez and other Church officials devoted considerable attention to the question of domestic workers' legal rights, endorsing a shift within ANECAP toward a revolutionary vision of domestic service. In ways fully consistent with the base ecclesial community model endorsed by the Medellín conference and promulgated by the Chilean Diocesan Synod, the pastoral efforts directed toward empleadas after 1967 sought the *Christianization* of domestic service relations through consciousness-raising and structural change.

Encouraged by this support, and spurred on by a new spiritual adviser, Hugo Verdugo, over the next six years ANECAP hosted important workshops on liberationist approaches to domestic service, worked with SINTRACAP to organize new union groups in Santiago and the provinces, and supported evangelization efforts focused on domestic workers, which fostered greater domestic worker militancy and enhanced the visibility of Church efforts to further enhance the dignity of domestic service. As ANECAP militants fanned out across the country in the late '60s, expanding the educational and legislative work of provincial hogares and promoting the creation of ANECAP unions, they carried this message of the empleada nueva throughout Chile, joining forces with the secular empleadas' union and secular trade unions as they went. This expansion is of interest not only because it reflected growing active membership in the association but also because it relied on a rhetoric of transformation—of empleadas to trabajadoras—to strengthen empleadas' integration into national politics. Relying heavily on Catholic liberationist rhetoric, the domestic workers' movement succeeded, at least for a time, in erasing some of the differences that had marginalized empleadas from workers' politics since the 1950s, and in so doing came closer than ever before—and closer than any other regional domestic workers' movement—to laws that would regulate domestic service relations by treating empleadas as workers.

These changes really began in June 1967, when the ANECAP directorate convened its First National Conference for Leadership Training and Preparation in Santiago. This conference brought together ANECAP's leaders for nine days to hear presentations, hold workshops, and plan the association's future. Eager to respond to the country's deepening political crisis and strengthen ANECAP's presence in the provinces, meeting organizers called on attendees to reevaluate the organization's existing goals and activities. Starting with presentations on topics ranging from "national reality" to "apostolic movements," and lectures on the nature of voluntary and democratic organizations, Father Verdugo and ANECAP leaders debated the challenges facing domestic workers in a period of rapid political and social transformation of Cold War Chile. ANECAP leaders received lectures from scholars and other activists about the nature of Chile's revolutionary moment and the possibilities for workers' movements. The conference's first two presenters emphasized the importance of the revolutionary moment, advocating the increased involvement of domestic workers in revolutionary politics. The presentations, which explained the state of Chile on the brink of socialist revolution, are less interesting than the general discussion that followed. In those sessions, organizers posed leading questions that pressed for domestic workers' greater political involvement, such as "How can the empleada get more involved when faced with the changes happening in this country?" According to the conference report, participants responded that "we must struggle for structural change and to bring an end to the class differences that exist today," and that "ANECAP's goals should be revolutionary so that change can happen":

> We must give some thought to what we mean by "revolutionary." In today's world, everyone—facing such misery—everyone, including the Church (and we, who are a Christian organization) is calling for us to get involved in the revolutionary process, not in a process of hate, but one of change. The world demands insistently that we struggle for these changes, it is the only way to end this situation of misery and marginality.[3]

The question following the second presentation, "The reality of the domestic employee," by Fernando Tapia A., was similarly rhetorical: "Do you see that it is necessary to achieve unity among all the empleadas, in order to create a revolutionary movement? If you understand this, how would you explain this to a fellow empleada so that she would feel the same way?"[4]

By contrast, the remaining six presenters at the conference addressed historical and structural questions about the association, and most were delivered by domestic worker activists themselves. Emphasizing ANECAP's traditional values of unity and dignity, these presenters reproduced some of the tensions between moral and political arguments for domestic workers' activism. In "La Asociación Nacional de Empleadas de Casa Particular, ANECAP," for example, the association secretary Rudy Urzúa asserted that, as a movement, ANECAP was neither political (nor evangelical) in orientation: "The association allows each person to have her own beliefs and militancies, but prevents anyone from using the Association to make propaganda or any kind of campaign: the association is only interested in the empleada as a person and as a group."[5] Like several other participants, Urzúa in her presentation emphasized the association's representative, democratic structure, clarifying for her audience the group's national organizational structure and suggesting changes to ANECAP statutes. Nevertheless, the lengthy summary conclusions recorded at the conference included several indications that organizers sought to strengthen the class and union identity of ANECAP, in keeping with the revolutionary flavor of the opening presentations.

Instrumental in this ongoing shift was the leadership of ANECAP by Father Hugo Verdugo, who served as asesor to the group from 1967 to 1979. As Aída Moreno later noted, ANECAP's religious directors had always played an important role in shaping the political attitudes of empleada activists: "So I think that there are times when the Church goes a certain way—depending on the priest who's there—and this was the way ANECAP went. If there was a priest who was more socially involved, there were better relations between ANECAP and the unions. If there was a priest who was just pro-church, the union was more marginal."[6] In an article published in the Jesuit magazine *Mensaje* in late 1968, Verdugo and his coauthor, Fernando Tapia, took up Father Piñera's vigorous defense of empleadas, reiterating arguments for their dignity and safety but also calling out the revolutionary state and organized labor for failing to address their exploitation:

> At first glance, it seems like this large sector of society has been stalled, absent from the whole dynamic process of participation that other sectors have experienced. It seems as though the 385,000 empleadas are a social sector that is prolonging a certain mentality, that of servility and dependency, which really belonged to and upheld society at a different time. This mentality has nothing to do with the current situation in which we push for the liberation and self-determination of peoples, popular participation that will transform an underdeveloped and oligarchic society into a developed and democratic one, made up of new values and structures.[7]

Although the article presented fairly standard explanations for the problems faced by empleadas, Verdugo and Tapia were more explicit than their predecessors about what should be done to improve the situation of domestic workers in Chile: organization, education, self-representation, and unity with organized labor. But empleadas would also have to struggle to change the very "labor system" in which they worked:

> This is not just about changing the occupation's name, or passing laws about work hours, or even improving wages. You must understand that a whole process and a massive struggle are needed to establish a new work process (*estilo de trabajo*). The basic ideas for this new work process are the following: change the relationship between the patrón and the empleada. Put an end to the existing vertical relation and replace it with a horizontal one. . . . This new humanistic and Christian relation requires a change in perspective on the part of employers, which we know will not come about through spontaneous generation, but rather it is the empleadas who will have to win and establish this new work process.[8]

In addition to ascribing agency and power to empleadas, Verdugo and Tapia linked the permanent transformation of domestic service to the transformation

FIGURE 4.1. Directorate of ANECAP Concepción, circa 1970

of Chile's social and economic relations, including the elimination of the poverty and underemployment in the rural sector that pushed young women into
urban domestic service. As ANECAP's asesor in these critical years, Father Verdugo used the existing national presence of ANECAP to unionize the domestic
workers' movement, seeking to educate members about the advantages of union
organization and, in 1970–1973, sponsoring the spread of union activity through
ANECAP Centers in cities throughout Chile.[9]

ANECAP's activities following the 1967 conference continued to blend
outreach through Catholic parishes with the transmission of more militant
messages for empleada liberation. In parishes throughout the country, priests
continued to organize domestic workers for catechism classes and send them
to the Hogar for services and skill training. But the organization's leadership
became increasingly radicalized through contact with pastoral efforts that criticized domestic workers' marginality and patronas' abuse, and stressed the need
for pastoral responses that would advance the cause of social justice (and for
some, socialism) in Chile. Again, ANECAP leaders relied on strong Church
leadership to support their efforts. Following the December 1968 meeting of
the Synod of the Church of Santiago, in which Church leaders affirmed a vision
of the Church as leading the quest for social justice, a commission to draw up a
pastoral plan for Santiago's empleadas was created. The following year Monsignor José Ismael Errázuriz Gandarillas, Auxiliary Bishop of Santiago, appointed

fifteen "Christian empleadas" and four spiritual directors to the newly created "Pastoral Commission on Domestic Empleadas." Even as ANECAP worked with Verdugo to expand ANECAP unions throughout Chile in this period, Errázuriz sought funding for a separate pastoral project for Santiago that "would make possible the Arrival of the Kingdom of God among the domestic empleadas of our Church."[10] Citing the 1968 meeting of the Synod, Errázuriz pointed to the clergy's consensus that "we are facing a gravely unjust situation, perhaps the most alienating condition of our society." In his proposal, Errázuriz went on to examine the multiple reasons for empleadas' disaffection with the Catholic Church and propose a post-conciliar vision of how the Church might respond, based primarily on clergy's engagement with empleadas' particular material and spiritual reality.

The explicit charge of Bishop Errázuriz' commission was to design and implement a new pastoral plan for 1970–1971 for Santiago that would do much more than reach empleadas with the catechism: "This Pastoral work should train Christian empleadas, not only so that they can carry out further evangelization but also so that they can act within worldly structures and struggle for a change to more human living and working conditions."[11] And in addition to developing "a specific kind of pastoral work . . . adapted to the mentality and conditions of domestic workers," the pastoral plan included catechism toward employers, noting that "this is not easy, because this sector's bourgeois and comfortable mentality usually presents an obstacle to this kind of work."[12] Like contemporaneous Catholic outreach efforts, this pastoral plan specifically required collaboration between Church leaders and domestic workers' associations, "in order to achieve the goals of a changed labor system, professionalization of the domestic worker, and improvement of her economic status and dynamic integration into society."[13] Finally, Bishop Errázuriz' pastoral plan for Santiago mandated the formation of seventeen base communities in the eastern sector of Santiago, to be supervised by three empleadas employed half-time by the Church. Although the pastoral proposal acknowledged the existing outreach and services provided by the Hogar, Errázuriz sought funding for salaries and operational expenses separate from that structure. However, ANECAP references to the project in June 1971 lamented its limited effect: "There is a Pastoral Commission that only partly functions. They formulate plans that aren't executed, because they aren't 'realistic.' Sometimes little things get done. There is a PASTORAL PLAN that doesn't work, at least in terms of the creation of core teams."[14]

Meanwhile, ANECAP's directorate held its own pastoral campaigns in 1969 and 1970 to convene and educate domestic workers, which successfully boosted

FIGURE 4.2. ANECAP Concepción beauty contest, circa 1970

membership and increased local Church support for the association. These efforts, concentrated in eastern Santiago, Concepción, and Talca, expressed the liberationist wing of Chilean Catholicism, and sought to form permanent base ecclesial committees (*comités eclesiales de base*) among domestic workers that would address empleadas' religious as well as trade-based needs. The Concepción pastoral campaign was typical of these efforts: ANECAP leaders arrived and divided the city into sectors, mobilizing domestic workers for gatherings of Christian reflection and discussion, and meeting as a team every eight days to coordinate efforts. In the end, these leaders managed to established six parish-level groups (including a basketball team and a chorus!), which became the basis for ANECAP Concepción.[15]

The working document for the Concepción campaign explicitly referenced the Marxist foundations of liberation theology:

Every step towards integral development is a step towards God. <u>Any class of men, a people, or a world</u> that leads the way is seriously failing if it does

FIGURE 4.3. Day of the Empleada, Concepción, 1971

not answer God's call, which posits that all of humanity must engage in development. Man's historic creations (slavery-servility-capitalism-un-derdevelopment-misery-interests-oligarchy-structures-individualism, etc.) unfairly inhibit development and create obstacles to millions of men's ability to respond to growth and progress, which we are destined and obligated to pursue in life.[16]

The product of collaboration between ANECAP and the Concepción Professional Union of Household Employees (Sindicato Profesional Empleada de Casas Particulares or SIPECAP) founded in 1970, the Concepción pastoral literature included summaries of empleada working conditions, lack of legal protections, information about ANECAP unions, and instructions on theology, as well as an extensive analysis of rural versus urban religious practices. By 1970, as Allende's election accelerated social transformation, economic crisis, and US intervention in Chile, ANECAP and its priestly allies were also poised to enter a new phase of mobilization, grounded in the apostolic mission of the association but newly invigorated by the prospect of the growing unionization of domestic workers across the country.

ANECAP Unionization and the "New Empleada"

ANECAP activists were key participants in the pastoral initiatives described above, but the Association had also generated its own more radical vision of domestic service by the early '70s. In June 1971, Verdugo and officers of the directorate reflected on their achievements to date: "We want to see the new empleada transformed into a new kind of domestic worker (*trabajadora de hogar*): with dignified, fair, and respectful relations between the empleada and her employer, with a fair economic situation in which the value of the empleada's work is reflected in her personal well-being."[17] In this, perhaps the first reference to the title by which domestic workers would fight to be recognized in the 1980s—trabajadoras de casa particular or TCP—ANECAP militants argued that domestic workers needed more free time not only to enjoy personal lives, continuing education, and recreational activities, but also in order to participate more fully in Chile's political transformation. As social workers researching ANECAP in this period, Cecilia Guiraldes, María del Pilar Ibieta, and Patricia Dávila opined that "the empleada nueva will be a person who . . . has consciousness of her membership in the working class."[18] Such invocations of the empleada nueva, however incipient, were directly tied to the association's struggle to codify and implement empleadas' legal rights as workers, which made the association amenable to new political alliances in the age of revolution, from the Central Labor Confederation (CUT) to the Socialist Party. Reflecting decades later on the changes in ANECAP in this period, Father Piñera offered that "in Chile in the time of the Popular Unity, but even earlier under Frei, then under Allende, then the workers' whole world was politicized and even among the empleadas leaders appeared who were more political, that is to say they were more involved in the struggle, they wanted things to get better, and there came a time in which the Hogar de Empleadas became more a bit more belligerent in a political sense."[19]

Like other workers' and popular groups, ANECAP in the 1960s responded to the structural reforms and political conflicts of the day, leading to dramatic national expansion and the political reorientation of domestic worker activism. As an agent of historical transformation, however, one of the most dramatic effects of the "revolution in socialism" was the attempt by ANECAP activists—here working closely with Santiago's small, independent union SINTRACAP—to redefine domestic service as an occupation, and empleadas as "workers," in ways consistent with the political incorporation of their unions into the revolutionary project. The national expansion of domestic workers' unions via ANECAP

FIGURE 4.4. ANECAP Santiago anniversary celebration, 1970

fostered the continuing reorientation of empleada identity from the rhetoric of proper service and human dignity to a union challenge to employers' unchecked abuse.

According to interviews with ANECAP's national directorate in 1970–1971, these activists were implementing a plan to transform the ANECAP centers and hogares into local union halls, then creating provincial and national union federations for domestic workers, and culminating in the incorporation of the domestic workers' unions into the CUT.[20] Although ANECAP's institutional archive is weakest for the Popular Unity period, the 1971 social work thesis by Catholic University students Cecilia Guiraldes, María del Pilar Ibieta, and Patricia Dávila recounts the association's legislative activities in detail. Their thesis, "The empleada *de casa particular:* realities and perspectives" was directed by none other than Hugo Verdugo and combines class analysis of contemporary Chile with feminist analysis of women's exploitation and a familiar social work assessment of empleadas' struggle against social anomie and psychological dependency. The authors trace the history of ANECAP from the early 1950s, focusing on the association's efforts to "create trade consciousness, with the goal of unionizing the empleada." More important than the authors' analysis, however, is their account and transcription of a document produced by

ANECAP in 1972: "What we want." This document, approved at ANECAP's
June 1971 national training, built on the conversations held with empleadas active in ANECAP throughout the country, and identified serious obstacles to
expanding ANECAP membership and enhancing union activities: from domestic workers' lack of interest and information to "the issue that was common
to all problems and mentioned as the main problem was the lack of time."[21]
ANECAP leaders then laid out a five-part strategy to massively expand and
strengthen empleadas' unions:

STAGE ONE

1. Educate the centers' boards of directors throughout the country.
2. Study unionization and the legalization of unions with experts.
3. Study the approval of legislation with experts.

STAGE TWO

Educate the members in the different centers.

STAGE THREE

Organize union trainings in different centers and districts.

STAGE FOUR

Constitute district unions with legal status.

STAGE FIVE

1. Establish the PROVINCIAL FEDERATIONS for the empleadas' unions.
2. Establish the NATIONAL CONFEDERATION of empleadas' unions.
3. Incorporate the unions into the CUT.[22]

Building on the prior work of SINTRACAP activists outside of Santiago, as
well as recent pastoral campaigns, ANECAP was very successful in building
new union groups throughout the country in 1971–1972, creating three new
ANECAP-sponsored unions in Santiago and a total of fifteen unions in provincial cities by 1973.

Among the significant accomplishments of this ANECAP-promoted union
expansion was the founding of union locals in three wealthy eastern neighborhoods of Santiago (Nuñoa, Providencia, Las Condes) that were home to largely
live-in domestic workers. According to Aída Moreno, this union expansion at

TABLE 4.1. ANECAP Chapters and Membership in 1976

Unions	Founded	Membership	Active Members
Number 2, Santiago (later SINTRACAP)	1947	1,050	40
Viña del Mar	1964	200	50
Copiapó	1969	45	
Concepción	1970	290	55
Las Condes–Santiago	1971	40	35
Providencia–Santiago	1971	51	25
Ñuñoa–Santiago	1971	35	18
Talca	1971	90	35
Temuco	1971	130	50
La Serena	1971	66	28
Antofagasta	1971	104	20
Curicó	1972	82	25
Chillán	1972	85	28
Osorno	1972	80	20
Valdivia	1972	120	50
Puerto Montt	1972	42	16
Ancud	1972	35	
Arica	1972	52	20
Angol	1973	38	
Total		**2,675**	**515**

SOURCE: *Boletines Informativos ANECAP*, 1968-1976, in Humberto Bravo Navarrete, "Régimen jurídico laboral de trabajadores de casa particular," Law Thesis, Universidad de Concepción, 1976, 65.

the local level was possible only because of significant cooperation between SIN-TRACAP and ANECAP that began in 1970, which encouraged many of the association's members to work with the local unions, and union representatives were elected to official positions within ANECAP.[23] Although membership numbers for ANECAP and SINTRACAP in this period vary considerably, the period 1970–1973 represented the period of most effective outreach and

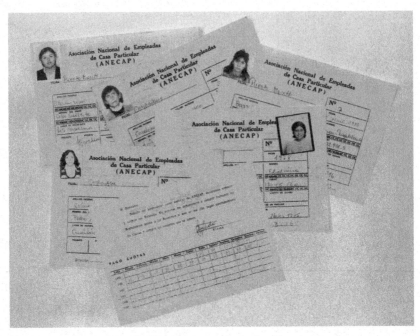

FIGURE 4.5. ANECAP Nacional membership cards, 1980s

mobilization among domestic workers. The first issue of the *Boletín* published that year, for example, ran out after 1,000 copies were distributed; the second number was published in a run of 1,500.[24] In the "Information" pages of those two issues, ANECAP leaders provided names, contact information, and membership numbers for the fledgling unions, emphasizing the communication among regional groups, leadership, and training provided by leaders from Santiago, and the success of several unions in joining the CUT and voting in their 1972 elections.

While the new provincial unions remained small, their activities and rhetoric of domestic workers' rights *as workers* represented a significant turn from the social services, vocational training, and pastoral activities sponsored by ANECAP in provincial hogares in the past. Particularly in Santiago, the multiplication of ANECAP unions—including their location in the northeastern sector of the city, where the most privileged domestic workers were employed—favored the emergence of more militant discourse in support of domestic workers' class identity. The 1972 ANECAP bulletin offered a report on the presentation of Antonio Camacho, professor of anthropology at the Universidad de Chile, to

Association members: after tracing the historical expansion of domestic service under industrial capitalism, Camacho vaunted the role of domestic workers—and the transformation of their occupational structure—in the coming revolution. Domestic workers would, according to Camacho, "help to build a new society, where this exploitation would not be possible. The woman and the Empleada must help to organize a new society, where she will have a just and humane labor system." Domestic service would itself be collectivized in this new society:

> The Empleada of a particular family should not exist. There should be people with professional skills who wash, watch children, clean, prepare meals, etc. and in this manner play a role in society. They should not work for a family, but rather for society. A society that does not allow for efficient empleadas, but rather efficient persons whose labor and freedoms should be respected.[25]

It was in this same issue of the bulletin that the president of the Providencia union Ivania Silva argued that ANECAP should seek affiliation with the CUT, writing, "Girls: we have to decide whether or not we are workers like all the rest of them, because we work with our hands. . . . If we do not take this step, our Union has no reason to exist, because we will not free ourselves on our own."[26] The radicalization of ANECAP union strategies opened spaces for greater discussion of the class relations of domestic service, as well as Camacho's critical assessment of domestic service in relation to reproductive labor in the family.

The inauguration of Allende's Popular Unity government in 1970 provided both ANECAP and SINTRACAP activists with their best hope of thoroughgoing legislative reform to redress empleadas' historic exclusion from Chilean labor law and marginalization within its union movements. As the work of ANECAP at the national level came to focus more squarely on unionization and labor demands in the late 1960s, cooperation between Church and secular activists became more marked, in some cases embodied in the double militancy of activists like Aída Moreno. With Allende's victory in the 1970s, SINTRACAP leaders moved quickly to demand that existing labor law be changed to better address the exploitation of empleadas, building as they did so important new linkages between the domestic workers' movement and political leaders on the Left. In two letters sent to government leaders in 1970—the first to the Minister of Labor and the second to "the Popular Unity parties"—SINTRACAP leaders demanded the modification of Article 62 and other sections of the Labor Code relevant to domestic workers.[27] Couching their appeal in terms of the international defense of human rights, this proposal treated at great length the importance of changing the legal terminology of the occupation from that stated in the Labor Code—"empleados domésticos"—to "empleados de casa particular." Citing the dictionary definition of "domestic" as those animals raised in a home or the "maid or servant" who serves there, the union proposal explained that:

> Now from this lofty point of examination, and considering ourselves part of the world of today, we find that, as human beings who think and analyze, we are shocked to find that we live in the age of the cavemen, and that, those beings defended their right to survive with dignity, given their time and means. Because of this, we believe that respect for human rights, in which every person should be considered dignified no matter what his social condition, especially in reference to his labor activity, we ask you educated people to abrogate Article 62 of the Labor Code.[28]

The SINTRACAP proposal demanded that Article 62 be repealed because employers regularly disregarded contracts and social security payments and because girls under age eighteen (a significant proportion of those employed in domestic service) were not allowed to sign contracts or make social security contributions in any case. In its place, the union proposal argued that the president of the Republic should institute a professional license (*carnet profesional*) for domestic workers, invoking a 1962 law (No. 14,890) that mandated the credentialing of workers in certain professions. This license would be of particular use in "our trade . . . made up of professionals who are intimately involved with people and children," and would allow prospective employers to rely on bona fide certification rather than recommendations of previous employers. A tripartite commission—made up of representatives of the Ministry of Labor, employers, and the union—would oversee accreditation, wage levels, and working conditions appropriate to each domestic service occupation (cook, nanny, etc.). In addition to its insistence on what had likely become the longest-standing request of Chilean domestic workers in the twentieth century—the declaration of November 21 as domestic workers' national day of rest—the proposal recommended that the workday be defined as 7 a.m. to 9 p.m., with two hours of rest from 2 to 4 p.m. Pointing out that this work schedule of 12 hours was modest—and in fact exceeded international norms for length of workday—the union proposal mandated time off of one half day per week and a Sunday rest every two weeks, with 50 percent overtime pay for hours worked above the proposed schedule. The proposal also stipulated that employers should pay severance to any domestic worker employed for more than six months in the amount of one month's pay per year served in the household. Finally, the proposal laid plans for a 2 percent tax on wages—paid by the employer—to fund education, social services, and vacation sites for domestic workers; these funds would be administered by Social Welfare Services and managed by a tripartite commission.[29]

Lobbying for Change: Deputy Lazo and the Empleadas

Even as ANECAP leaders moved to embrace more unionist strategies, the Sindicato No. 2 de Santiago was seeking closer integration into national union politics, seeking a short-lived membership in the Asociación Sindical Chilena (ASICH) in 1967, later with the Federación Gremial Chilena (FEGRECH) and, in 1970, in the Central Unitaria de Trabajadores (CUT).[30] According to the history of the Santiago union produced by Aída Moreno in 1983, at this point "a new era began, of strengthening and active participation in other unions: protest marches with demands; a legislative proposal is drafted expressing the pressing needs of the trade, with demonstrations when the bill was discussed in the Chamber of Deputies."[31] Here Moreno was referring to a bill on domestic service proposed by Socialist deputy Carmen Lazo in August 1970, based explicitly on the plan proposed to the Popular Unity coalition by SINTRACAP in March 1970. Lazo brought a modified version of the SINTRACAP bill before the Chamber of Deputies, where her introductory remarks again foregrounded the question of terminology: "I consider this name [of domestic employee] humiliating for a trade that deserves our full consideration and respect." Citing domestic workers' long hours, random firings, and lack of free time, Lazo proposed a bill made up of nine articles:

1. Changed name;
2. Professional licensing;
3. Tripartite regulatory commission;
4. Eight-hour day, with twelve hours permissible only with overtime pay;
5. National day for empleadas (November 21);
6. Severance pay of one month's salary for each year employed;
7. Weekly half day and two days per month off;
8. 2 percent tax on salaries, paid by employers, for domestic workers' services;
9. *Reglamento* to enforce provisions.

FIGURE 4.6. Socialist Deputy Carmen Lazo

The main innovation in Lazo's proposal compared with that of SINTRA-CAP was the bill's insistence on an eight-hour workday, which would bring regulation of domestic work into line with international and national labor norms. In every other respect, the Lazo bill reproduced the SINTRACAP proposal of March 1970.

According to the account of the legislative proposal and its reception among domestic workers by Guiraldes et al., ANECAP and SINTRACAP activists worked tirelessly to bring the proposed legislation before domestic workers' groups throughout the country in the early months of 1971. This process resulted in a proposal for extensive modifications to the bill, which was brought to Deputy Lazo in a public meeting of more than 400 domestic workers on July 25, 1971.[32] These "modifications" articulated a more radical vision of domestic workers *as* workers and as revolutionary citizens, and dramatically expanded the bill's contents from nine to seventeen articles. In contrast with the more paternalistic framing of Lazo's presentation, the revised text of the bill situated domestic workers' exploitation within the larger frame of class struggle and revolutionary transformation: "The situation of servitude in which the household employee now lives must not be prolonged: we must struggle to liberate all of the household employees, and to this end the empleados [sic] should use their strength and struggle to organize with government support to achieve their liberation as human beings and as workers." The revolution in domestic service relations instituted by the bill would, its (activist) authors promised, bring about a "new type of household worker," one who enjoyed dignified and fair employment as well as "a new personal situation," with sufficient free time to improve professional skills, participate in trade associations, and lead a normal life.[33]

The text of the revised bill went on to explain the need for the "liberation" of domestic workers on multiple levels: in relation to their status as free human beings, "and as such they must be free"; as citizens of Chile, where "we have begun a process of revolutionary change"; and, finally, "because those household employees must stop acting as the men and women who serve only the fulfillment and liberation of other men and women, without reaching their own fulfillment, and they should become the men and women who are motors of change from within the very base of society."[34] In addition to granting domestic workers full status as workers and citizens, this third justification seems to refer to those domestic workers serving in the employ of *other* revolutionary citizens. Perhaps, as Bernardino Piñera recalled, the legal defense of domestic workers' dignity was needed in the households of the revolutionary leadership as much as anywhere else in Chile: "There were even empleadas who worked in the homes of socialist and communist leaders, and these houses were the same: the señora might be very socialist or communist, but she didn't want the empleada living under her roof to take on an attitude of resistance."[35]

In the revised bill itself, the additional articles proposed by domestic worker activists, asesores, and legal advisers also increased domestic workers' representation on commissions supervising professional credentialing and the distribution of the 2 percent tax (specifying, moreover, their democratic election by representative organizations) and eliminating employer representation. These revisions also clarified base salary and overtime pay, specifying that room and board should be included, as well as cash payments, in such calculations. The revised text of the bill expanded the services to be financed by the 2 percent tax—including both job placement services and "technical-professional training so that they can incorporate themselves into the process of Chilean industrial production"—and added domestic workers employed puertas afuera to the group eligible for subsidized housing. These revised articles reflect the complexity of domestic employment and its regulation in ways not captured by Deputy Lazo's proposed bill.

Another outcome of the July 1971 meeting between Deputy Lazo and the domestic workers' associations was that it pushed Church leaders to openly support the proposed legislation. At that meeting, Father Verdugo promised to carry the group's concerns to Archbishop Raúl Silva Henríquez, one of Chile's most important architects of liberation theology and human rights in the region. The resulting September 1971 pastoral letter, signed not only by the Archbishop but also by Auxiliary Bishop Errázuriz and Rafael Maroto Pérez, Episcopal Vicar of Santiago's Central zone, gave the Church hierarchy's explicit support to the union and legislative projects pursued by the empleadas. In an opening statement, the authors affirmed a resolution passed with near unanimity at the 1967–68 Synod: "Since the Church serves the world. . . . It should remind all Christians, and the entire society, that it is extremely urgent and necessary to change the structures of the empleadas' life and work so that they may mature as people, as women, and as Christians; and so that they can be allowed full liberation."[36] Referencing the liberationist goals inherent in the Medellín documents, the 1967–1968 Synod, and recent Temuco meetings, the letter reminded both empleadas and their employers about the grave injustices pertaining to domestic service in Chile, including the low marriage and high single-motherhood and abortion rates among domestic workers. Lamenting the absence of adequate social legislation, the letter even alluded to Marxian notions of economic backwardness in domestic service: "Relations between the empleada and the housewife are more typical of a feudalistic society than a capitalist industrial society, and resemble even less what one would find in a socialist society." Describing the "absolute dependency" of empleadas' relationship with their employers, the authors drew a stark contrast with the factory worker, who could mix with other workers and form associations: "in the case of the Empleada who works as a live-in, this situation is fundamentally different: she has no real liberty."[37]

The most radical aspect of the 1971 pastoral letter, however, was the full expression given to the liberationist argument in the final section on "The LIBERATION OF THE EMPLEADA, as a WOMAN and as a WORKER." In promoting Church support for associations and stronger labor laws, the authors articulated a vision of the new labor relations of domestic service with the empleada nueva as the key protagonist: "the Empleadas who, through the force of their solidarity and organization, can create a new structure and system of work, in which there will be no dependency or scorn, but only competent work,

which is respected and carried out in liberty." The authors were careful to clarify, however, that they were not competing with union or party efforts to work
with empleadas: "Our contribution does not aim to compete with the attempts
to reach a solution currently underway, and much less do we reject or ignore
these attempts." In this respect, whether it referred to the activism of ANECAP
militants or the broader revolutionary project of the UP regime, the pastoral
letter clarified the Christian mission as complimentary to, but still distinct from,
revolutionary objectives.[38]

The pastoral letter of 1971 concluded with an emphatic assertion of the
need for labor legislation, supporting by inference the bill for domestic service
protection proposed by Deputy Lazo in August 1970. In arguing concretely
for the eight-hour day, the authors commiserated with empleadas' fears that
this goal would be unattainable and costly, but nevertheless insisted that such
legislation would force positive changes in the organization of many Chilean
households:

> Difficulties will arise IN THOUSANDS OF HOMES where Empleadas
> work, where life's rhythms are organized in a traditional fashion, depen-
> dent on the permanent availability and continuous work, at any hour, of
> the Empleadas. When this situation ends because an eight-hour workday
> is established, the homes, the family, and especially the housewives will
> have to imagine and create a new regime for family life that will certainly
> affect the family's customs, conveniences, schedules, etc. This is a sad situ-
> ation, but one that's necessary to make possible the liberty of thousands of
> women, women who deserve our respect in their struggle to achieve their
> personhood. It's a situation that will provide an opportunity for Christian
> families to update their values and actions in relation to family collabora-
> tion, children's responsibilities, and the role of men in the home, which for
> the sake of convenience have been lost.[39]

In taking this position the Church leaders also acknowledged, if only in
passing, how recognition of empleadas' labor rights would present challenges,
such as the reorganization of household labor and greater unemployment for
empleadas. The pastoral letter of 1971 made its call not only to empleadas and
señoras but also to organized labor and legislators, to support the creation of the
NUEVA EMPLEADA: "a free person, competent because of her education and
professional training, organized and unified among themselves and with the
rest of the country's workers; who has a normal life; who has a just salary and
real benefits."[40] In addressing a key constituency of the Church—including both

empleadas and their employers—Silva Henríquez and his coauthors significantly altered in the Church's historic discourse on domestic service in Chile.

Despite empleada mobilization and visible support from Church leaders in 1971, Deputy Lazo's bill failed to advance quickly through the legislative process. Though the Congressional record reveals little about the bill's fate, ANECAP representatives who met with Aída Figueroa, deputy director of the Labor Ministry in early 1972, reported that, although Figueroa encouraged the empleadas' continuing struggle, Lazo's bill was unlikely to pass: "She warned us that the proposed bill was unlikely to be approved, because it is a double-edged sword for the empleadas: the bill has good and bad things in it, but if it passed it might cause a lot of unemployment."[41] In July of the same year, Deputy Luis Espinoza met with union leaders, "and expressed his interest in bringing the proposed bill, a copy of which we sent him, to the Parliament. The proposed bill joins the ideas from Deputy Carmen Lazo's bill with ANECAP's changes."[42] While there is no record of Espinoza's bill, we do know is that on November 16, 1972, the Chilean congress legalized the term "empleados de casas particulares," a partial victory for domestic workers' longstanding objections to the term empleada doméstica.[43]

Whatever the shortcomings of Lazo's original bill from the point of view of domestic worker activists, the increasing interactions of domestic workers' leadership with political leaders of the Popular Unity further facilitated incorporation of domestic workers into the national union structure. In the months before the final coup, Aída Moreno has recounted, TCP leadership worked closely with CUT representatives to form the Unified National Union of Household Employees (Sindicato Único Nacional de Empleadas de Casa Particular) in 1972, which represented the nineteen domestic workers' unions the active in Chile. Closer relations with the CUT formalized domestic workers' access to activities enjoyed by other unionized workers:

> Yes, a lot was achieved in that period: we made agreements with help from the CUT, we got workers' vacations, the [household] workers participated a lot. We bought household goods, refrigerators, stoves, heaters, all those things that have been privatized back then we did everything through the unions, and for that reason it was excellent work. We worked with a lot of university students, the guys came from the University of Chile to train us, to give us workshops, there was great participation.[44]

The Sindicato Único was given an office alongside the CUT in the government UNCTAD building, and in January 1973 celebrated a national congress there with over 800 domestic workers, and representatives of the CUT and

Labor Ministry in attendance. Moreno has frequently recounted how the Sindicato Único enjoyed the attendance of President Allende and Sra. Moy de Tohá (wife of Allende Minister of Interior José Tohá) at the opening of a child care center for domestic workers.[45] In tandem with the syndicalization and expansion of ANECAP, the leaders of Chile's oldest domestic workers' union—Sindicato No. 2—saw their efforts applauded and promoted at the highest level of national union politics.

In addition to the increased visibility of domestic worker activists in political and union venues, oral history accounts of the period invariably note the change in workers' attitudes—and employer responses—because of workers' increasing sense of labor rights. If, on the one hand, these changes made it harder for activists staffing the Hogar de las Empleadas to find jobs for leftist domestic workers, Elba Bravo pointed out that employers were more restrained in Allende's time:

> I can tell you this because it was my job to place the girls, to talk to them, with the señora up in los Dominicos, and I got this sense that "look, it's like this: I'm not going to say no if she's very UP (Popular Unity), but you know how things are, that it's hard to buy things, you know, poor people, that if we're suffering how must it be for them?" But they were treated with a lot of care, I don't know if it was superficial . . . with a lot of care because they were afraid that they would get reported for this and that. It was different from how things were under Pinochet, very different, a very big change. I personally suffered under both [leaders], so I don't support either of them, but I value some of the positive things about Allende.[46]

Conclusion

This chapter has examined how the increasing strength of popular mobilization in late 1960s Chile invigorated the small domestic workers' unions and associations of Santiago, leading to their expansion at the national level, turning even Catholic associations into centers for the politicization of women domestic workers. In 1970, domestic worker activists gained unprecedented access to government offices, reaping the benefits of visibility and legislative activism that further incorporated them into formal union and party politics. The military coup of 1973 radically altered this trajectory, shrinking union rolls and creating new solidarities of surviving groups with Catholic and international religious agencies, as well as with the middle-class feminist organizations.

The study of domestic workers in this short period sheds new light on key questions in the study of Cold War Chile and the Allende period. From Church as well as ANECAP records, we can see how transformations integral to the Catholic Church in this period, and the explicit embrace of Catholic leaders of liberation theology, dovetailed easily with the Church's historic commitment to empleadas. Without skipping a beat, Catholic leaders moved from promoting a jocist ideology of the dignity of work and association for all workers to one that incorporated Marxist analysis of class relations and even quasi-feminist critiques of female exploitation. This shift allowed the Church's considerable resources dedicated to the defense of empleadas to be channeled into a series of grassroots campaigns, in Santiago and the provinces, which in turn laid a foundation for increased domestic worker mobilization. This, in combination with Church leaders' greater advocacy for ecumenical cooperation with non-Catholics and continuing recognition of the secular union as a sister organization to ANECAP, proved auspicious for expanding the reach of ANECAP—and the Church—into new parishes and activities. In the years prior to the increased polarization over socialism within the Chilean Church, such strategies offered Church leaders opportunities to advance "the preferential option for the poor," and advocate for structural change in ways consistent with liberationist Catholic discourse of the post-conciliar age.

Although we have far fewer details about what might have motivated Carmen Lazo, Moy de Tohá, and other Leftist politicians to support domestic workers' political aspirations, it should not be too surprising that their political gaze—long expanded to include workers in informal sectors and land or neighborhood *tomas*—should come to incorporate empleadas in this period as well. Although the most formal and masculine of Chilean trades remained at the head of national union and political party efforts (copper, truckers, industrial workers), the tent of the Chilean left had broadened to include other workers and their specific strategies to exert political pressure on formal politics. It tells us a great deal that it took a successful Socialist electoral bid to open up these spaces for empleada activists, when their votes—largely female, many rural—had been there for the getting since female suffrage was instituted in the 1940s. As studies of rural women and work have also demonstrated, even as the Chilean left broadened its mantle to usher in women and their "issues," or rural families and theirs, it remained an electoral strategy hindered by deeply preconceived notions of gender, citizenship, and modernization. Notwithstanding the misogynistic cast of Chile's Cold War left parties, the existence of a growing empleadas' movement, and the evident labor rights enshrined in their demands for corresponding legislation, brought at least some sectors of the Socialist Party into cooperation with those movements under Allende.

CHAPTER 5

Women's Rights, Workers' Rights

Military Rule and Domestic Worker Activism

T HE MILITARY INTERVENTION OF September 11, 1973, not only violently truncated the Chilean road to socialism, beginning one of the longest periods of state violence in Chile's history, but also transformed the landscape of political mobilization, especially for those who participated in unions and other forms of collective organization. Compared with those workers whose labor rights had been violently suspended by the military junta, however, Chile's domestic workers experienced not so much the reversal of their political and legal status—which they had not yet obtained—as they did the frustration of their most recent efforts to pass new protective legislation for their trade under the Popular Unity regime. In this respect, the military's abrogation of the Labor Code in 1973 had little direct impact on how employers hired and fired, compensated, and treated their domestic workers. Like workers in other sectors, over the next seventeen years empleadas suffered the shocks of the military's neoliberal economic turn, as well as the furious violence of a civil-military regime bent on the destruction of the political Left and all mobilized resistance to authoritarian rule.[1]

However, in the midst of the military's campaign of systematic violence against workers and their organizations—which accounts for a high proportion of the many thousands tortured, killed, and/or "disappeared" by the military government—Chilean domestic workers' organizations actually flourished under military rule. After a hiatus of several months imposed by the most severe violence following the coup, in January 1974 ANECAP members got back to work, continuing to provide support, legal services, employment training, and pastoral services to domestic workers throughout Chile. Making only occasional reference in meeting minutes to the ongoing state of siege and military decree-laws on censorship and association, leaders in ANECAP organized with care, always aware that they were subject to military surveillance and possible arrest. Over the course of the 1970s, however, and with support from Chilean university students and international aid organizations, ANECAP was able to significantly expand its services and increase the participation of domestic workers. And unlike other unions that were crushed and disbanded in the months following the coup, SINTRACAP's leaders were also able to offer services through ANECAP, whose affiliation with the Church offered them greater legitimacy and protection under the new regime.

ANECAP proved an especially enduring site for mobilizing domestic workers in spite of the dictatorship for two key reasons, the first of which was their status as an association founded by and enjoying the protection of the Catholic Church. The Archbishopric of Santiago, after all, held the title to the Hogar de la Empleada; appointed ANECAP's spiritual director from among its clergy; and within months of the coup had helped to form the Committee for Peace (*Comité Pro-Paz*), an ecumenical group of religious leaders who intervened on behalf of those persecuted by the military regime that laid the foundation for the Catholic Church's creation of its own enduring human rights organization, the Vicariate of Solidarity (*Vicaría de la Solidaridad*).[2] But under military rule domestic worker activists finally reaped a certain benefit from their relative *invisibility as workers:* unlike the male mining, factory, and rural workers who bore the brunt of the military's campaign of state violence and surveillance, Chile's predominantly female domestic service workforce had little in the way of labor rights to lose, and in a perverse way benefitted from the persistent invisibility of their work as "labor." Carefully curating their status as an association "of Christian inspiration," ANECAP's leaders continued their legal, housing, educational, and religious services for domestic workers throughout Chile, a project that attracted significant grant funding from foreign churches and aid organizations as the dictatorship (and the deepening inequality its policies fostered) wore on. In this way, and in a fashion reminiscent of contemporaneous mothers' movements for human rights in Argentina and Guatemala, domestic workers remained strategically illegible as workers and activists to a military regime committed to the suppression (or elimination) of both.[3]

Significantly, ANECAP then emerged as a prominent national organization in the wake of the regime's consolidation—enacted through the 1978 referendum on Pinochet and the 1980 Constitution—offering important support to the emerging, broad-based mobilization of women against the dictatorship. As public opposition to the regime grew in the 1980s, the domestic workers' movement expanded and fostered greater politicization, advancing members' concerns in tandem with Catholic, feminist and democratic protests against the seventeen-year Pinochet regime. At this juncture, the regime's patriarchal, traditionalist propaganda also inspired collaboration between feminists and domestic workers in the 1980s, not only popularizing a feminist critique of domestic service, but also spurring the creation of financial and technical networks that would transform the outreach and ideology of domestic workers' movements. Despite this new alliance, the older strand of empleada activist discourse—e.g., the social Catholicism of the JOC and early ANECAP—remained foundational for the movement in the 1980s, as Catholic leaders continued to play an active and prophetic role in protesting the regime's anti-democratic and repressive practices. As political opposition to the regime gained momentum after 1983, domestic workers frequently combined feminist and progressive Catholic arguments and alliances, joining the broad politics of *concertación* that animated Chile's return to democracy via plebiscite in 1989.[4] Along with the human rights, anti-poverty, student and religious organizations that had emerged under military rule, under the aegis of ANECAP domestic worker activists advanced their agenda of service and unionization, building a movement for empleadas' rights—as workers and women—that would long outlast the dictatorship and survive to the present day.

Finally, through the lens of the domestic workers movement, we can see how the violently anti-political regime actually provided new opportunities for political alliance, and for collaboration across class and political lines, networks that would install domestic workers' rights as an irrefutable aspiration of the emerging democratic regime. Theirs is a story of resilience and persistence in the face of repression, as well as one of continuity and adaptation: by continuing to participate in religious, social, and trade union activities, and cultivating new international donors and domestic allies, empleadas built a sustainable national movement that would in time contribute leadership and symbolic resources to the broad-based movements that ultimately toppled the regime. This complex web of alliances is not unique to domestic workers, but rather representative of the broader processes shaping human rights, labor, feminist, party, indigenous and religious activism in the same period.[5] Though scholars have tended to emphasize how ideological differences have historically divided Chilean activists on the Center-Left and within the Left, an analysis attentive to a wider range of social movement actors (such as the Church and women's movements) provides important context for how political alliances and movements were reconstituted in the transition to civilian democracy in the 1990s. Only by understanding the diverse identities and intersections at the heart of the domestic workers' movement under dictatorship can we appreciate the success of resulting labor rights legislation for domestic workers passed in the 1990s.

Beyond Survival: Empleada Activism after the Coup

Like other mass movements and union organizations, domestic workers' associations were immediately impacted by the military intervention of 1973. In their early morning coup against the elected socialist government of Salvador Allende, the Chilean Armed Forces stunned the world by bringing Allende's government to a violent end and installing a national security regime, much like those recently imposed elsewhere in Latin America. In the first three months of military rule, tens of thousands of civilians were detained and tortured, several thousand "disappeared," and many others driven into exile. The military junta (including Gen. Augusto Pinochet) declared a state of siege, imposing a curfew and press censorship, closing schools and universities, suspending the Congress and banning Left political parties. Although widespread evidence of human rights abuses prompted protest from within and without the country—inspiring one of the Cold War's most powerful human rights movements—military leaders and their civilian allies nevertheless succeeded in violently overcoming their political opposition, crushing vibrant unions and political parties, jailing, torturing, and exiling political opponents, and consolidating rule by force and military decree. The "culture of fear" imposed through force and threats, later supplemented by Pinochet's legal and political maneuvers to consolidate military rule, provides the context in which domestic workers continued to associate and struggle for labor rights under military rule.

In the upheaval following the September 11 coup, SINTRACAP lost its rented union hall, asked to leave because the owners feared reprisals from security forces.[6] Rather than sharing offices with a national federation (FEGRECH, Chilean Workers' Federation), SINTRACAP moved on after a year with no offices to share space with the Construction Workers' Union, where their meetings were monitored by police.[7] Subjected occasionally to police raids, the union nevertheless continued, receiving authorization from the government to run an employment bureau, organizing a cultural collective, publishing the bulletin SINCOOP (*Sindicato y Cooperativa*), and maintaining contact with the weakened provincial unions. The biggest challenge to the union's continuing work was the generalized fear of repression leveled by the military regime against any form of organization: Aída Moreno was arrested twice, once when she went to City Hall to register her status as an officer of ANECAP, and again during a speech to women assembled on International Women's Day. Union leaders recognized the impact of these fears when they tried, in 1975, to convene domestic workers for the National Day of the Empleada, when the union only filled ten of the twenty busses contracted for the event, signaling what would become a long period of decline and dormancy for the secular union: "Over time, we lost this tradition and the right we had already won: the right of thousands of workers to enjoy a single day of relaxation and sociability."[8]

Activists affiliated with the Catholic Church, on the other hand, were better positioned to continue their work, almost uninterrupted, and some union activists became prominent leaders within ANECAP in this period.[9] Within four months of the coup, domestic workers had resumed their yearly National Assembly and monthly Board meetings, declaring the following goal for 1974: "To build the brotherhood of Christ (*fraternidad en Cristo*) among domestic workers in Chile, in order to strengthen the trade and contribute to national reconciliation."[10] Within the first year of military rule, ANECAP not only received authorization from the military junta to publish the monthly *Boletín de la Empleada* (financed by the Catholic Church, and subject to military review), but also held their annual cultural celebration—complete with presentations on the group's trade and religious activities—in the Don Bosco auditorium.[11] In what would later become a sustained effort, the earliest meetings of the board after the coup included plans to survey their membership about "the reality of the domestic servant," information activists considered vital to their efforts to secure funds, work with employers, and continue to press for labor legislation for their trade.

ANECAP's historic affiliation with the Catholic Church provided not only relative protection from direct repression, but also access to a network of Catholic professionals and institutions that advocated for empleadas' basic legal rights: in some ways the military regime and its policies increased public attention to those hardest hit by military repression and economic policies, strengthening ties between ANECAP on the one hand, and universities, NGOs, and churches on the other. As agreed the year before the coup, the ANECAP Board started working with faculty and students at the Catholic University in early 1974, first by inviting the Catholic University Law School's Department of Legal Practice and Assistance (Departamento de Práctica y Asistencia Legal or DEPAL) to provide courses orienting members to empleadas' legal rights, and later through sustained internships of law and social work students with the Association. These were not casual arrangements, but rather formal relationships established between the two institutions: law interns offered classes for domestic workers in Santiago and provincial centers, while two students helped the Hogar staff to provide childcare, job placement, and professionalization workshops to empleadas.[12]

With its continuing close ties to the Catholic Church, ANECAP also ben-
efited from the relative protection offered by its religious directors and legal
counsel provided by the Workers' Pastoral Office housed in the Vicariate of
Solidarity.[13] This collaboration was expressed through ANECAP's partnership
with DEPAL, which allowed attorneys and law students to provide legal advice
and collect data for their 1976 study, "The Reality of Chile's Domestic Workers."
This study, which included empleadas' working and living conditions, attitudes
of employers, and a proposal for new legislation, would serve the board as important evidence for their work with employers, empleadas, and government
officials in the years ahead.[14]

Even under the constraints of military rule in the 1970s, domestic worker
activists and their allies returned to the question of empleadas' exclusion from
basic labor protections as a starting point for improving their trade. Out of AN-
ECAP's collaboration with university law programs came a succession of interns
and tesistas who supported the group's continued attempts to introduce new
labor legislation. Humberto Bravo Navarette, for example, in 1976 wrote his law
thesis for the University of Concepción, an exhaustive review of the legal status
of domestic workers in Chile that drew on ANECAP as well as state records.
According to Bravo Navarette, ANECAP leaders worked with union leaders
and representatives from DEPAL to draft materials relative to domestic work
contracts, and together presented them to officials at the Ministry of Labor—
with a particular emphasis on the need for minimum wage regulations—in
June 1975.[15] In a proposal subsequently drafted in September 1975, "Project for a
Legislative Statute for Domestic Workers," activists drew on both DEPAL and
Bravo Navarette's work in their appeal to military leaders for better regulation of
their trade: "we hope our petition will be well-received by the Government both
because it asks for a just recognition for this group of long-suffering workers, and
because it will allow for their more effective integration into the process of our
country's development."[16]

Significantly, ANECAP's proposal differed in tone and substance from the
legislative proposals of earlier decades: stressing ANECAP's ties to the Church
and its fundamentally associative (versus syndicalist) nature, and eschewing demands for labor rights per se, the proposal suggested measures through which
the military regime could assist empleadas: by helping ANECAP to promote
trade certification, self-help organizations, and a national registry of empleadas. Shying away from any details for any change to existing law, the document
went on to elaborate the limited scope of ANECAP's request, stipulating that
"the change that we hope the Project will produce will in no way be forced,

but rather we will allow this to be slowly produced over time."[17] Moreover, the costs of these changes would be assumed only by the workers themselves, so that "the State and employers remain free of any burden." Finally, the document also stipulated that the "pleasure, well-being, and privacy of the family" would continue to be respected, allowing for example an employer of a pregnant domestic worker to choose between granting her maternity leave (and reserving her position) and ending her contract (with an unspecified severance package that would help her survive until she found new work after the birth of the child). The plan for professional certification—in stark contrast with the 1970–1972 proposals—watered down this provision to the point of insignificance; any person seeking employment as a domestic worker might carry a *carnet* (license), but would not need prior experience or training to obtain it. Instead, the carnet signified the worker's commitment to continuing her professional training after obtaining work: in this fashion, "the Professional License that would be granted does not interfere directly or indirectly with the freedom of labor."[18] In their proposal to implement a system of professional certification, but establishing a loophole through which employers and employees could operate without it, activists showed caution and restraint, fitting their request for rights within the parameters of the free market relations favored by the neoliberal regime.[19]

On the other hand, even as activists approached military officials with evident caution, the principles of ANECAP remained very similar to those guiding the association throughout its history: in its internal report of activities for 1976, ANECAP leaders called for "the liberation of the empleada as a woman and as a worker [and recognition] of her active and free participation in the development of our country." As an association, they wrote, ANECAP responded to the needs of empleadas as women—essentially, the need to affirm their humanity and rights to marriage and family—as Christians, and as workers.[20] Significantly, empleadas' labor rights were based here in a familiar trope of their importance to the function and happiness of families, but also went on to state that ANECAP sought to advance their rights to association and protection *as workers*:

- the Empleadas can, through unity and organization, build a new labor structure or system, where there is no dependency or disrespect, but rather competent, respectable and free work.
- they can organize in unions, so that through consciousness and unity, along with the other women workers, they contribute to the social and economic transformation of our country.

• they make employers obey social laws, paying a just wage and corresponding benefits, and fundamentally improve current domestic service and welfare laws.[21]

Echoing familiar union themes of solidarity and rights, as well as the importance of pastoral work with empleadas, the report went on to detail the range of
activities supported by ANECAP in 1976, from training classes in professional
skills and outreach to needy empleadas to trade mobilization and campaigns to
change labor regulations.[22]

Several years after the coup, and under the new leadership of the former
SINTRACAP president Aída Moreno, ANECAP's records attest to an developing relationship between ANECAP and other empleadas' associations, such
as SINTRACAP and the Housing Cooperative, which ANECAP leaders repeatedly noted "are failing . . . we have to support them so that they become
active again."[23] President Aída Moreno and Secretary Ana Colluquín reported
meetings with the union and the cooperative, where they discussed "whether we
can work together."[24] The following month, ANECAP hosted a May Day event
featuring a panel of workers' and religious organizations, attended by about fifty
empleadas.[25] Moreno also represented ANECAP, along with representatives
from the retirees' and textile workers' unions, in their attempts to build a "wom-
en's department" within the Coordinadora Nacional Sindical. When this group
celebrated International Women's Day in 1976, Moreno and the SINTRACAP
sought permission for a mass gathering of women at the Caupolicán Theater,
one of the first mass meetings held under military rule that was later known
as the "Gran Caupolicanazo." Though Moreno was almost arrested during her
speech—and was later warned to stay out of politics—the event steeled Moreno's
resolve to continue her activism and marked a new phase in the development of
the Chilean women's movement.[26]

The year 1976 was also a watershed year for ANECAP with respect to the
extent and permanence of its presence as a national association. Responding to
new requirements by local military commanders that all associations "normalize" their statutes, membership, and elected leadership, the ANECAP Board
inaugurated a registry with twenty-five dues-paying members in June 1976, and
began to report its leadership and statutes to the Municipality.[27] In Santiago, a
Dutch-funded initiative allowed activists to inaugurate new buildings for the
Hogar de la Empleada, a ceremony attended by the Dutch ambassador and the
Chilean archbishop. In July, the National Directorate signed several agreements
with Chilean service NGOs, in particular with CEDAP (Permanent Council of

Institutions for Private Adult Education), which provided training workshops
in archives and human resources for ANECAP leadership. And with support
from Father Cornelio Wolff, ANECAP leaders organized outreach to multiple
provincial organizations, offering leadership training, pastoral activities, and
other services regularly available to empleadas in Santiago. All of these efforts,
together with a greater degree of planning and assessment visible in the 1976
report, constituted a high-water mark for the organization under military rule,
suggesting that the protection and support of the Catholic Church, resources
provided by foreign churches and governments, and constant effort by paid
leadership and a strong network of volunteers, had placed the organization on
excellent footing by 1976.

Three years after ANECAP sent its recommendations to the Ministry of
Labor, the articles regarding domestic service contracts contained in the 1978
Labor Code (Decree-Law 2,200) were innovative—establishing for the first time
a legal obligation for written contracts for empleadas—but were very limited
insofar as they regulated domestic work as a kind of "special contract." Building
on a more ample definition of domestic workers than previous legislation—including, for example, part-time workers as well as those engaged in cleaning or
caretaking activities in charitable institutions—the "domestic workers' contract" established minimal protections to domestic workers, reaffirming some of
the more paternalistic articles of the 1931 labor code (and the Civil Code before
that). In the case of the death of an employer, for example, the domestic worker's contract passed to the control of the remaining family, "who will in solidarity be responsible for fulfilling the obligations established by the contract."
The law also reversed past progress toward limiting domestic workers' hours,
establishing only an absolute minimum rest of ten hours daily, and one day off
per week. Gone were the concerns about carnet, education, organization embedded in Popular Unity-era proposals and alluded to in ANECAP's request to
the Ministry of Labor in 1975. Once again, the contract of the domestic worker
constituted the bare minimum of state regulation but was defined in such a way
as to preserve employers' mandate to set wages, determine working conditions,
and terminate employment.[28]

Domestic workers' aspiration to a more robust recognition of their labor rights
clearly suffered a setback in the military's 1978 Labor Code, as did the rights of
all workers in this and subsequent decree laws on labor.[29] However, a significant
contribution of this legislation was that it legalized the terminology "trabajadoras de casa particular" ("workers in private homes" or domestic workers) for the
first time. It was the Popular Unity law of November 1972 that had first changed

the terminology of the Labor Code, transforming "empleados domésticos" into "empleados de casas particulares." But, as Bravo Navarette pointed out, the Labor Code of 1978 went further, eliminating the longstanding distinction in Chilean labor law between categories of white-and blue-collar workers (empleados and obreros, respectively), using "trabajador" to refer exclusively to workers engaged in any form of paid work. Thus, although the critical transition away from the demeaning term "domésticos" had been codified by the socialist government, it was the military government that renamed domestic workers, eliminating the long-standing contradiction in the 1931 labor code by which "domestic employees" were denied rights ascribed to salaried "empleados." Of course, in the context of the violent marginalization of organized labor and national economic development that deepened income inequality for workers, domestic workers' semantic victory—known at last as "workers"—provided little cause for celebration.[30]

Politics and Religion in an Expanding Movement, 1978–1988

Regardless of the military government's failure to protect domestic workers in the new Labor Code, 1978 also marked the beginning of an expansion and increasing complexity of both the Catholic and the secular wings of the domestic workers' movement. First, as summer waned in Chile, members of the ANECAP National Board fanned out throughout the country, meeting with activists and former leaders in Valdivia, Puerto Montt, Talca, and Concepción, garnering support for the board's plan to stimulate Christian base communities among *empleadas* in the year ahead.[31] The National Directorate minutes record a period of intensified work, including a revision of the association's statues, scheduling extra national assembly meetings, and board members' work to found new chapters of ANE-CAP in provincial cities like Coyaique.[32] The question of activists' political engagement—submerged since the Popular Unity period in the organization's survival strategies—also reemerged that year, as the board reaffirmed the authority and independence of the ANECAP president, a move that may explain the resignation of spiritual director Father Cornelio Lemers in August, which the board secretary asserts was because "he wasn't clear on pastoral work with empleadas. And he was not comfortable with the the [illeg] of the Board."[33] The following year, politics was also the focus on one funding agency's caveat about its grants for empleadas to study at ANECAP: board minutes record that "The agreement we have stipulates that the grants will end if any political activity is detected."[34]

Also in 1978, with support from Bernardino Piñera, activists in the secular union managed to reorganize Santiago and provincial unions into a national union, the National Commission of Domestic Workers' Unions (Comisión Nacional de Sindicatos de Trabajadoras de Casa Particular or CONSTRACAP).[35] Also known as the Coordinating Commission of the Organizations of the Domestic Worker Trade, the organization responded to the regime's efforts to limit union activities through minimum membership requirements. Monthly meetings of the executive committee of CONSTRACAP convened delegates from SINTRACAP, ANECAP, and the savings and housing cooperatives. The commission was established to coordinate these organizations' efforts to promote the common cause of domestic workers, while at the same time clarifying distinctions among participant organizations: "We will elaborate a common pamphlet in which the importance of each organization is clarified, making the specific function of each organization very clear, to avoid any confusion."[36] At the first meeting of the commission, in July 1979, representatives of ANECAP (1), the union (4), the savings cooperative (3) and housing cooperative (2), expressed high hopes that the leaders could find common ground, not only advancing their cause but also "that we come to be a real team, we should define who will participate in this meeting regularly.... Go over the diverse points of view, to avoid any prejudices or misunderstandings that might exist among the organizations' leaders, in order to clarify and eliminate them." In this group, at least, various appeals to their unity as "real Christian militants" indicated the common roots of this leadership in the jocist era of ANECAP.[37] As the mimeographed bulletin *Caminando* published by CONSTRACAP in the 1980s demonstrated, the commission functioned essentially as a clearinghouse for information on the various organizations, disseminating information on their various anniversaries, planned events, and proposed changes to labor legislation.[38]

The burst of independent activity by the Executive Board in 1978 led to further changes in ANECAP the following year: members elected a new directorate and the Church appointed the organization's first lay asesor, Fernando Orchard, who proved to be very effective at mobilizing international religious support for the association via specific proposals for ANECAP projects. These projects foregrounded catechism and vocational as well as leadership training, taking explicit distance from the more syndicalist stance of the 1969–1973 period and reviving the Catholic worker agenda of the 1950s. According to a 1983 internal account of the domestic workers' movement, the period after 1979 represented a

... return to origins. The association seeks to generate a group of militants who, in the spirit of social Catholicism (jocismo), will pursue the revival of the trade; that is, the association seeks to recover the feeling of a specialized movement within Catholic Action. Catechetical activity increases. The services provided to the trade are reorganized and strengthened . . . the relationship to the unions is redefined: we combine mutual autonomy with plans for collaboration.[39]

The Santiago pastoral campaign of 1979 articulated a very different vision of ANECAP objectives than the efforts of the ANECAP Board and union activists the year before, directing pastoral efforts through parish structures and avoiding links to union organizations and activities that had developed under Father Verdugo's leadership prior to 1973.[40]

In 1979, SINTRACAP and the remaining unions organized by ANECAP faced a common institutional crisis: the military decree-law 2,756 demanded that unions show significant active membership to remain legal. In a petition to the Ministry of Labor dated June 1981, SINTRACAP's president Aída Moreno pled the domestic workers' special case:

> As you surely understand, Mr. Minister, our occupation presents such special characteristics that it is extremely difficult to unionize, since the workers exercise their trade very spread out and normally live in their employers' homes; the worker who is puertas afuera works more occasionally. . . . we ask your grace (*usía*) to consider our special circumstances and modify the law that demands such a high number of members, and consider lowering this to the same number that was demanded before, that is, 25 members.[41]

The petition went on to request greater ministerial oversight of domestic service labor relations (including contracts stipulated by the 1978 labor code), and asked again for recognition of November 21 as a National Day of the Domestic worker.

Like many other trades and social movements, the period following the approval of the 1980 Constitution, and on the eve of the impending financial crisis that would spark bank intervention and street protests in 1983, domestic worker activists experienced another movement revival. In June of 1982, for example, SINTRACAP joined with other unions in printing, construction, and mining to rent a shared meeting space in Santiago, which allowed them greater stability. At the same time, SINTRACAP leaders also published a new bulletin that offers a glimpse into the activities sponsored by the union in their new downtown office: the group held multiple talks (on economy, union organizing, and social legislation), as well as workshops on personal development and basic education classes. While the union could in no way compete with the range of

FIGURE 5.1. Religious service, ANECAP retreat, n.d.

basic services offered by ANECAP at the Hogar de la Empleada (offering only a lunch service for members), the bulletin documents the spirit of working-class alliance that infused the group in the early 1980s, which included a round-table event with other workers; discussions of the effects of economic crisis on workers' wages and employment; and promoting their members' participation in the Savings Cooperatives and ANECAP.

The close relationship between SINTRACAP and ANECAP leaders in the early 1980s is reflected in an anonymous "testimony" published in SINTRACAP's first bulletin in 1982, which recounted a domestic worker's journey through the trade's associations: after celebrating the Day of the Empleada (to which she was invited by a nun), this "worker" found her way to the Hogar, where she got help from the ANECAP President and the group's spiritual advisor, joined the group, and took courses on cooking. Once in ANECAP, the worker learned about and joined the union: "I became a member of the Union, and I continue as a member today, because I believe this is something valuable for the woman worker to do. I participate on a committee and I am glad to be able to help my working-class *compañeras*."[42] In fact, SINTRACAP and ANECAP worked so closely together at this point that much of their correspondence was signed jointly, and several key activists rotated through leadership roles in both groups.

For its part, in this period ANECAP experienced its own revival, publicized in a twenty-page bulletin called *Amistad y Esperanza* (Friendship and Hope), which was distributed to members bimonthly well into the 1990s. *Amistad y Esperanza* disseminated information about the Institute housed at the Hogar, which in 1984 boasted twenty-three teachers and five hundred students, as well as a library, kitchen, and cultural-recreational programs. In addition to short histories of ANECAP, religious reflections, and reports on celebrity, religious, and literary figures, *Amistad y Esperanza* published domestic workers' own poetry, testimony, and interviews. In 1984, María Castillo, talked about the terms used to refer to women in her trade, in a poem entitled "Neither slaves nor managers!":

> "Twentieth-century slaves"
> Some luminaries call us;
> Others call us "managers"
> Have you ever seen anything so absurd?
> Neither slaves nor managers,
> I assure you,
> Just a woman who works
> Taking care of a home
> My god! Why can't you agree
> When you want to call us something,
> *Yes, we are workers*
> *Like all the rest of them.*[43]

Nestled in the bulletin's twelve mimeographed pages, amid news from the provinces, an interview with a soap opera star, an advice column, and a page of cartoons and puzzles, readers also found another poem, this time several modified stanzas drawn from "The Pleasure of Serving," by the Chilean Nobel laureate Gabriela Mistral:

> There is joy in being healthy and righteous.
> But above all, there is the
> beautiful and immense task of serving.
> . . .
> Great works are not all that matter;
> There are small services:
> Setting the table, organizing books . . .
> Serving is not the chore of inferior people.
> God, who gives both fruit and light, serves.

And he has his eyes fixed on our hands
and he asks us each day:
Did you serve today?[44]

Particularly in reports and editorials about contemporary events, ANECAP leaders also connected domestic workers' continuing struggle for labor rights with the economic hardships and political authoritarianism affecting all Chileans, evidenced by articles protesting the expulsion of three foreign priests, supporting street protests against the regime, critiquing political leaders' efforts to dialogue with military leaders, and promoting domestic workers' participation in the 1988 plebiscite on Pinochet's continued rule.[45] In a pointed editorial at the height of the 1983 street protests that damaged the regime, organizers took aim at the violent and anti-democratic nature of the Pinochet regime:

> We all know that Chile is in a bad way. We know it and we feel it. It's too much: the unemployment, the economic insecurity, the anxiety of not having enough to live with dignity and tranquility. Ten years is too much for those Chileans who love their homeland, they are afraid to speak out or they do it anyway at great risk. It has been too long that only one group makes decisions for all Chileans. They can give us lots of explanations for these things; they can blame the recession or the communists. But what is certain is that Chileans want this to change. And at last we dare to say so. We say it with peace with order, and with firmness.[46]

Perhaps more significant than this explicit political expression, in 1984 ANECAP also distributed a pamphlet on domestic workers' rights, "We invite you to learn your labor rights," complete with drawings of a kindly empleada and succinct explanations of the requirements (and limitations) of the labor code and social security. Asserting that "We propose that all of us together can turn our trade into work like that of everyone else," organizers provided a menu of their continuing demands: "Work schedules, freedom to go out when daily work is finished, our own space, private and family life, to be treated as equals at work, and time to exercise our rights as citizens." The theme of labor rights, ever present in the multiple organizations formed by domestic workers in previous decades, remained key to ANECAP's activities in this period as well.[47]

The first ten years of military rule restricted the arena for activities of domestic worker activists as they retreated from the political and union allies that had radicalized their struggles for dignity under Popular Unity, causing them to rely once again on the movement's historic links to the Catholic Church.

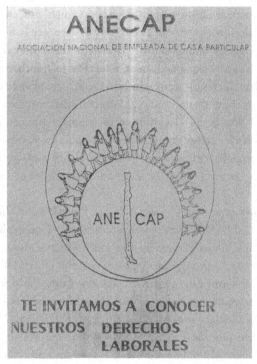

FIGURE 5.2. ANECAP training pamphlet,
"We invite you to learn about our labor rights," 1984

And though their efforts bore little fruit, activists were able to maintain their organizations under the repressive and anti-union policies of the military regime, even appealing at times to officials' paternalism to address the continuing marginalization of domestic workers. Rather than complete demobilization, however, the anti-political regime pressed this movement to seek new kinds of allies to support the expansion and reinvigoration of domestic workers' politics in the 1980s.

Democracy in the Home? Empleadas and Patronas Unite

Having survived some of the worst years of state violence, by 1980 the domestic workers' associations were well positioned—like other popular women's organizations—to attract the attention of leaders in Chile's middle-class feminist movement. Within the now familiar story of Chilean women's vigorous mobilization against military rule is a lesser known chapter that highlights middle-class feminists' confrontation with the politics of class privilege, as a handful of patronas and empleadas forged common cause in defense of the rights of domestic workers. This alliance can be explained through local factors, such as the solidarities forged across class and political party lines in the furnace of violent military rule, but it also reflects common tendencies among feminist movements during Latin America's Cold War period. In addition to synergies and conflicts generated over questions of race, ethnicity, sexuality, and politics, feminists also turned their attention to global debates on reproduction, labor, and family, debates that not infrequently centered the problems of domestic service and unpaid domestic labor.[48]

This cross-class experiment between domestic worker and feminist activists in 1980s Chile had little precedent in over a century of women's mobilization. While studies of Chilean feminism—like much of Latin America and indeed the world—have privileged the emergence of middle-class and liberal sectors in the late nineteenth and early twentieth century, women also formed associations, unions, and other movements as part of the labor and revolutionary movements, as well as ancillary to the Catholic Church.[49] If women's alliance across class has any clear precedent in Chile, it would be the MEMCH or Chilean Women's Movement of the Popular Front era (discussed in Chapter 3), which actively sought to bring women together to champion issues of working-class women and families.[50]

Cold War Chile, as elsewhere in Latin America, saw women's increasing engagement in both partisan and movement politics: women were instrumental in mobilizations to bring an end to both the Allende presidency in 1973 and the Pinochet dictatorship in 1989.[51] The installation of violent military rule and a neoliberal economic project provided a backdrop and stimulus for the expansion of a diverse array of women's movements—from neighborhood soup kitchens and health education projects to women's Left, indigenous, and feminist organizations—which pursued radically different agendas for "women's rights" but also converged in public demonstrations and coordinated efforts to challenge the authority of the military regime.[52] In the midst of the ever-shifting politics of the women's movement, therefore, two groups—the empleadas' movements and the Women's Study Circle (Círculo de Estudios de la Mujer)—pursued a radical project of consciousness-raising and collaboration across the divide that had historically separated empleadas and patronas.

Since its founding in a crowded women's meeting in 1979, the Women's Study Circle had over several years sought to convene larger, more diverse representation of women in Chilean society, and in 1981 the group turned its attention to domestic service as an arena of feminist concern. Originally founded under the aegis of the Catholic research center known as the Academy for Christian Humanism, the Circle became a primary locus of middle-class women's organizing against gender inequality, "in the country and in the home," by convening working groups, promoting feminist research, and sponsoring public protests in alliance with a range of women's organizations.[53] The Circle—later separated from the Church because of its vocal engagement with questions of sexuality and women's rights—served as a space and a springboard for a variety of research and political initiatives for Chilean feminists, thereby strengthening the web of women's NGOs and women's public protest that would later contribute to the downfall of the military regime.

In August 1981, representatives of the Circle met with leaders from ANECAP and SINTRACAP out of what feminist participants later described as "each group's spontaneous desire to discuss the topic of paid domestic work." One of the key organizers of the event, the feminist economist Thelma Gálvez, explained her group's interest in working with the empleada activists:

> We women of the Circle were speaking up for THE WOMEN of 1980s Chile, we discussed various topics related to how we could discover and understand women's lives from perspectives. We were (and we continue to be) women who were bourgeois and petit bourgeois, middle class and even some elites, Catholics and former Catholics, atheists, women of Santiago and from the Provinces. We were all probably raised at home by "nanas" (empleadas, nannies, servers, and what we now call "domestic workers"— TCP—a term we learned at that conference) and we were not very adept at domestic tasks, sometimes hating them, fleeing them for the university, paid work, political work, feminism, etc.

Gálvez, who with fellow economist Rosalba Todaro would go on to spearhead the Circle's research and collaboration with the empleadas, continued reflecting on the feminist motivations:

> In that context we set up the conference. . . . The visions that we, the hosts, presented on the theme [of domestic service] were diverse, but we wanted to be good feminists and stand alongside of, and not in charge of, the TCP. Certainly at the conference our ideas were out there, but they were diverse and anecdotal. As for the rest—there were about twenty-five or thirty-five of us—everyone relied on TCP to meet their own family obligations, and

Rosalba and I were really interested in this subject, from the perspective of considering them working women and understanding their working (and other) lives.[54]

For their part, union and ANECAP activists contributed their own insights to the conference, where they discussed the conditions of domestic service work in Chile, the history of domestic worker organizing, and activists' specific demands (enforcement of contracts, employer respect for work hours, proper use of Social Security booklets, etc.). A month later, the presidents of ANECAP and SINTRACAP signed off on a joint letter of support to commission an external consultancy, and by September, Gálvez and Todaro initiated their first study of Chilean domestic service.[55] They would go on to employ sociological surveys, feminist economic analysis, and ethnographic research and publication in their effort to raise feminist awareness of the condition of domestic workers in Chile.[56]

A clear expression of Gálvez and Todaro's approach to domestic service—one fairly common in the debates on housework and inequality underway in global feminist circles in the 1970s—can be found in Todaro's presentation at the conference, titled "Domestic work: women's work?" After describing the nature of domestic service, its status as "female occupation," and the role of domestic workers in the reproductive and affective life of the families they served, Todaro expressed some of the questions that had motivated women of the Circle to examine the phenomenon of domestic service in Chile:

> To what degree does [professional women's reliance on paid domestic labor] imply the liberation of women? In the first place, what women are we talking about? Could this be the liberation of some women at the price of the greater oppression of others? And in the second place, to what degree does the reliance on domestic workers limit and retard women's consciousness, allowing them to believe the fiction of a liberated couple, free of family confrontations and maintaining untouched the sexual division of labor? Does this not lead to a society polarized into two spheres, the public sphere with visible work monopolized by men and a few women and the private sphere with invisible work completely occupied by unpaid housewives or salaried domestic workers?[57]

Todaro's presentation reflects how the encounter with domestic workers challenged these feminist intellectuals to reflect on how their own professional lives, and relative freedom from reproductive labor, depended on the availability of other women to work for them. Circle participants readily confessed their mixed feelings about their reliance on domestic workers: "There's a feeling of guilt for paying someone else to do [the housework], but there's also a certain relief: it's not just that society doesn't value domestic work, but also that we women also do not value it." In addition to learning more about the discrimination and marginalization experienced by domestic workers, feminist professionals began to incorporate domestic service (even in their own homes) into their feminist analysis of women's choices with respect to reproductive labor. These revelations were highly personal, revealing feminists' own choices about family, work, and politics:

> In the end, the conference was also an encounter about individual choices, about personal experiences with domestic labor. These experiences included everything from sharing housework among family members, hiring a worker puertas afuera to complete certain tasks and limited hours, the desire to hire impersonal [cleaning] services, the nanny hired by the hour to watch the children when the adults are not at home, to the worker-cook-nanny-manager who assumes responsibility for our entire domestic role.[58]

Feminist professionals not only made domestic service a focus of scientific research, but also confronted (as they had at other moments) the class and ethnic tensions that shaped women's mobilization in this period. A few of these feminists embraced collaboration with domestic workers as a new arena for feminist activism, as well as an opportunity to engage in theoretical and political discussions about the relationship between paying other women to work in their homes, on the one hand, and maintaining their feminist commitments to equality and sisterhood, on the other. Again, according to Thelma Gálvez:

> I don't remember a lot of details about the conference, but I do remember that [the TCP] told their stories, made their proposals to these women who looked like patronas but were not playing that role in that moment. There was dialogue, there were speeches, there were questions, there were promises. For us, at least for myself and Rosalba, it was a real encounter, since after that we later developed the project [of the cleaning business] and we began to understand some things. And above all it allowed us to make contact [with the TCP].[59]

According to a later report, the conference ended with mutual pledges of future collaboration: "We said good-bye with the promise to dedicate this issue of the bulletin to the topic, to investigate further the reality of salaried domestic work in Chile, to support the idea of organizing a cleaning service business. Bit by bit, all of this will be come to be."[60]

For domestic worker activists of ANECAP and SINTRACAP, the sustained encounter with the Women's Study Circle influenced the movement's rights-based discourse, providing as it did training and tools for addressing domestic service as a "women's issue." While the heterogeneous domestic workers' movement did not embrace a feminist label, these experiences, resources, and opportunities did add the powerful critique of gender inequality to the potent mix of class and religious discourse that had sustained the movement since the 1950s. As early as December 1981, the framing of domestic workers' demands began to reflect a greater interest in and reflection on their status as women, and the desire to participate in broader women's pro-democracy movements. In "Problems of the trade," for example, a piece authored by domestic worker activists and published in the Circle's special issue on the domestic worker conference, the description of domestic workers' struggles included typical demands for greater labor protections and unionization, but also described domestic workers' struggles as part of broader agendas of women's rights and democratization: empleadas, it said, should "make an effort to form a women's organization that is broad and democratic, that brings together large numbers of women whether or not they are organized, where the struggle for our rights as women is active and in solidarity, and serves to bring about change in our society so that it is more just and democratic."[61] Another concrete outcome of this encounter between domestic workers and their feminist middle-class allies was the creation of an industrial cleaning company, Quillay: with Gálvez and Todaro as consultants, Quillay obtained contracts primarily with nongovernmental organizations (including feminist ones). Collaboration with women of the Circle provided new opportunities for empleadas to press their case—among other workers as well as journalists, professionals, and political leaders—about the working conditions, poor labor protections, and the movement of domestic workers.

The collaboration of feminists—particularly the feminist economists at the Circle—and domestic workers extended beyond the leaders of their principal associations. From the numerous ephemeral publications circulating in the mid-1980s, the impact of this collaboration is evident in the double seal of CEM and SINTRACAP or ANECAP on these publications as well as their content. CEM and SINTRACAP together produced, for example, a series of ten pamphlets for educating groups of domestic workers, "Guide for group learning," through which facilitators would address topics ranging from the identity of empleadas as workers and women to exercises for learning their legal rights and

FIGURE 5.3. Teatime at an ANECAP training, 1985

developing critical awareness about their relationship with employers. In "Our Legal Rights," for example, a group facilitator would display posters outlining domestic workers' rights to a labor contract and other rights, then lead the group in a card game designed to help workers' share their experiences, clarify their rights, and explain how to access the union and/or the ministry of labor when those rights were violated. Through playing cards that quizzed participants about their legal rights, the game sought to provoke the workers' critical reflection on their own experience of the gap between law and regulation, as well as critical evaluation of the adequacy of labor legislation.[62]

From the start, therefore, the alliance of domestic workers and feminist activists not only served their organizations' respective interests, but also generated significant effects on both movements. Working closely with key domestic worker activists, Círculo feminists generated new research on domestic service relations, turning the international feminist agenda on domestic labor of the 1970s to the critical study of reproductive labor with respect to class, gender, and ethnic inequality in Chile. In addition to the ways it informed women's movements within Chile, this research produced a raft of important publications in testimony, sociology, and economics that quickly reached an international

FIGURE 5.4. Meeting of feminist and domestic worker groups, August 1981

activist and scholarly audience, particularly through Chaney and Castro's edited collection, *Muchachas No More*.[63]

Cooperation between empleadas and patronas in the early 1980s also provided an opportunity for some feminists to simultaneously reflect on the deeper limitations and meanings of cross-class collaboration or "sisterhood." One poem published in the Circle's special *Boletín* four months after the conference provides some critical insight into tensions underlying this new alliance. In "Auto-pregunta," a title with the double-meaning of "self-questioning" and "questions about cars," Circle member Patricia Crispi assessed the conference:

> How did I like the encounter?
> It was more like a mis-encounter.
> A kind of highway that had
> Faster and slower cars running
> On different levels and directions
> Over here, the "scientific" car.
> Talking about the cultural construction of
> Domestic service as women's work
> Going back to gendered roots.
> Poking around in role assignments.

Crispi's poem went on to describe the "encounters" over Chile's long history between domestic workers and others, including employers, the Church, Marxists, and foreigners: as previous chapters have noted, domestic service has regularly provoked public scrutiny of the working conditions, labor market, and moral effects of such employment on working-class women. In a verse dedicated to the domestic workers participating in the conference, however, Crispi added:

> At last, we have the domestic employee's own car.
> It's on a suspension bridge.
> Flying and passing over this whole ocean
> Of ideas and contradictions.
> Being expressed and expressing herself
> through her condition.
> Explaining her oppression.

For Crispi, then, the Círculo's feminist "encounter" at the 1981 conference was neither entirely new or unproblematic: rather, it was just one of the many perspectives that Chileans had brought to the subject of "la empleada doméstica," in representations ranging from paternalistic and social Catholic to legal, charitable, and revolutionary.[64] Asked to comment on Crispi's poem twenty-five years later, Thelma Gálvez offered the following context:

> Reading it today, it is a good description of the different visions at the conference—I won't say "could be found" (*"se encontraban"*). Maybe [Crispi] . . . captured best what others preferred to overlook in order to "encounter each other." . . . In the background for all of us well-intentioned women who convened the conference were the multiple motives and choices that Crispi described, maybe by listening carefully to what was said. Maybe we were a bunch of women's stories facing the reality of other women who had been near us our whole lives, but whom we had not seen as women.[65]

Conclusion: *Limpieza* en sus derechos (cleaning house)

In the political effervescence of the 1980s, but particularly in the years leading up to the 1988 plebiscite on Pinochet, domestic workers' activism converged around the multiple alliances fortified since 1967. Building on a decade of enhanced funding from foreign religious groups, research and outreach with feminists, as well as the coordinated efforts among domestic workers' multiple associations, activists engaged in direct challenges to the regime and the public's view of domestic service, launching a petition drive to demand greater labor protections and—in a letter signed by fifteen ANECAP groups, twenty parish-level groups,

FIGURE 5.5. ANECAP leadership training, 1988

the Housing Cooperative, and SINTRACAP—protesting the national TV station's recent portrayal of domestic workers.[66] Emboldened by the promise of an electoral path to democracy, domestic worker advocates struggled to establish the legitimacy of their long-postponed claims to legal protection and social standing.

In the months following the victory of the "No"—the national plebiscite that ended Pinochet's bid for "reelection" for another eight-year term in 1988— SINTRACAP presented the empleadas' demand for basic labor protections to the Ministry of Labor.[67] In contrast to earlier petitions submitted to military officials, the 1988 document listed fourteen demands for the regulation of domestic workers, without apology, religious references, or deference to military authority. In addition to the basic demand for limited work hours, regulation of contracts, vacation pay, health care (specifically for the "professional diseases" like neurosis, varicose veins, early arthritis, and back problems), and official recognition of November 21, the petitioners demanded maternity leave and union representation in the face of employer noncompliance. Unlike earlier petitions, the 1988 demands were announced in a public press conference and widely reported.[68]

When the labor ministry failed to respond to the petition, six months later activists re-submitted their appeal, adding eight additional demands to the original fourteen, insisting among other things that they be referred to as "trabajadoras de hogar."[69] This time leaders from SINTRACAP, CONSTRACAP, ANECAP (National and Regional-Santiago) presented their petition in a meeting with a labor ministry official, Ernesto Deval, who informed them that not only had their petition arrived too late to be included in an ongoing labor reform but also that the labor ministry would not recognize their specific demands, largely because of the informal nature of domestic service labor. In their August 1989 report on their interactions with labor ministry officials, domestic worker activists summed up the minister's position as

> in order for our working conditions to improve, they must be regulated by the Free Market system, that is, by the law of supply and demand. This means that under the current political and economic system, we cannot have laws that regulate working conditions. All that is left is to hope that, when we return to Democracy, our demands will be considered, and to this end we must strengthen our organizations to keep demanding our rights as women and as workers.[70]

The leaders of Chile's major domestic worker associations together issued a press release denouncing the military regime for its failure to address their concerns, taking advantage of the space for public dissent opened by the transition to democracy then underway in Chile. While the domestic workers' movement had matured and expanded politically under dictatorship, both the ministry officials and some press coverage continued to treat their labor, and demands for protection, as outside the legitimate boundaries of labor politics and state regulation.[71] Not only did association and union leaders work closely together to bind both groups into pro-democracy movements but this activism also reflected a synergy of religious, women's, and union objectives. In March 1989, for example, the ANECAP directorate sent a letter to the association's membership, noting the group's recent participation in International Women's Day celebrations in the Santa Laura stadium, the CUT Congress, and national Church meetings.[72] Collaboration between feminists and domestic workers in the 1980s produced a critical vision of class politics among middle-class feminists as well as providing the financial and technical networks that would transform the outreach and ideological structures of domestic workers' movements. During the transition to democracy in 1990, these collaborations would also bear fruit in the form of laws for maternity leave and other benefits for domestic workers, which relied equally on the legacy of empleadas' struggles for labor rights and the newfound discourse of women's rights and solidarity. Together with SINTRACAP, the association continued to work on a proposal for domestic worker legislation, which would be addressed by the incoming democratic Congress in 1990.[73]

The development of domestic workers' alliance with the women's movement did not, however, signify the eclipse of Catholic influence on the empleadas' movement. Not only did ANECAP remain highly relevant as a service provider for empleadas, but the prophetic stand of Catholic leadership against the neoliberal Pinochet regime in the late 1980s continued to draw attention to the plight of domestic workers. For example, the 1989 pastoral letter by Bishop of Copiapó Fernando Ariztia Ruíz, "Pastoral Letter to Domestic Workers," detailed the need for religious, legislative, and union activism to address the continuing injustices of Chilean domestic service relations.[74] This attention from the Church hierarchy formed the basis for the ANECAP leaders' affirmation that "Anecap will always be distinct from the union, but its members may belong to the unions, while Anecap remains faithful to its own charisma."[75]

Despite the military regime's attempt to reinscribe domestic service within paternalist labor relations, domestic worker activists kept their movement alive through innovative strategies to protect their associations and form new alliances in the struggle against dictatorship. As the activist Aída Moreno wrote in 1989:

> In our trade, the greatest success has come from continuing training that raises the level of consciousness; so that the workers value themselves as people, and in addition to having duties, they have inalienable rights; they understand their responsibility as workers and as citizens to participate in the destiny of their country. We have not grown much in number, but we believe that the quality of the movement is far superior to that of 1973."[76]

Like the broader women's movement, Chile's transition to democracy in 1990 resulted in part from the success of grassroots mobilization and new political alliances in Chile. Drawing on old and new paradigms, Church and feminist allies made the super-exploitation of empleadas a prime example of Chile's oligarchic, patriarchal, and anti-democratic past and dictatorial present. But it would take more than political transition to obtain labor rights "like all the rest of them" for domestic workers the. The project of fully recognizing empleadas' labor rights, advanced in fits and starts over the last thirty years, remains a challenge for the movement's current and future activists.

The Inequities of Service, Past and Present

> It's disappointing because [the employers] say you're part of the
> family and it's not true, because when something happens we are
> the first to be let go and there they are forgetting that we were their
> friends, their family. They've never asked me if I needed something
> and they haven't called me.... They don't realize that we are workers
> like all the rest of them. We are not just the woman who comes to
> help with the housework, we are workers just like them.
>
> —"Marcela," speaking to *La Tercera*, July 31, 2020

P ART OF WHAT I have done in this book is show, through the stories
recovered from Chilean archives and activists, that history influences
how we think about domestic workers' rights in the present. Although
"Marcela" said she was "disappointed" to have been dismissed by her employers because of COVID-19—like 70 percent of Chile's domestic workers were
in 2020—she insists to reporters on the real problem: her employers' failure to
recognize her status as a worker.[1] Echoing the refrain voiced by domestic workers in Chile since the 1920s, and codified in the domestic legislation of thirty
countries since the passage of the International Labor Organization's Domestic
Workers Convention in 2011, "Marcela" joins the more than fifty-five million
domestic workers worldwide who have lost income—with little or no access to
employment and health insurance—as a result of the global pandemic.[2]

Recovering the longer history of this inequality matters not only because it
is useful and affirming for living activists, but also because, if we do not, the
persistent story that the exploitation of women through domestic service is an
unchanging reality will continue to obscure more than it reveals about domestic service: who performs it, under what conditions, and what forms of resistance and change were and are therefore now possible. Histories of domestic
service that reify the subjects and structures of inequality as "beyond history"

(or somehow fixed in colonial social relations) have served as useful narratives for a whole range of political projects—from conservative and neoliberal to Left and feminist—but can also systematically erase the creative and bold work of activists and allies who have struggled for domestic workers' labor rights in Latin America for more than a century.[3] By demonstrating the complexity and historical contingency of domestic service relations, and centering domestic workers' claims to rights and citizenship since the early twentieth century, *Workers Like All the Rest of Them* allows us to better identify the real historical causes of social inequality against which generations of workers continue to struggle.[4]

Contrary to the claims found in some social science research that focuses on recent local and global conditions, the struggles and debates about regulating domestic service have meaningful roots in the early decades of the twentieth century, when domestic workers first mobilized for their labor rights, and the Cold War period, when social Catholicism, socialism, and feminism converged to elevate attention to the marginal status of domestic workers. Rather than a timeless vestige of colonialism, domestic service in Chile expressed and transformed the social relations of inequality in which it was embedded, and then as now demonstrated both the persistence of inequality and domestic workers' creative, stubborn resistance to it. These deeper historical roots allow us to raise critical questions about how, contrary to teleologies of modernization and progress, domestic workers' demands became politically salient through the discourses of Catholic dignity, revolutionary citizenship, and women's rights long before the twenty-first century and the rise of global care activism. The persistence of domestic workers' frustrated aspirations to dignity, safety, and wages should not obscure the important temporal and political differences that enabled and obstructed those efforts over time. As domestic worker activists repeatedly expressed in their interviews and publications, knowing this history offers activists lessons for the present. For historians and social scientists, this history is also crucial for analyzing the forces that continue to facilitate and obstruct progress toward domestic workers' rights in Chile, Latin America, and the world.

The legacy of interdisciplinary and activist engagement of scholars with domestic workers, inaugurated by Chaney and Castro's *Muchachas No More* in the 1980s, has left an important mark on this study. Principally through my conversations and interviews with Aída Moreno (Q.E.P.D.), I came to better understand the complexity of domestic workers' political mobilization in Chile over time: divided not only by deep ethnic, regional, and in some cases religious differences, domestic workers have fought an uphill battle to establish the basic legitimacy of their rights *as workers* over the course of the past century. Upon closer examination of ANECAP's records, and in combination with precious union archives dating back to the 1920s, I found that tipping points in domestic workers' mobilization corresponded with dramatic political externalities, that is, with the increasing resonance of progressive Catholic and revolutionary discourses on human rights and social transformation. Without such formulations, and the access to organizational and legislative power that they facilitated, Chilean domestic workers could scarcely lay claim to the representations and social legislation that—as late as 1992—would lead eventually to regulation of their labor contracts, working conditions, and social entitlements. The evidence presented here shows conclusively that the regulation of domestic service *as labor* was not, at least in Chile, solely the product of social and political conditions prevalent in late twentieth-century Latin America. Rather, the construction of "servants" as *workers* in Chilean public discourse (if not law) has a long historical trajectory, rooted in domestic workers' own mobilization, as well as the expansion of the welfare state, in the early-to-mid-twentieth century. In comparative terms, we learn from these Chilean sources that legislatures and social movements elsewhere in Latin America were engaged in similar debates over the incorporation of domestic workers into labor relations systems.[5] However, even when the 1931 Labor Code recognized servants as workers, it had a limited impact on domestic workers' entitlements, in part because so many of them were employed part-time or informally, without contracts or social security payments. In the end, the pernicious combination of custom and lack of regulation limited access to benefits available to domestic workers, many of whom remained ignorant of new laws granting them access to health care as well as maternity services and pensions.

The politicization of domestic service associations in Chile during the 1960s, and the ensuing overlap between women's and domestic workers' movements in the anti-dictatorial struggles of the 1980s, left a legacy of labor mobilization which, like other social movements spurred by the dictatorship, declined dramatically in the decades immediately following the transition to democratic rule in 1990. Domestic workers' associations, once capable of bringing thousands of women into the street and sustaining vibrant educational, cultural, and political activities, dwindled to a few hundred active members (at least in Santiago) and had very little public presence until a new wave of mobilization that emerged with the ILO's Convention 189 in 2011.[6] Thus we see that the progressive transformations in labor relations characterizing domestic service employment—changes reflecting the rise of live-out over live-in service, the growth of neighborhoods that concentrate men and women working in service trades, the passage of maternity and severance legislation in the 1990s—did not necessarily provide better conditions for domestic workers' politicization and organization. A question that links both historical and presentist concerns is: what conditions permit or provoke domestic workers, particularly women, to mobilize in pursuit of their occupational interests?

Throughout this history, I have reconstructed one of the most important sectors of Chile's working class, and demonstrated the importance of their legal exclusion to the creation of modern labor systems over the course of the twentieth century. The legal exclusion of domestic workers from the labor relations regulated by the Chilean state was built into Chile's earliest legal codes and practices. As the Chilean state began to address the first topics highlighted by the social question in the early twentieth century—the protection of working women and children—domestic workers and other women belonging to informal labor markets (selling, prostitution, etc.) were explicitly excluded from proposed legislation.[7] This exclusion was driven by legislators' and officials' assumptions about domestic service relations: despite abundant evidence to the contrary, political leaders described domestic workers' relationships with their employers as paternalistic and familial. Starting in the 1920s, Chilean domestic workers mobilized to protest these exclusions, bringing their concerns about employer abuses (overwork, firing without cause, etc.) to the attention of the media, Labor Office officials, and party representatives, demanding that their trade be incorporated into emerging legislation. Their protests influenced parliamentary debates and the content of a series of legislative proposals considered between 1923 and 1931, which defined limited rights and protections for empleados and their employers: while domestic workers were granted the status of salaried workers and therefore included in the social welfare system, the creation of a separate article for domestic service effectively separated them from the regulatory apparatus linked to the main provisions of the Labor Code. In effect, the 1931 Labor Code recognized domestic service as employment, describing the respective rights of employers and empleadas, but excluded domestic workers from the key provisions that regulated other labor sectors through the requirement for contracts, minimum wage, severance pay, accident protection, and a host of other rights. The ensuing struggle for recognition and incorporation demonstrates not only how class identities and radical labor ideologies circulated among domestic workers in the 1930s but also the ways that some state officials and legislators accepted the logic of their most basic claim: that domestic workers were in fact *workers* deserving of the rights and protections accorded to other laborers in the emerging Chilean labor relations system.

The mobilization and visibility of Chilean domestic workers since the 1920s contributed to the steady transformation of legal and political discourse concerning paid domestic labor, a transformation reflected in the semantic journey from "servants" to "workers." In the 1930s and '40s, domestic workers' advances along this road were enabled by the Popular Front project for "Chileanization," a campaign of public health and anti-poverty initiatives that represented the steady advance of the Chilean welfare state.[8] Working closely with domestic workers who accessed the state's maternity wards, family assistance programs, and labor office, state officials repeatedly protested domestic workers' exclusion from the Chilean labor code, joining domestic worker activists and the Popular Front women's organization Movimiento pro-emancipación de la mujer chilena (MEMCH) in campaigns to legislate paid domestic labor. These developments illustrate the relative ease with which, their legal exclusion notwithstanding, empleada activists joined with other unions and worked closely with labor and welfare officials to lobby for equal protection under Chilean law.

The expansion of the domestic workers' movement in the late 1940s illustrates the central role of the Catholic Church in Chilean social relations, as well as radical Christianity's capacity to adapt and innovate in this time. The sustained popularity of the JOC de las Empleadas at midcentury demonstrates the great potential of a Church-supported movement, the importance of lay activism, and the provision of social services to a population characterized by recent migration, social isolation, and hard working and living conditions. This history allows us to better understand why it was the Catholic Church—not the welfare state or organized labor—that touched the lives, defended working conditions, and advanced the "dignity" of so many empleadas in Chile in the second half of the twentieth century. Church leaders had the disposition—particularly after working with Acción Católica—the resources, and the access to advocate for empleadas. With a discourse of self-help and dignity, Catholic leaders centered domestic servants in the project of class uplift—and defense of women—nearly two decades before major socialist parties or women's organizations would attempt the same. At the same time, as the ritual celebrations of Santa Zita and the longevity of aging empleadas demonstrated, the Church-led movement also drew on long-standing tropes of loyalty, service, and honor, values that would later dominate conservative religious strategies for organizing empleadas.

At the most basic level, whether or not domestic workers or their allies recognized empleadas' labor as *work* shaped the identities, ideologies, rhetoric, and political alliances available to domestic workers active in the Federation. On the one hand, Father Piñera and several long-time activists have continued to insist on the original premise that motivated—and in their view made successful—the Church's foray into the world of domestic service: they argued that, as rural migrants isolated by their employment in elite homes, bereft of formal labor protections and subject to the patronage of employers, practicing the popular religiosity of their rural origins, empleadas were neither workers nor proletarians. According to this view, failure to recognize the domestic worker's fundamental difference and alienation from the world of the urban proletariat would have doomed empleadas' associations, inspiring fear of politics in empleadas and hostility from employers.

On the other hand, the transformation of pastoral action in Chile during and after the Vatican II conference (1962–1965), as well as the politicization of key empleada leaders through their exposure to Christian Democratic and Left politics, transformed the social Catholicism of the JOC into the liberationist, dependency-oriented, revolutionary activism that reflected the predominant spirit of the Popular Unity period. Movement leaders tended increasingly to view paid household labor as *work*, but also as an occupation that history and tradition had conspired to marginalize from proletarian struggle and state regulation. The 1967–1973 period, marked as it was by the increasing political organization of Catholics and the political ascendency of popular leftist movements, activist empleadas transformed not only the means and scale of their movement but also the Catholic discourse of service and dignity that had dominated their efforts for more than a decade. Post-Vatican II leadership of the Chilean Church relied on liberation theology and its analysis of "structural sin" to diagnose and address the problem of domestic service. That this liberationist discourse and associated pastoral plans produced little lasting change in domestic workers' legal status is less important than the fact that such arguments were entertained and promoted by Church authorities in the first place. As politicization invigorated and divided empleada activists, the Catholic domestic workers' movement continued to harbor members of both viewpoints, as well as those who articulated conciliatory positions in between. Through the Federation, and its successor ANECAP, Catholic militants and their spiritual directors fundamentally shaped these choices, employing social Catholic notions of human dignity, community, and liberation to create movements intended for the temporal as well as spiritual salvation of Chilean empleadas. In ways not always appreciated sufficiently in the historiography of Latin American labor, the changing methods, doctrines, and leadership of the Catholic Church made key contributions to the discourse of twentieth-century labor movements in Latin America.

Beyond the vital contributions of state, professional, and religious allies, however, Chile's feminist movement also made its mark on empleada movements,
providing what has proven to be lasting political support necessary for the incorporation of domestic workers in Chilean labor law and provision of a public
education campaigns about this form of women's work. From the August 1981
meetings between middle-class feminists and domestic worker activists to the
subsequent wave of collaborative projects, as elsewhere in Latin America the
focus on domestic service has provided a crucial platform for feminist challenges
to gender and racial inequality. In the Chilean case, such collaborations were
strengthened in the crucible of anti-dictatorial political movements, which further surfaced in public discourse the marginality of domestic service as a demon-
stration of the regime's patriarchal and anti-democratic structures.

THE VERY NATURE of this study as twentieth-century history constitutes both
its primary strength and a limitation because it does not—as colleagues in other
disciplines have done—address the question: how has the status of domestic
workers in Chile changed over the last thirty years? Chilean society itself has
undergone dramatic transformations in political and social organization since
the defeat of General Pinochet at the polls in 1989, governed for twenty years
by a Center-Left coalition committed to neoliberal economic growth and enhanced anti-poverty measures, and thereafter alternating in power with conservative regimes. The political transition of 1990 inaugurated a new landscape
for domestic worker activists, as for the many social movements that had propelled anti-dictatorial politics past the 1988 plebiscite to the installation of civilian democratic rule. Scholarship on the Chilean transition has repeatedly
emphasized the demobilizing effects of this transition on social movements for
women, the poor, organized labor, and human rights, pointing to the dramatic
decrease in international funding and solidarity established under military rule,
as well as the incorporation of leading activists into party and government roles
in the Concertación.[9] The 1990s in particular were characterized by political
and cultural "destape," a period of sudden openness and new political alliances
that facilitated the emergence of powerful new indigenous, student, and sexuality rights. In this context of jarring political and social change, however, the
position of domestic workers—as well as the social and cultural expectations
ascribed to that occupation—remained surprisingly stable.

From the perspective of domestic workers' labor rights in Chile—the focus
of struggle, legislative efforts, and social reform for much of the twentieth century—the transition to civilian democracy in 1990 quickly shifted the legal

ground. In 1991, President Patricio Aylwin granted domestic servants severance pay and health benefits in 1991 (Decree-Law 436); in 1993, Law 19.250 regulated salary, limited daily work hours to twelve, and mandated rest; and Congress finally granted these workers maternity leave in 1998 (Law 19.591). The state official most responsible for these changes, Aída Figueroa, was someone whose participation in the UP government of the '70s, and in women's movements in the 1980s, had nurtured her contacts with ANECAP and other domestic worker activists, making her a ready supporter of domestic workers' lobbying efforts with the new government. Finally, in 2007, national holidays were extended to domestic workers; in 2008 they were included in broader reforms to the law governing minimum wage; and in 2009 domestic workers were granted vacation days on national holidays. In 2010, domestic worker activists formed a national association (la Coordinadora Nacional de Organizaciones de Trabajadoras de Casa Particular) to lobby government officials for additional regulations such as written contracts, a forty-five-hour workweek, and age sixty-five retirement, with limited success. Under the second Bachelet government in 2014–2018, activists fared better, securing Congressional support for the International Labor Organization's Convention 189 and final ratification of a law regulating the workday, rest periods, and salaries—and prohibiting employers from requiring that domestic workers wear uniforms in public—in June 2015 (Law 20.786).[10] Significantly, the reason such changes came about in this period has less to do with changing perspectives on domestic service, and more to do with the specific political alliances carried over and nurtured from the military period.

Another important development in the domestic service sector at the dawn of the twenty-first century also revealed enduring patterns of mistreatment and discrimination of domestic workers, notwithstanding the new rights codified in the above series of laws. Economic crises in neighboring Peru and Bolivia stimulated an uptick in migration toward Chile's urban centers in the 1990s. Official counts of Peruvians living in Chile grew from 7,500 in 1992 to 60,000 in 2000, and the area around Santiago's Plaza de Armas became a "little Lima," where restaurants, money wiring and long-distance phone services dominate the landscape, and the streets around the Plaza de Armas filled with Peruvian workers every weekend.[11] Bolivian women's migration to Chile's northern cities experienced similar growth in this period.[12] Most of the Andean women of this migration are employed in domestic service, often working as live-in maids and nannies, and as undocumented workers they enjoyed no labor protection and faced overt racial discrimination. This influx of Peruvian nanas since the early 1990s has complicated Chilean women's trajectory toward fuller labor rights, providing employers with a robust market of undocumented Andean workers who accept lower wages, require no social security payments from employers, and make fewer demands of their employers than their Chilean counterparts. Immigrant women—more recently including significant numbers of Venezuelan and Caribbean migrants—Chilean activists have been known to complain, are even *harder* to mobilize than Chilean women, and undermine the achievements of domestic workers by reminding employers of the "servants" of yesteryear.[13]

Domestic service relations, albeit subject to a variety of social pressures and changing educational and employment opportunities for working-class and migrant women in the late twentieth and early twenty-first century, remain a flashpoint for cultural representations of service, tradition, and paternalism in Chilean society. Even as 1940s representations such as González's Desideria were seen as reminders of an earlier time, Chilean middle-class family economies relied just as heavily as ever on the availability of live-in and part-time domestic labor. These continuities (and some important changes) were on full display in the highly acclaimed 2009 feature film *La Nana*. Marketed as a dark comedy, *La Nana* focuses on the daily life of a live-in domestic worker who has served a Santiago middle-class family for over twenty years, revealing the social isolation and resulting psychosis of the protagonist, a woman who defends her terrain against additional hired help with singular focus on self-preservation. Her schemes include driving away a younger Peruvian nanny hired to "help out," mostly by locking the girl out of the house until she surrenders and quits.

In *La Nana* as in the recurring representation of Chilean domestic workers in soap operas, films, and popular culture, we continue to see stereotypes and challenges that reflect the long history of domestic service and its representation over the course of the twentieth century. Like Mama Rosa, La Nana's existence consists of household labor, child care, and the narrow confines of her employers' home: this is an updated, neoliberal form of *convivencia,* one that preserves traditional notions of service and class hierarchy that are a poor fit with the middle-class family's pretense of social equality and familial intimacy. La Nana also preserves the rebellion and humor on display for so many decades by La Desideria, playing tricks and sticking up for herself when she finds her employer does not. In the film's final scene, La Nana has achieved independence and self-care through jogging and friends, but her home life and employment remain in the confines of the middle-class home she serves. In this way, the modern figure of La Nana seems to exist almost in a bubble, devoid of reference to the legal protections, social mobility, occupational training, and other advantages slowly achieved since the transition to democracy.[14]

As *La Nana* illustrated, stereotypes and social prejudice about women's domestic work have remained strong in Chile. This can also be seen in repeated, highly publicized incidents of domestic workers' mistreatment as they travel to work elite neighborhoods. In January 2012, news media reported several incidents that occurred in wealthy Santiago neighborhoods, gated communities of sprawling private homes developed in the early 2000s. The most scandalous event involved Felicita Pinto, a domestic worker employed in the elite Santiago housing community in Chicureo, who was stopped by the neighborhood association's private guards as she traversed the sidewalk en route to her employer's house: "the guards told me that 'nannies' can't walk through the community, because they make it look bad."[15] The association's internal rules required empleadas and hired help to use the shuttle service and stay off the street; such restrictions echoed a controversy at a nearby elite sports club a month earlier, where nannies had been prohibited from entering the pool area with their charges unless they were in uniform.[16] In the ensuing controversy, neighbors invited further media scandal and social media reaction by offering opinions about how empleadas and other workers should not be allowed to walk "their" streets; endangered their private homes by sharing information about owners' schedules; and threatened the safety of young children in the neighborhood. These restrictions on empleadas' mobility and freedom were denounced not only by Pinto's employer (who gave her title to part of his land so she could not be challenged on the street), but also by the minister of labor, Evelyn Matthei, the president of SINTRACAP Ruth Olate, and multiple scholars and pundits, all of whom deemed the Chicureo homeowners to be vestiges of racist and classist relations of an older time, one that is "unacceptable in 2012 Chile."[17]

Even as domestic workers remain ubiquitous in Chilean media coverage and popular culture, domestic worker activists have themselves continued to make the same demands they have fought for since early in the last century, among them: better pay, fair treatment, limited hours, and effective leave protections. After a decade of declining membership and limited activism linked mostly to the regional network CONLACTRAHO (Confederación Latinoamericana y del Caribe de Trabajadoras del Hogar or Latin American and Caribbean Confederation of Domestic Workers), in 2010 SINTRACAP Santiago and the national union SINDUCAP (Sindicato Nacional Unitario de las Trabajadoras de Casa Particular) spearheaded efforts for legislative reform.[18] Their struggle has, meanwhile, become global: when the International Domestic Workers' Network met in Uruguay in October 2013 to plan for the future of global struggle for domestic workers' rights, it culminated a century's long struggle and began another. A mere two years after the ratification of the historic ILO Convention 189 on the rights of domestic workers, Chilean leaders joined activists from dozens of countries across the globe to celebrate that victory and seek ratification and expansion of the convention's provisions, a goal partially achieved when Chile ratified the ILO convention in 2015. Most recently, in 2018 SINTRACAP and SINDUCAP joined with ANECAP to petition the Ministry of Labor to provide greater enforcement of Law 20,786, increase employers' contributions to severance funds, and augment state contributions to domestic workers' social security and health insurance.[19] And before the effects of the COVID-19 pandemic brought even greater challenges in 2020, movement activists had turned their attention once again to recovering the organization's history, supporting the recent archival project undertaken by students at the University of Chile to donate and catalog a collection of CONLACTRAHO documents to Chile's National Archive.[20] On the long road to recognition of their rights as workers, Chilean activists have stopped to collect, preserve, and narrativize their struggle, leaving an instructive legacy for contemporary leaders and scholars alike.

Introduction

1. The archival records of domestic workers' unions are contained in four volumes of union minutes held in the Archive of the Union of Household Workers (SINTRACAP), hereafter SINTRACAP, and at the Chilean National Archives. Santiago, Archivo Nacional de la Administración (hereafter ARNAD), Santiago, Fondo Organizaciones Sociales, "Libros de Actas: Reuniones Generales," four volumes, 1926–1964. Hereafter Actas. The author thanks Jorge Rojas Flores of Chile's Catholic University for depositing a photocopied set of the Actas at the ARNAD and for bringing their existence to the author's attention.

2. Santiago, Archivo de la Asociación Nacional de Empleadas de Casa Particular (hereafter ANECAP). With the able assistance of María Fernanda Caloiro F., research assistant and graduate in history from Chile's Catholic University, much of the ANECAP archive—including the organization's magazine *Surge*, 1958–1962—was photographed and preserved in digital format before the ANECAP National Directorate lost access to its own archives. Digital reproductions of these materials were returned to ANECAP officers in 2005, and also remain in the author's possession.

3. Studies of domestic service have long emphasized employer narratives of paternalism and fictive kinship. See Grace Esther Young, "The Myth of 'Being Like a Daughter,'" *Latin American Perspectives* 14, no. 3 (Summer 1987); Emma Marie Pérez, "'She Has Served Others in More Intimate Ways': The Domestic Servant Reform in Yucatán, 1915–1918," *Aztlán* 20, nos. 1–2 (Spring-Fall 1991): 11–37; Lesley Gill, *Precarious Dependencies: Gender, Class, and Domestic Service in Bolivia* (New York: Columbia University Press, 1994); Elsa M. Chaney and Mary Garcia Castro, eds., *Muchachas No More: Household Workers in Latin America and the Caribbean* (Philadelphia: Temple University Press, 1988).

4. The quest to produce a critical historical record of working conditions in Chilean domestic service (and other "female" occupations) began in the 1980s, when Chilean feminist scholars—triggered both by critical currents in global feminism and their own contact with domestic workers in women's movements against the dictatorship—produced brief studies that relied on testimony and photographs to describe domestic workers' stories of migration, poverty, overwork, isolation, and sexual abuse. Some of those works include Thelma Gálvez and Rosalba Todaro, *Trabajadoras de casa particular:*

Tábita, Clementina, Lidia (Santiago: CEM, 1984); Rosabla Todaro and Thelma Gálvez, *Trabajo doméstico remunerado: Conceptos, hechos, datos* (Santiago: CEM, 1987); Thelma Gálvez and Rosalba Todaro, *Yo trabajo así, en casa particular* (Santiago: CEM, 1985); Macarena Mack, Paulina Matta, Ximena Valdés, *Los trabajos de las mujeres entre el campo y la ciudad, 1920–1982: Campesina, costurera, obrera de la costura, empleada doméstica, cocinera de fundo, temporera* (Santiago: CEM, 1986).

5. International Labor Organization, "C189, Domestic Workers Convention, 2011 (No. 189)," https://www.ilo.org/dyn/normlex/en/f?p=NORMLEXPUB:12100:0::NO::P12100_ILO_CODE:C189.

6. G. Labarca Hubertson, "La abuela," *Nuevos Horizontes*, January 1, 1904; Daniel de la Vega, "La antigua criada," *Zig-Zag* 15, no. 776 (January 3, 1920), n.p. Two popular songs mentioned in empleada interviews include Nicanor Molinare, "Rosita de Cachapoal," and Tito Fernández, "Muchacha de Domingo."

7. The phrase "trabajadoras, como todas las demás" is drawn from Ivania Silva's 1972 article urging ANECAP members to unionize: ANECAP, Ivania Silva, "Afiliación a la CUT," *ANECAP Boletín* 1 (April 1972): 5–6.

8. Eileen Boris, *Making the Woman Worker: Precarious Labor and the Fight for Global Standards, 1919–2019* (New York: Oxford, 2019).

9. Jocelyn Olcott, "Researching and Rethinking the Labors of Love," *Hispanic American Historical Review* 91, no. 1 (2011): 1–27.

10. Eileen Boris and Jennifer Fish, "Decent Work for Domestics: Feminist Organizing, Worker Empowerment, and the ILO," in *Towards a Global History of Domestic Workers and Care Workers,* ed. Dirk Hoerder, Elise Van Nederveen Meerkerk, and Silke Neunsinger (Leiden: Brill: 2015), 530–552.

11. A growing body of interdisciplinary research on domestic workers in contemporary Latin America led to the formation in 2018 of the Network of Research on Domestic Work in Latin America (Red de Investigaciones sobre el Trabajo del Hogar en América Latina or RITHAL), which promotes the dissemination of research findings, interdisciplinary projects, and collaboration with domestic workers' associations throughout the region. https://www.facebook.com/Rithal-Red-de-Investigaci%C3%B3n-sobre-Trabajo-del-Hogar-en-Am%C3%A9rica-Latina-106986504419062/?ref=page_internal.

12. Gill, *Precarious Dependencies.*

13. Elizabeth Quay Hutchison, *Labors Appropriate to Their Sex: Gender, Labor and Politics in Urban Chile, 1900–1930* (Durham, NC: Duke University Press, 2001), chap. 2; Lucía Pardo, "Una revisión histórica a la participación de la población en la fuerza de trabajo: Tendencias y características de la participación de la mujer," *Estudios de Economía* 15, no. 1 (April 1988): 25–82.

14. The earliest history of this movement was written using archival sources by the domestic worker activist Aída Moreno Valenzuela, in a mimeographed account, "Cuadernillo de antecedentes históricos de Sintracap" (August 22, 1989), in the SINTRACAP archive. This work was later published in English as "History of the Household Workers' Movement in Chile, 1926–1983," in *Muchachas No More,* ed. Chaney and Castro,

407–416. See also Aída Moreno Valenzuela, *Evidencias de una líder: Memorias de una trabajadora de casa particular* (Santiago: LOM Ediciones, 2012).

15. Sonia Montecino and Loreto Rebolledo, *Diagnóstico sobre inserción laboral de mujeres Mapuche rurales y urbanas* (Santiago: Universidad de Chile and SERNAM, 1993); SINTRACAP, "Realidad de las Trabajadoras de Casa Particular en Chile: Resumen Ejecutivo" (Spring 1993), photocopy, Archivo SINTRACAP; Ximena Díaz and Iris Delgado, *Personal de Servicio Doméstico: Estudio Diganóstico, Chile 2001* (Santiago: Centro de Estudios de la Mujer, 2001); Silke Staab and Kristen Hill Maher, "The Dual Discourse About Peruvian Domestic Workers in Santiago de Chile: Class, Race, and a Nationalist Project," *Latin American Politics and Society* 48, no. 1 (Spring 2006): 87–116.

16. Ivonne Szasz, *Mujeres inmigrantes y mercado de trabajo en Santiago* (Santiago: CELADE, 1994) and David E. Hojman, "Land Reform, Female Migration and the Market for Domestic Service in Chile," *Journal of Latin American Studies* 21, no. 1 (1989): 120–121.

17. Cristobal Kay, "The Development of the Chilean *Hacienda* System," in *Land and Labour in Latin America*, ed. Kenneth Duncan and Ian Rutledge (Cambridge: Cambridge University Press, 1977), 103–40; Arnold Bauer, *Chilean Rural Society from the Spanish Conquest to 1930* (Cambridge: Cambridge University Press, 1975); Brian Loveman, *Chile: The Legacy of Hispanic Capitalism* (New York: Oxford University Press, 1979); Gabriel Salazar, *Labradores, peones y proletarios: Formación y crisis de la sociedad popular chilena del siglo XIV* (Santiago: SUR, 1985); Heidi Tinsman, *Partners in Conflict: The Politics of Gender, Sexuality, and Labor in the Chilean Agrarian Reform, 1950–1973* (Durham. NC: Duke University Press, 2002).

18. Elba Bravo, Aída Moreno, and Father Bernardino Piñera, in particular, gave generously of their time to allow me to collect their stories on multiple occasions in Santiago between July 2002 and June 2005. Since then, however, all three have passed away, most recently Aída Moreno on June 2, 2021.

19. Elba Bravo, interview, Santiago, Chile, July 5, 2002.

20. Bravo, interview, July 5, 2002.

21. Bravo, interview, September 8, 2004.

22. Bravo, interview, September 8, 2004.

23. Heidi Tinsman has also documented the risks and benefits of female migration and rural labor with respect to sexual abuse and income in "Reviving Feminist Materialism: Gender and Neoliberalism in Pinochet's Chile," *Signs* 26, no. 1 (Autumn 2000): 165–167.

24. Bravo, interview, July 5, 2002.

25. Studies of these particular migrant flows are available only in the 1950s forward. Szasz draws on a variety of statistical sources to demonstrate the predominance of young, poorly educated, migrant women employed in the Santiago domestic service sector between 1952 and 1982, while David Hojman's 1986 survey of household workers in Santiago showed that a minority (thirty out of 112) had been born in the Metropolitan Region; most migrant empleadas came from rural communities south of Santiago, and

over time migration originated in the southern regions even more distant from Santiago. Szasz, *Mujeres inmigrantes,* and Hojman, "Land Reform," 120–121.

26. Bravo, interview, September 8, 2004.

27. Bravo, interview, September 8 2004.

28. Bravo, interview, September 8, 2004.

29. A radio and television character created by the actress Ana González Olea in the 1940s. María Elisa Ruiz Vera, *Ana González: Primera Actriz* (Santiago: Edebé, Editorial Don Bosco, 2002).

Chapter 1

1. El Porvenir de Empleados de Casas Particulares, "Los empleados domésticos," *La Nación*, November 1923.

2. ANECAP, Ivania Silva, "Afiliacion a la CUT," *ANECAP Boletín* 1 (April 1972): 5–6.

3. Steve J. Stern, *Reckoning with Pinochet: The Memory Question in Democratic Chile, 1989–2006* (Durham. NC: Duke University Press, 2010); Peter Winn, ed., *Victims of the Chilean Miracle: Workers and Neoliberalism in the Pinochet Era, 1973–2002* (Durham, NC: Duke University Press, 2004); Edward Murphy, *For a Proper Home: Housing Rights in the Margins of Urban Chile, 1960–2010* (Pittsburgh: University of Pittsburgh Press, 2015).

4. Alvaro Jara, *Guerra y Sociedad en Chile: La transformación de la Guerra de Arauco y la esclavitud de los indios* (Santiago: Editorial Universitaria, 1971).

5. David J. McCreery, "Debt Servitude in Rural Guatemala: 1876–1936," *Hispanic American Historical Review* 6, no. 4 (1983): 735–759; Donna Guy, "Women, Peonage, and Industrialization: Argentina, 1810–1914," *Latin American Research Review* 16, no. 3 (1981): 65–89.

6. Heidi Tinsman, "Rebel Coolies, Citizen Warriors, and Sworn Brothers: The Chinese Loyalty Oath and Alliance with Chile in the War of the Pacific," *Hispanic American Historical Review* 98, no. 3 (2018): 439–469; Julio Pinto Vallejos, *Trabajos y rebeldías en la pampa salitrera: el ciclo del salitre y la reconfiguración de las identidades populares (1850–1900)* (Santiago: Universidad de Santiago, 1998); Mario Góngora, *Orígen de los inquilinos de Chile Central* (Santiago: Universidad de Chile, 1960).

7. Nara B. Milanich, *Children of Fate: Childhood, Class, and the State in Chile, 1850–1930* (Durham, NC: Duke University Press, 2009); Ann S. Blum, *Domestic Economies: Family, Work, and Welfare in Mexico City, 1884–1943* (Lincoln: University of Nebraska Press, 2009); Christine Ehrick, *The Shield of the Weak: Feminism and the State in Uruguay, 1903–1933* (Albuquerque: University of New Mexico Press, 2005); Sol Serrano, *¿Qué hacer con Dios en la República? Política y secularización en Chile, 1845–1885* (Santiago: Fondo de Cultura Económica, 2008).

8. Sergio Paolo Solano and Roicer Flórez Bolívar, "Política y trabajo: Debates sobre las normas jurídicas y las relaciones laborales de servidumbre en el Bolivar Grande (Colombia) en el siglo XIX," *Revista de Estudios Sociales* 45 (January-April 2013): 16–28.

9. Manuel Abrantes, "A Matter of Decency? Persistent Tensions in the Regulation of Domestic Service," *Revista de Estudios Sociales* 45 (January-April 2013): 110–122.

10. Nara Milanich, "From Domestic Servant to Working-Class Housewife: Women, Labor, and Family in Chile," *E.I.A.L.* 6, no. 1 (2005): 11–39.

11. Peter DeShazo, *Urban Workers and Labor Unions in Chile, 1902–1927* (Madison: University of Wisconsin Press, 1983); Brian Loveman, *Chile: The Legacy of Hispanic Capitalism* (New York: Oxford University Press, 1979); Michael Monteon, *Chile in the Nitrate Era: The Evolution of Economic Dependence, 1880–1930* (Madison: University of Wisconsin Press, 1982).

12. In 1991, President Patricio Aylwin granted domestic servants severance pay and health benefits (Decree-Law 436); in 1993, Law 19.250 regulated salary, limited daily work hours to 12, and mandated rest; and Congress finally granted these workers maternity leave in 1998 (Law 19.591).

13. For an extended reflection on activists' understandings of these diverse terms, see José A. Vidal Yañez, "ANECAP como agente de cambio social frente a las Trabajadoras de Casas Particulares," (Social science thesis, Alberto Hurtado University ILADES, 1990), 3–4.

14. On empleados, see J. Pablo Silva, "The Origins of White-Collar Privilege in Chile: Arturo Alessandri, Law 6020, and the Pursuit of a Corporatist Consensus, 1933–1938," *Labor* 3, no. 1 (2006): 87–112; Azun Soledad Candina Polomer, ed., *La frágil clase media: Estudios sobre grupos medios en Chile contemporáneo* (Santiago: UREDES, Universidad de Chile, 2013).

15. Bernadino Piñera, interview by Pamela Aróstica Fernández, in "Sindicato de empleadas de casa particular (1930–1960)" (Undergraduate thesis, University of Chile, 1997), 137–138.

16. Consider, for example, the National Domestic Workers' Alliance (NDWA), the International Domestic Workers' Federation, and the "Domestic Workers' Convention" adopted by the International Labor Organization in 2011. Some scholars, such as Nadasen, have chosen instead to use the variant "household worker," to avoid the theoretical and political implications of the term "domestic." Premilla Nadasen, *Household Workers Unite: The Untold Story of African American Women Who Built a Movement* (Boston: Beacon Press, 2015).

17. Recent studies outside of Latin America that have likewise placed domestic service at the center of historical analysis include Swapna M. Banerjee, *Women, Men, and Domestics: Articulating Middle-class Identity in Colonial Bengal* (New York: Oxford University Press, 2014); Shireen A. Ally, *From Servants to Workers: South African Domestic Workers and the Democratic State* (Ithaca, NY: ILR/Cornell University Press, 2009); Nadasen, *Household Workers Unite.*

18. Grace Esther Young, "The Myth of 'Being Like a Daughter,'" *Latin American Perspectives* 14, no. 3 (Summer 1987); Emma Marie Pérez, "'She Has Served Others in More Intimate Ways': The Domestic Servant Reform in Yucatán, 1915–1918," *Aztlán* 20, nos. 1–2 (Spring-Fall 1991): 11–37; Lesley Gill, *Precarious Dependencies: Gender, Class, and Domestic Service in Bolivia* (New York: Columbia University Press, 1994); Elsa

M. Chaney and Mary Garcia Castro, eds., *Muchachas No More: Household Workers in Latin America and the Caribbean* (Philadelphia: Temple University Press, 1988).

19. Heidi Elizabeth Tinsman, "The Indispensable Services of Sisters: Considering Domestic Service in United States and Latin American Studies," *Journal of Women's History* 4, no. 1 (1992): 37–59.

20. Chaney and Garcia Castro, *Muchachas No More*.

21. Sandra Lauderdale Graham, *House and Street: The Domestic World of Servants and Masters in Nineteenth-Century Rio de Janeiro* (Cambridge: Cambridge University Press, 1988. Another example of continuity in master-servant relations is Young, "Myth of Being 'Like a Daughter,'" 365–380.

22. Gill, *Precarious Dependencies*. For Mexico, see Pérez, "'She Has Served Others.'"

23. Cecilia Allemandi, *Sirvientes, Criados y Nodrizas: Una historia del servicio doméstico en la ciudad de Buenos Aires (fines del siglo XIX y principios del XX)* (Buenos Aires: Teseo and Universidad de San Andrés, 2018); Inés Pérez, Romina Cutuli y Débora Garazi, with Santiago Canevaro, *Senderos que se bifurcan: Servicio Doméstico y derechos laborales en la Argentina del siglo XX* (Mar del Plata, Argentina: EUDEM, 2018); María Julia Rossi and Lucía Campanella, eds., *Los de abajo: Tres siglos de sirvientes en el arte y la literatura en América Latina* (Rosario, Argentina: UNR Editores, 2019); Louisa Acciari, "Paradoxes of Subaltern Politics: Brazilian Domestic Workers' Mobilisations to Become Workers and Decolonise Labor" (PhD diss., London School of Economics, 2018).

24. Beyond the landmark collection *Muchachas No More*, key works in this generation include Graham, *House and Street*; Gill, *Precarious Dependencies*; Mary Goldsmith, "Female Household Workers in the Mexico City Metropolitan Area" (PhD diss., University of Connecticut,1990); Tinsman, "Indispensable Services"; Carlos Zurita, *Trabajo, servidumbre y situaciones de género. Algunas acotaciones sobre el servicio doméstico en Santiago del Estero, Argentina* (Santiago del Estero: Universidad Nacional de Santiago del Estero, 1997).

25. Merike Blofield, *Care Work and Class: Domestic Workers' Struggle for Equal Rights in Latin America* (University Park, PA: Penn State Press, 2013); Encarnación Gutiérrez Rodríguez, *Migration, Domestic Work and Affect* (New York: Routledge, 2010); Rhacel Salazar Parreñas, *Servants of Globalization: Women, Migration, and Domestic Work* (Stanford: Stanford University Press, 2001).

26. RITHAL, https://www.facebook.com/Rithal-Red-de-Investigaci%C3%B3n-sobre-Trabajo-del-Hogar-en-Am%C3%A9rica-Latina-106986504419062/?ref=page_internal.

27. Carolina Stefoni and Fernanda Stang, "La construcción del campo de estudio de las migraciones en Chile: notas de un ejercicio reflexivo y autocrítico," *Íconos* 58 (2017): 109–129; Carolina Stefoni, "Migración, género y servicio doméstico," in *Mujeres peruanas en Chile. Trabajo doméstico: un largo camino hacia el trabajo decente,* ed. María Elena Valenzuela and Claudia Mora (Santiago: OIT, 2009), 191–232; Carolina Stefoni and Rosario Fernández, "Mujeres inmigrantes en el trabajo doméstico: entre el servilismo y los derechos," in *Mujeres inmigrantes en Chile ¿Mano de obra o trabajadoras con derechos?* ed. Carolina Stefoni (Santiago: Ediciones Universidad Alberto Hurtado, 2011),

43–72; Irma Arriagada and Marcela Moreno, "La Constitución de Cadenas Globales de Cuidado y las Condiciones Laborales de las Trabajadoras Peruanas en Chile," in *Mujeres inmigrantes*, ed. Stefoni, 151–191; Irma Arriagada and Rosalba Todaro, "Cadenas globales de cuidado. El papel de las Migrantes," in *Mujeres inmigrantes*; Sandra Leiva and César Ross, "Migración circular y trabajo de cuidado: Fragmentación de trayectorias laborales de migrantes bolivianas en Tarapacá," *Psicoperspectivas* 15, no. 3 (2016): 56–66.; Sandra Leiva, Miguel Ángel Mansilla, and Andrea Comelin, "Condiciones laborales de migrantes bolivianas que realizan trabajo de cuidado en Iquique," *Si Somos Americanos* 17, no. 2 (2017): 11–37; Andrea Comelin and Sandra Leiva, "Cadenas globales de cuidado entre Chile y Bolivia y migración circular," in *Migración e Interculturalidad: perspectivas contemporáneas en el abordaje de la Movilidad*, ed. José Berríos-Riquelme and Idenilso Bortolotto (Santiago: Fundación Scalabrini/INCAMI, 2017), 181–213; Verónica Correa Pereira, "Más allá de la racionalidad económica: una nueva aproximación para la comprensión de la emigrante latinoamericana que llega a Santiago de Chile," *Revista de Estudios Sociales* 49 (May 2014): 176–189; Kristen Hill Maher and Silke Staab, "Nanny Politics. The dilemmas of working women's empowerment in Santiago, Chile," *International Feminist Journal of Politics* 7, no. 1 (2005): 71–88; Silke Staab and Kristen Hill Maher, "The Dual Discourse about Peruvian Domestic Workers in Santiago de Chile: Class, Race, and a Nationalist Project," *Latin American Politics and Society* 48, no. 1 (2006): 87–116.

28. Parreñas, *Servants of Globalization*.

29. Blofield, *Care Work and Class*.

30. Robyn Allyce Pariser, "The Servant Problem: African Servants and the Making of European Domesticity in Colonial Tanzania, 1919–1961," in *Towards a Global History*, 271–295; Andrew Urban, "Imperial Divisions of Labour: Chinese Servants and Racial Reproduction in the White Settler Societies of California and the Anglophone Pacific, 1870–1907," in *Towards a Global History*, 296–322.

31. For an astute analysis of the continuing ideological work of the "crisis de cuidados" discourse in contemporary Chile, see Rosario Fernández, "Mujeres de elite y trabajo doméstico remunerado en Chile: ¿crisis de cuidados o de la familia?" *La manzana de la Discordia* 12, no.1 (2017): 33–47.

32. On the iterations of the "servant crisis" in Europe and the United States, see Faye Dudden, "Experts and Servants: The National Council on Household Employment and the Decline of Domestic Service in the Twentieth Century," *Journal of Social History* 20 (Winter 1986): 269–90; and Rose Holmes, "Love, Labour, Loss: Women, Refugees and the Servant Crisis in Britain, 1933–1939," *Women's History Review* 2, no. 2 (2017), 288–309.

33. "Sabados del Hogar," *El Porvenir*, September 4, 1907.

34. M. De Avila, "Crónica Doméstica. Sirvientes," *El Mercurio*, March 29, 1905 (emphasis added).

35. E.B., "El servicio doméstico. Exijencias exajeradas de las sirvientes," *El Chileno*, April 20, 1907.

36. Jours, "Pro-sirvientes domésticas," *El Ilustrado*, March 1, 1914.

37. F., "La Huelga doméstica," *El Chileno*, June 15, 1907.

38. Ramón Escudero, "Tratado de moral," *La Federación Obrera*, January 10, 1911.

39. Elizabeth Quay Hutchison, *Labors Appropriate to Their Sex: Gender, Labor and Politics in Urban Chile, 1900–1930* (Durham, NC: Duke University Press, 2001), chap. 3; Lorena Godoy Catalán, "'Armas ansiosas de triunfo: Dedal, agujas, Tijeras . . .': La educación professional femenina en Chile, 1888–1912" (undergraduate thesis, Universidad Católica de Chile, 1995).

40. J.E.S., "Sirvientes Domésticas," *El Ilustrado*, March 11, 1914.

41. X., "Sirvientes," *El Ilustrado*, August 26, 1908.

42. X., "Sirvientes," *El Ilustrado,* January 16, 1911.

43. X., "Sirvientes," *El Ilustrado*, January 7, 1911.

44. Una dueña de casa, "Crisis de servidumbre," *El Ilustrado*, March 10, 1914.

45. "El problema de los servicios domésticos," *El Chileno*, July 11, 1911.

46. "El problema de los servicios domésticos," *La Unión*, July 21, 1911.

47. Malek, "La Crisis de la servidumbre," *El Ilustrado*, Apri 29, 1907

48. Like the "servant crisis," the proliferation of private employment agencies in Chile during this period has been a pattern in early industrial societies elsewhere. See Felice Batlan, *Women and Justice for the Poor: A History of Legal Aid, 1863–1945* (New York: Cambridge University Press, 2015).

49. Archivo de la Dirección General del Trabajo (Labor Office Archive), hereafter ADGT. "Sindicato Señoritas Empleadas de Comercio y Oficinas," June 19, 1925, and "Sindicato señoritas empleadas de comercio y oficinas," June 19, 1925.

50. "Empleados y obreros," *La Nación*, January 19, 1930, 45.

51. P.P.H., "Agencias de Empleos," *La Nación,* May 30, 1939, 3.

52. "Empleados y empleadas de casas particulares ofrece el Sindicato Profesional-Garantiza el servicio y honradez de sus miembros," *El Mercurio,* November 15, 1939, 26.

53. Francisco J. Zuñiga Reyes, "Los sirvientes domésticos," *La Reforma*, November 17, 1907. *La Reforma* tracked activities of resistance societies, including men and women employed in industry. Hutchison, *Labors Appropriate*, chap. 3.

54. "Los sirvientes en huelga," *La Reforma*, January 31, 1908.

55. *La Reforma*, June 23, 1907.

56. S. Sala E., "Sangre Obrera: Salud!," *La Socialista*, May 27, 1916.

57. "El drama de muchas madres proletarias," *La Opinión*, April 26, 1917.

58. Elizabeth Quay Hutchison, "'El Fruto Envenenado del árbol capitalista': Women Workers and the Prostitution of Labor in Urban Chile, 1896–1925," *Journal of Women's History* 9 (1998): 131–150.

59. "Manifiesto a las compañeras del servicio doméstico," *Acción Directa*, May 1, 1921.

60. "Una joven escapa por los tejados. En donde se verá como tratan los burgueses la servidumbre," *La Federación Obrera*, March 25, 1922.

Chapter 2

1. A growing body of scholarship examines how national political context shapes different regimes of exclusion in Latin America. See, for example, Inés Pérez, Romina Cutuli, and Débora Garazi, with Santiago Canevaro, *Senderos que se bifurcan: Servicio Doméstico y derechos laborales en la Argentina del siglo XX* (Mar del Plata, Argentina: EUDEM, 2018) and Sara Hidalgo, "The Making of a 'Simple Domestic': Domestic Workers, the Supreme Court, and the Law in Postrevolutionary Mexico," *International Labor and Working-Class History* 94 (Fall 2018): 55–97.

2. "La situación de los empleados domésticos," *El Ilustrado*, October 23, 1923.

3. "Radiotanda 1 Radioteatro de humor," https://www.cooperativa.cl/noticias/entretencion/radio/el-recuerdo-de-radiotanda-el-popular-programa-de-radioteatro-de-la/2018-08-13/040239.html.

4. ADGT, "Descanso Quincenal," February 25, 1918.

5. The Spanish term *convivencia* can be translated as cohabitation, but also connotes a social relationship of tranquility and mutual respect. Its deployment in legal arguments against state regulation of employer-domestic worker relations echoes a discourse of kinship and intimacy that obscured the social, and often racial, hierarchies embedded in domestic service labor relations. See Inés Pérez and Santiago Canevaro, "Languages of Affection and Rationality: Domestic Workers' Strategies before the Tribunal of Domestic Work, Buenos Aires, 1956–2013," *International Labor and Working-Class History* 88 (2015): 130–149.

6. Elizabeth Quay Hutchison, *Labors Appropriate to Their Sex: Gender, Labor and Politics in Urban Chile, 1900–1930* (Durham, NC: Duke University Press, 2001), 217–220.

7. Peter DeShazo, *Urban Workers and Labor Unions in Chile, 1902–1927* (Madison: University of Wisconsin Press, 1983); Julio Pinto and Verónica Valdivia, *Revolución proletaria o querida chusma? Socialismo y Alessandrismo en la pugna por la politización pampina, 1911–1932* (Santiago: LOM, 2007); Jorge Rojas Flores, *El sindicalismo y el estado en Chile, 1924–1936* (Santiago: Colección Nuevo Siglo, 1986).

8. "Los empleados domésticos," *La Nación*, November 1923. A later newspaper report refers to the association as the Sociedad de Empleados Particulares "El Porvenir" José Miguel Infante, linking the union to the leader of Chilean independence credited with the country's abolition of slavery in 1823. "La situación de los empleados domésticos," *El Ilustrado*, October 23, 1924.

9. Hutchison, *Labors Appropriate*, chap. 7. See also Linda Gordon, ed., *Women, the State and Welfare* (Madison: University of Wisconsin Press, 1990); Susan Pedersen, *Family, Dependence, and the Origins of the Welfare State: Britain and France, 1914–1945* (Cambridge: Cambridge University Press, 1995).

10. "La situación de los empleados domésticos," *El Ilustrado*, October 23, 1923. The petition was later discussed at length by union leaders of the time: "Por propias y ajenas necesidades, de bien y de justicia, ha luchado con ejemplar tesón el Sindicato de Empleados de Casas Particulares," *La Nación*, March 31, 1930, 25.

11. "Los empleados domésticos."

12. "Los empleados domésticos," *La Justicia*, March 17, 1925.

13. "Por propias y ajenas necesidades," 25.

14. Decree Law 4054, Article 14 c, http://bcn.cl/1xxi7.

15. Hutchison, *Labors Appropriate*, chap. 7; Jadwiga Pieper Mooney, *The Politics of Motherhood: Maternity and Women's Rights in Twentieth-Century Chile* (Pittsburgh: University of Pittsburgh Press, 2009); María Soledad Zárate Campos, *Dar a luz en Chile, siglo XIX. De la "ciencia de hembra" a la ciencia obstétrica* (Santiago: Ediciones Universidad Alberto Hurtado, 2007); Lidia Casas and Tania Herrera, "Maternity protection vs. maternity rights for working women in Chile: a historical review," *Reproductive Health Matters* 20, no. 40 (2012): 139–147.

16. In the example provided by a guide for employers in 1941, a domestic worker in Santiago who received 80 pesos monthly in salary, and the equivalent of 120 pesos in *regalía*, would contribute 4 pesos (2 percent), while the employer provided 10 pesos (5 percent). *Libreta recibo de la dueña de casa. Cumplimiento y resguardo con los Empleados domésticos de acuerdo con la ley* (Santiago: Talleres Graficos Artuffo, 1941).

17. María Elisa Ruiz Vera, *Ana González: Primera Actriz* (Santiago: Edebé, Editorial Don Bosco, 2002).

18. Fernando Debesa, *Mama Rosa* (Santiago: Editorial Universitaria, 1995), 66.

19. ADGT, July 28, 1928, 2.

20. ADGT, January 7, 1928.

21. Jorge Arancibia Muñoz, *El contrato de trabajo de los empleados domésticos* (Santiago: Dirección general de prisiones, 1939), 60.

22. Eileen Boris and Jennifer N. Fish, "Decent Work for Domestics: Feminist Organizing, Worker Empowerment, and the ILO," in *Towards a Global History*, 530–552; Louisa Acciari, "Decolonising Labour, Reclaiming Subaltern Epistemologies: Brazilian Domestic Workers and the International Struggle for Labour Rights," *Contexto Internacional* 41, no. 1 (January/April 2019): 39–63.

23. "Consulta No. 340 (M.C.) Empleada Doméstica (Ley Social que le corresponde)," *La Nación* January 28, 1930.

24. ADGT, Ministry of Foreign Affairs Official Letter to Labor Office, August 24, 1927.

25. The first volume of this collection bears a seal that gives the founding date of the Sindicato Autónomo as January 1, 1926, although the regular minutes prior to January 6, 1931, are not contained in the volume. ARNAD, Fondo Organizaciones Sociales, "Libros de Actas: Reuniones Generales," vol. 1, 1931–1942.

26. CNCD, "Sesión General Extraordinaria," July 7, 1931; Actas, vol. 1, 54. The proposal was debated several times in the House of Deputies (ordinary sessions, June 17, 1930, September 10, 1930, July 14, 1931) and proposed in the Senate on September 16, 1936.

27. Actas, "Sesión ordinaria celebrada por el Sindicato de empleados de Casas particulares," [June or July] 1936, 68.

28. "El Problema de los empleados domésticos debe considerarse," *El Mercurio*, March 17, 1927.

29. The inspection team of the Labor Office was created in 1919, and female inspectors were added in 1926, under the leadership of key reformers including Moisés Poblete Troncoso and the feminist Elena Caffarena de Morice. Hutchison, *Labors Appropriate*, 224–230.

30. ADGT, "Informa consultas sobre sindicatos de empleados de casas particulares," January 12, 1928.

31. Senator Ayala had also been a key player in debates over a proposed modification to DL 4053 to include industrial home workers. Hutchison, *Labors Appropriate*, 223.

32. CNCD, *Boletín de Sesiones Ordinarias*, July 23,1928: *Diario de Sesiones de la Cámera de Diputados 1923*, Cámara de Diputados, 621–629.

33. The proposal received no further debate and was ignored by the press. CNCD, "Salario minimo de las obreras," February 9, 1931, *Boletín de Sesiones Extraordinarias*, vol. 2, 1931, 2067–2068.

34. Arancibia Muñoz, *El contrato de trabajo*, 49.

35. This date is an estimate, based on where the undated document is located: ADGT, "Ante-Proyecto de Título sobre Domésticos que presenta a la Sub-Comisión de Organización Sindical y Contrato de Trabajo el Secretario, Sr. Patricio Santander Denis," vol. 198, 1929.

36. Jorge Rojas Flores, *La Dictadura de Ibáñez y los sindicatos (1927–1931)* (Santiago: Dirección de Bibliotecas, Archivos y Museos, 1993); Juan Carlos Yañez Andrade, *La intervención social en Chile y el nacimiento de la sociedad salarial, 1907–1932* (Santiago: RiL editores, 2008); Brian Loveman, *Chile: The Legacy of Hispanic Capitalism* (New York: Oxford University Press, 1979), chap. 7.

37. President Ibáñez, quoted in Arancibia Muñoz, *El contrato de trabajo*, 54.

38. Ministerio de Interior. *Recopilación de Decretos con Fuerza de Ley. Año 1931. Dictados en virtud de las facultades otorgadas al Ejecutivo por la Ley numero 4945 de 6 de febrero de 1931* (Santiago: Talleres Graficos "La Nación" 1933), 233.

39. "Un dirigente obrero que renunucia," *El Diario Ilustrado*, January 7, 1931, 20.

40. "Un dirigente obrero," 20.

41. CRAC also endorsed candidates for parliamentary elections, including Luis Moreno Fantanes and Humberto Martonez, two legislators who would later propose legislation for domestic workers. The domestic workers' union also singled out the socialist (Partido Demócrata) politician Malaquías Concha—long a proponent of more stringent labor protections—for special praise. The union sent Malaquías Concha a letter congratulating him on his election to the Senate. "Sesión General celebrada el 15 de Septiembre de 1932," Actas, vol 1. For Malaquías Concha's role in generating early social legislation, see Hutchison, *Labors Appropriate*, chap. 7.

42. "Alcanzo brillante caracteres la concentración que ayer celebro la CRAC," *La Nación*, January 27, 1930, 17.

43. Actas, "Sesión General celebrada el 15 de Septiembre de 1932," vol 1.

44. "Modelo de contrato de trabajo para empleados domésticos" [1939], Arancibia Muñoz, *El contrato de trabajo*, 128–130.

45. Arancibia Muñoz, *El contrato de trabajo*, 58.

46. In theory, these contracts could be made verbally, but only if the employer provided workers with a signed declaration of the verbal agreement, with a copy also to be sent to the Labor Office. Arancibia Muñoz, *El contrato de trabajo*, 68–69.

47. Arancibia Muñoz, *El contrato de trabajo*, 70.

48. Sentence of the Supreme Court of the Labor Tribunal, Iquique, August 1, 1934, quoted in Arancibia Muñoz, *El contrato de trabajo*, 57.

49. "Análisis numérico comparativo sobre el movimiento de la oferta y la demanda de Obreros, Empleados Particulares y Empleados Domésticos . . ." *Revista de Trabajo* 3, no. 8 (August 1933): 19.

50. *Revista de Trabajo* 6, nos. 1–2 (January-February 1936): 251–252 and 6, no. 3 (March 1936): 53–54.

51. *Revista de Trabajo* 10, nos. 6–7 (June-July 1940): 34–35.

52. Olga Maturana Santelices, *Revista de Trabajo* 3, no.10 (October 1933): 68–72.

53. *Revista del Trabajo* 22, nos. 8–9 (August-September 1952): 24. See also *Revista del Trabajo* 21, nos. 2–3 (Februrary-March 1951): 27–28.

54. *Revista del Trabajo* 14, nos. 9–10 (September-October 1944): 22–23.

55. Karin Rosemblatt, *Gendered Compromises: Political Cultures and the State in Chile, 1920–1950* (Chapel Hill: University of North Carolina Press, 2000). See also Ricardo López-Pedreros, *Makers of Democracy: A Transnational History of the Middle Classes in Colombia* (Durham, NC: Duke University Press, 2019).

56. As a clinician and administrator, Dr. Vizcarra drew on data collected from a variety of clinics within the CSO Medical Center in the port of Valparaíso between 1926 and 1942. Dr. J. Vizcarra C., "Servicio Doméstico," *Boletín Médico-Social de la Caja de Seguridad Obligatorio* 9, nos. 98–99 (August-September, 1942): 15–19.

57. Rosemblatt, *Gendered Compromises*, 127.

58. Rosemblatt, *Gendered Compromises*, 129.

59. Rosemblatt, *Gendered Compromises*, 137–141.

60. Juana Concha, *La Empleada Doméstica y sus problemas* (social work thesis, Escuela de Servicio Social "Elvira Matte de Cruchaga," 1940), 26.

61. Julio Bustos A., José Vizcarra, and Manuel de Viado, "La aplicación del Seguro Social a los Trabajadores Agrícolas, a los independientes y al personal doméstico," International Welfare Conference (Santiago: Imprenta Universitaria, 1942), 11.

62. Bustos et al., "La aplicación del Seguro Social," 13.

63. Vizcarra, "Servicio Doméstico," 446–455.

64. Vizcarra, "Servicio Doméstico," 14.

65. Vizcarra, "Servicio Doméstico," 16–21.

66. Vizcarra, "Servicio Doméstico," 20–23 (emphasis mine).

67. Violeta Paez Boggioni, "Empleada doméstica y maternidad" (social work thesis, University of Chile, Valparaíso, 1948), 5–7.

68. Paez Boggioni, "Empleada doméstica y maternidad," 10–12.

69. Paez Boggioni, "Empleada doméstica y maternidad," 42.

70. Paez Boggioni, "Empleada doméstica y maternidad," 105.

71. Paez Boggioni, "Empleada doméstica y maternidad," 110.

72. Before launching her commentary on this data, Pérez Monardes dismissed both ahistorical understandings of domestic service and the notion that domestic service will wither away: "domestic service will remain an endless source of problems for legislators, sociologists, psychologists, etc." Gladys Pérez Monardes, "La empleada doméstica de casa particular" (social work thesis, School of Social Work, University of Chile, 1954), 75.

73. Pérez Monardes, "La empleada doméstica," 105–116.

74. Pérez Monardes, "La empleada doméstica," 117–118.

75. Manuel Rojas and Ramon Reyes, for example, were leaders in both unions. Actas, May 30, 1936, vol. 1.

76. Arancibia Muñoz, *El contrato de trabajo*, 104.

77. "Se reorganiza el 'Sindicato de Empleados de Casas Particulares: Acuerdos tomados en la primera sesión," *La Opinión*, June 9, 1936, 4.

78. "El sindicato de empleados particulares," *Últimas Noticias: La Hora*, June 15, 1935, 10; also in *La Opinión*, June 14, 1936.

79. This list included Provincial Labor Inspector Avila, head of the Department of Associations Amengual, Labor Inspectors Montecinos and Aristodemo Escobar, and members of the press and labor leaders from other unions. "Ganamos bajos salarios y trabajamos más de 15 horas diarias, declaro Manuel Rojas, Secretario del Sindicato de Empleados de Casas Particulares," *La Hora* 4, no. 1,435 (May 30, 1939), 16.

80. "Cena a la prensa ofrecerá el sabábado próximo sindicato de E.E, de Casas Particulares," *La hora*, November 17, 1939, 16.

81. "Reunión de Directorio celebrada el día 17 de Octubre de 1939 (Nocturna)," Actas, vol. 2, 21.

82. "Su tercer aniversario celebraron empleados de casas particulares," *La Opinión*, November 21, 1939, 4.

83. Actas, "Reunión de Directorio celebrada el 28 de mayo de 1940," vol. 2, 57–61.

84. Actas, "Reunión de Directorio, celebrada el Martes 14 de enero de 1941," vol. 2, 93.

85. Actas, "Reunión General celebrada el día 6 de agosto de 1941," vol. 1, 92.

86. CNCD, "Mensaje de S.E. el Presidente de la República," Boletín de Sesiones Extraordinarias, 1934, October 23, 1934, 77.

87. Actas, "Sesión ordinaria celebrada por el Sindicato de empleados de casas particulares," [July or August] 1935, vol. 1, 68.

88. For a detailed analysis of the feminization of domestic service in Argentina, including the recategorization of chauffeurs, see Inés Pérez, "Género y cambios en las definiciones legales del servicio doméstico: desmarcación y profesionalización de los choferes," in Inés Pérez et al, *Senderos que se bifurcan*, chap. 2.

89. Actas, "Reunión General celebrada el 25 de Noviembre de 1941", vol. 1, 98.

90. *La Mujer Nueva* 1 (November 1935): 1.

91. E. Román, "La empleada doméstica," *La Mujer Nueva* 2 (December 8, 1935): 1.

92. Delie Rouge, "Que esa ley sea un hecho," *La Mujer Nueva* 6 (March 1935): 4. Delie Rouge was the pseudonym of Delia Rojas Garcés (or Delia Rojas de White), a prominent literary figure, feminist, and member of MEMCH.

93. "A los enemigos del aborto," *La Mujer Nueva* 6 (May 1936): 4.

94. On MEMCH, see Corinne Antezana-Pernet, "Mobilizing Women in the Popular Front Era: Feminism, Class, and Politics in the Movimiento Pro-Emancipación de la Mujer Chilena (MEMCH), 1935–1950." (PhD diss., UC Irvine, 1996); Rosemblatt, *Gendered Compromises*, chap. 4.

95. The Chilean labor movement of the 1940s remained overwhelmingly focused on male-dominated trades and participation, despite the prominence of MEMCH and other women's movements affiliated with the Popular Front governments. Rosemblatt, *Gendered Compromises*, chap. 3.

96. "Reunión de Directorio celebrada el día 23 de enero de 1940," Actas, vol. 2, 41–43.

97. "Reunion de Directorio celebrada el día 2 de julio de 1940," Actas, vol. 2, 65.

98. "Reunion de Directorio celebrada el día 25 de marzo de 1941," Actas, vol. 2, 97–98.

99. "Los obreros domésticos y el carnet profesional," *Confederación de Trabajadores de Chile* (June 1946): 14.

100. "Acuerdos concretos sobre reinvindicaciones generales," *Confederación de Trabajadores de Chile* (January 1947): 4.

101. "Reunión de Directorio celebrada el día 9 de enero de 1940," Actas, vol. 2, 37–38.

102. María Soledad Zárate Campos and Elizabeth Quay Hutchison, "Clases medias en Chile: Estado, género y prácticas políticas, 1920–1970," in *Historia Política de Chile 1810–2010*, ed. Iván Jakšić, Juan Luis Ossa, Susana Gazmuri, Francisca Rengifo and Andrés Estefane (México: Fondo de Cultura Económica, 2017), 271–300.

Chapter 3

1. Scott Mainwaring, "The Catholic Youth Workers Movement (JOC) and the Emergence of the Popular Church in Brazil," Kellog Institute Working Paper 36 (December 1983), 16; Alejandro Cussiánovich, *Llamados a ser libres* (Lima: CEP, 1974); William Elvis Plata Quezada, "El Sindicato del Servicio Doméstico y la Obra de Nazareth: entre asistencialismo, paternalismo y conflictos de interés, Bogotá, 1938–1960," *Revista de Estudios Sociales* 45 (January-April 2013): 29–41.

2. *Catálogo de los eclesiásticos de ambos cleros, casas religiosas, iglesias y capillas de la República de Chile a fines del año 1939* (Santiago: Imp. Y Edit. "Sagrado Corazón de Jesús," 1940), 138–139, 157–158. Nara Milanich examines the treatment of families and children in nineteenth-century Chile in *Children of Fate: Families, Class and the State in Chile, 1850–1930* (Durham, NC: Duke University Press, 2009). See also Patience Schell's *Church and State Education in Revolutionary Mexico City* (Tucson: University of Arizona Press, 2003) and Christine Ehrick's *The Shield of the Weak: Feminism and the State in Uruguay, 1903–1933* (Albuquerque: University of New Mexico Press, 2005).

3. The European origins of the Young Catholic Workers are described in Michael de la Bedoyere, *The Cardijn Story: A Study of the Life of Mgr. Joseph Cardijn and the Young Christian Workers' Movement Which He Founded* (London: Longmans, Green,

1958). For an excellent firsthand account and analysis of the Young Christian Worker movement in the United States, see Mary Irene Zotti, *A Time of Awakening: The Young Christian Worker Story in the United States, 1938 to 1970* (Chicago: Loyola University Press, 1991).

4. The Chilean JOC was founded by two young priests, Larrain and Piñera, following their participation in the world JOC congress in Canada. María Antonieta Huerta M., *Catolicismo social en Chile: Pensamiento y praxis de los movimientos apostólicos* (Santiago: Ediciones Paulinas, 1991), 470.

5. Tracey Jaffe, "In the Footsteps of Cristo Obrero: Chile's Young Catholic Workers Movement in the Shantytown, Factory, and Family, 1946–1973" (PhD diss., University of Pittsburgh, 2009), 39.

6. Bernardino Piñera, interview, Santiago, August 29, 2004.

7. These "saritas" included Sara Espejo, Sara Marambia, Carmen Rojas, Alicia Molina, and Martina Guerrero. Bernardino Piñera, interview, Santiago, July 5, 2002.

8. Piñera commented that he "chose the leaders well," a group that included Anita de la Fuente, Dina Garrido, Marta Pino, Eliana Cid, Olfa Aceval, Ema Jiménez, Teresa Carillo, and Elba Bravo. Bernardino Piñera, interview, Santiago, June 20, 2005.

9. Aída Moreno Valenzuela, *Evidencias de una líder: Memorias de una trabajadora de casa particular* (Santiago: LOM Ediciones, 2012), 19.

10. Moreno, *Evidencias*, 38.

11. Elba Bravo, interview, Santiago, July 5, 2002.

12. Elena Prado (pseud.), interview, Santiago, June 19, 2005.

13. Rudy Urzúa, interview, Santiago, June 25, 2005.

14. *Surge* 24 (February-March 1960): 8.

15. Jaffe, "In the Footsteps of Cristo Obrero," chap. 3.

16. "Nuestra décima aniversario," *Surge* 26 (May 1960): 8–9.

17. Archive of the Archbishopric of Santiago (hereafter AAS), *A.C., 1955–1956*, 132:2, Bernardino Piñera C. to the Consejo de Administración del Arzobispado de Santiago, mimeo [1956]. The Federación de Empleadas also maintained the property with funds collected from its membership; see *Surge* 47 (June 1962): 13.

18. "Vale la pena ser socia?" *Surge* 24 (February-March 1960): 10; "Nueve años cumplió el Hogar de la Empleada," *La Voz* 119 (June 7, 1959): 11.

19. The proportion of women performing domestic service off-site and part-time increased sharply in times of economic crisis, reaching 35.3 percent in 1974 and 51 percent in 1981. Ivonne Szasz, *Mujeres inmigrantes y mercado de trabajo en Santiago* (Santiago: CELADE, 1994), 184.

20. Bernardino Piñera, interview by Pamela Aróstica Fernández, October 31, 1996, "Sindicato de empleadas de casa particular (1930–1960)" (undergraduate thesis, University of Chile, 1997), 131–132.

21. Piñera, in Aróstica, "Sindicato de Empleadas," 135.

22. Moreno, *Evidencias*, 32.

23. Moreno, *Evidencias*, 31.

24. Moreno, *Evidencias*, 36–37.

25. Rudy Urzúa, interview, Santiago, Chile, June 25, 2005.

26. Prado, interview.

27. Elena Prado worked for the same employer for 46 years. Prado, interview.

28. Piñera in Aróstica, "Sindicato de Empleadas," 129.

29. Piñera in Aróstica, "Sindicato de Empleadas," 138.

30. Piñera in Aróstica, "Sindicato de Empleadas," 139.

31. The Libros de Actas on which this reconstruction is based contain a gap in union minutes between October 1945 and January 1951, when a reconstituted, all-female empleadas' union appeared: the Sindicato Profesional de Empleadas Domésticas No. 2. Actas, "Santiago 3 de Mayo de 1953," vol. 4, 28–29; "Santiago 9 de Agosto de 1953," vol. 4, 32; "Santiago 11 de Septiembre de 1953," vol. 4, 33.

32. Actas, "En Santiago a 11 de Mayo de 1952," vol. 4, 17; "Santiago 5 de Octubre de 1952," vol. 4, 22.

33. Actas, "Santiago a 6 de julio de 1957," vol. 4, 73; "En Santiago 6 de Agosto de 1957," vol. 4, 74; "En Santiago a 7 de Agosto de 1958," vol. 4, 84; "En Santiago a 7 de Septiembre de 1958," vol. 4, 85; "Santiago 2 de Octubre de 1959," vol. 4, 100; "Santiago 6 de Diciembre de 1959," vol. 4, 102.

34. The level of activism sustained by the directorate in this period may be attributed in part to the greater availability of then-president Raquel Ortiz. On the heels of a dispute within the directorate over the advisability of opening the employment service on the basis of empleadas' voluntary contributions, President Ortiz provoked considerable controversy when she tried to reschedule a meeting of the directorate from a Wednesday to a Sunday; since all of the other officers worked puertas adentro, they objected to the change, saying that they were unable to secure permission to change their days off. Ortiz's desire to change, willingness to risk empleada funds on the employment office, and availability to give multiple recruiting talks in local parishes suggests that she was financially more secure and/or employed fewer hours than her fellow officers. Actas, "28 de Noviembre de 1962," vol. 4, 172.

35. SINTRACAP, Moreno, "Cuadernillo de antecedentes históricos," 8.

36. The end of archives for the Sindicato Profesional in 1964 leaves the fate of this organization unclear until its revival in 1979 under the aegis of the *Sindicato Interempresas de Trabajadoras de Casas Particulares*. In any case, both ANECAP and SINTRACAP currently claim the secular unions as their institutional precursors.

37. Piñera, interview, June 5, 2002.

38. Piñera, interview in Aróstica, "Sindicato de empleadas," 135.

39. Piñera, interview, June 5, 2002.

40. Because of its long association with the Catholic Church and its success in attracting members, the Federation (later ANECAP) has been the principal subject and source base for Chilean *tesistas* examining the experience, legal status, and social participation of domestic workers in Chile. One of the most valuable studies of domestic worker associations (including ANECAP and the union, SINTRACAP) was drafted in 1983 by the Executive Committee of ANECAP: ANECAP, Comité Ejecutivo Nacional de

Anecap, "Historia del movimiento de la trabajadora de casa particular de Chile, 1926–1983," mimeo, June 1983.

41. "Federación de Empleadas de Casa Particular," *Surge* 24 (February-March 1960): 8–9.

42. Jaffe, "In the Footsteps of Cristo Obrero."

43. Piñera, interview, August 29, 2004.

44. Piñera, interview, July 5, 2002.

45. "Domésticas tienen su código," and "Interesante folleto de divulgación social: 'La E. de Casa Particular,'" in *La Voz* 38, no.2 (December 24, 1955): 2, 10.

46. "Se unen en una agrupación para defenderse en forma colectiva," *La Voz* 3, no. 59 (October 12, 1956): 6; and "Las empleadas domésticas: 60 mil mujeres abandonadas en manos extrañas en la capital," *La Voz* 49 (May 20, 1956): 6–7.

47. B.P.C., "Empleada de casa particular y sus problemas en la profesión," *La Voz* 78 (September 8, 1957): 5.

48. Piñera, interview, August 29, 2004.

49. Piñera in Aróstica, "Sindicato de empleadas," 133–134.

50. "Llegan las vacaciones," *Surge* 53 (December-January 1962): 14–15.

51. "Festival: 12.000 Chilenos mostraron unidad obrera," *La Voz* 3, no. 60 (October 28, 1956): 16.

52. "El Congreso Jocista de Lima," *La Voz* 130 (November 8, 1959): 1.

53. Once in Chile, Cardijn attended Vargas's wedding and participated in JOC events and visits to various Centros de Empleadas. "Una Visita Ilustrada," *Surge* 22 (November 1959): 6.

54. Through JOC congresses and visits from Father Piñera, Vargas remained in close touch with the Federation. Marta Pino G., "Llegó carta de Lima," *Surge* 21 (October 1959): 10.

55. "Problemas de Canadá," *Surge* 31 (October 1960): 8–10 and *Surge* 32 (November 1960): 10. In August 1960, *Surge* published three letters celebrating the success of the Chilean Federation and requesting written materials: the Sindicato Unico de Servicio Doméstico, Bolivia; the JOC Femenina, Uruguay; and "Las Martas," a Colombian organization autonomous of the JOC Femenina. "Correspondencia," *Surge* 29 (August 1960): 10–11.

56. "La soledad de la empleada," *Surge* (September 1960): 5–6.

57. "María Madre de Jesús y Madre Nuestra," *Surge* 22 (November 1959): 8–9.

58. The life of the Virgin Mary was apparently still an attractive theme for group reflection in the 1980s, when ANECAP produced a pamphlet for pastoral reflection titled "María, mujer," in which Mary's suffering is presented as similar to the suffering of Chilean women. ANECAP, "María, mujer," pamphlet, n.d. [circa 1980]. On the historical evolution of marianismo in Latin America, see Linda Hall, *Mary, Mother and Warrior: The Virgin in Spain and the Americas* (Austin: University of Texas Press, 2004), as well as the critique of marianism as a paradigm for Latin American "womanhood" in Marysa Navarro, "Against *Marianismo*," in *Gender's Place: Feminist Anthropologies of Latin America,* ed. Rosario Montoya, Lessie Jo Frazier, and Janise Hurtig (New York: Palgrave MacMillan, 2002), 257–272.

59. "Zita, la sirvienta," *La Voz* 116 (April 26, 1959): 12.

60. "La empleada llegó a los altares," *Surge* (three undated numbers, 1961): 4–5. In some versions, she also performed extreme acts of penitence, including self-flagellation, and after death her body became a relic for devotion and pilgrimage. Bernardo Gentilini, *El libro del doméstico (o empleado) y el del artesano (u obrero)* (Santiago: Apostolado de la Prensa, 1935), 45–50.

61. Bravo, interview, July 5, 2002; "Empleada dignifico los quehaceres domesticos," *La Voz* 78 (September 8, 1957): 5. Other cases of lifelong service were regularly recorded in *Surge*: see, for example, "Emotivo caso de abnegación," *Surge* 21 (October 1959): 4 and "Ejemplo de vida," *Surge* 44 (April 1962): 16.

62. "La empleada llegó a los altares," *Surge*: 4–5.

63. While the annual pilgrimage was apparently conducted without incident, the "día nacional" regularly provoked conflicts between empleadas and their female employers. In line with its emphasis on seeking balance between domestic harmony and empleadas' dignity, each year *Surge* published vignettes about "good" and "bad" patronas' responses to empleadas' requests for a day off on November 21. See, for example, *Surge* 23 (December 1959-January 1960): 10–11.

64. "Nueve años cumplió el Hogar de la Empleada," *La Voz* 119 (June 7, 1959): 11. The following year (1960), *Surge* reported the existence of twenty-three parish-level "Federaciones en formación," each of which held weekly meetings (Tuesday through Friday). "Federación de Empleadas de C.P."

65. Elena Prado, Santiago, June 19, 2005. At age 93 Prado recalled—and recited—Gabriela Mistral's "La madrecita duerme," a tragic story of a mother's death as told by her orphaned child.

66. *Surge* 52 (November 1962): 1. Earlier in the year, Cardinal Silva Henríquez's first act as cardinal had been to address the leadership of the Federación de Empleadas at the JOC retreat center in Quisco, asking them to mobilize more workers in the movement. "Nuestro Cardenal," *Surge* 45 (April 1962): 1.

67. AAS, *Acción Católica 1956–1958*, Leg. 132 No. 2A, Ariztía to Tagle, May 31, 1958.

68. AAS, *Acción Católica 1956–1958*, Leg. 132 No. 2A, Ariztía, "Distribución de los Asesores de la AC Obrera," n.d., and Ariztía to Tagle, August 6, 1958.

69. *Surge: Publicación mensual de la Federación de Empleadas de Casa Particular* was created in 1958 and published monthly at least through 1962.

70. "Una militante en día de lluvia," *Surge* 48 (July 1962): 6–7.

71. "Un Apóstol de 'Surge,'" *Surge* 53 (December-January 1963): 4–5.

72. "El Trabajo," *Surge* 26 (May 1960): 1.

73. Carmen Rojas, "Todo trabajo es igualmente digno," *Surge* 36, no.12 (May 1961): 9.

74. "Our cover," *Surge* 52 (November 1962): 1.

75. "Una Empleada sana," *Surge* 24 (February-March 1960): 1.

76. "Sufrimientos y esperanzas," *Surge* 28 (July 1960): 8–10.

77. *Surge* published news of the Sindicato No. 2 de Empleadas Domésticas, such as the election of the union's new directorate in February 1962. *Surge* 44 (February-March 1962): 3.

78. Bravo, interview, July 5, 2002.

79. Bravo, interview, July 5, 2002.

80. Bravo, interview, June 26, 2005.

81. Beginning in 1958, at least half of the fourteen bishops' vacancies were filled by clergy formerly active in Acción Católica or with close ties to the Falange, including Silva Henríquez (of Caritas Chile) and Manuel Larraín (of Catholic Action). Brian H. Smith, *The Church and Politics in Chile: Challenges to Modern Catholicism* (Princeton, NJ: Princeton University Press, 1982), 112–114.

82. Stewart-Gambino documents how Church involvement in the rural sector in the 1950s—though trailing social Catholics' embrace of urban workers' issues—anticipated and propelled the broader agenda of liberation in the Chilean Church. Hannah W. Stewart-Gambino, *The Church and Politics in the Chilean Countryside* (Boulder, CO: Westview Press, 1992), chap. 5. Furthermore, Smith notes that the senior clergy who participated in the Vatican II Concilium were widely praised for their deep theological and practical experience with social Catholicism, Catholic political involvement, and questions of liberation, issues that became central to the Council's project. Smith, *Church and Politics*, 109–114.

83. Interviews with Fathers Bernardino Piñera and Carlos Camus, cited in Fernando Aliaga Rojas, *Itinerario histórico de los círculos de estudios a las comunidades juveniles de base* (Santiago: Equipo de Servidios de la Juventud, 1977), 132–133.

84. ANECAP, "Estatutos de la Asociación Nacional de Empleadas de Casa Particular" [1965] and related correspondence, mimeo, July 1965–May 1966.

85. With only 2,800 official members recorded in 1957, JOC statistics are sketchy at best; the JOC certainly involved much larger numbers of workers in its activities. These membership numbers come from an article reprinted in the Catholic press, "El Catolicismo en Chile," *Política y Espíritu* 199, no. 13 (May 1, 1958): 13–21, which also emphasized the JOC's influence on much greater numbers of workers. The author wishes to thank Tracey Jaffe for her original insights on this question, explored in greater detail in her dissertation, "In the Footsteps of Cristo Obrero."

86. Unlike progressive Catholic student organizations and political activists, domestic workers' explicit political engagement followed, rather than preceded, Vatican II and Medellín. For a detailed discussion of the Chilean hierarchy, organized laity, and the "political question" before 1964 (the year of Christian Democratic victory), see Stewart-Gambino's excellent treatment in *The Church and Politics in the Chilean Countryside*.

87. Smith, *Church and Politics*, chap. 6.

Chapter 4

1. Scholarship on Allende's brief presidency (1970–1973) is extensive, covering in great detail the politics, policies, and controversies of his government, including the forces leading to the successful military coup against him in 1973. See for example Peter Winn, *Weavers of Revolution: The Yarur Workers and Chile's Road to Socialism* (New York:

Oxford University Press, 1984); Tanya Harmer, *Allende's Chile and the Inter-American Cold War* (Chapel Hill: University of North Carolina Press, 2011); Marian E. Schlotterbeck, *Beyond the Vanguard: Everyday Revolutionaries in Allende's Chile* (Oakland: University of California Press, 2018); Heidi Tinsman, *Partners in Conflict: The Politics of Gender, Sexuality, and Labor in the Chilean Agrarian Reform, 1950–1973* (Durham, NC: Duke University Press, 2002).

2. See Anthony Gill, *Rendering Unto Caesar: The Catholic Church and the State in Latin America* (Chicago: University of Chicago Press, 1998); Kenneth Serbin, *Secret Dialogs: Church-State Relations, Torture, and Social Justice in Authoritarian Brazil* (Pittsburgh: University of Pittsburgh Press, 2000).

3. Archive of the National Association for Household Employees (ANECAP), "Primer seminario nacional capacitación y formación de dirigentes," mimeo, Santiago, June 1967, 10. Hereafter ANECAP.

4. "Primer seminario nacional," 19.

5. "Primer seminario nacional," 31.

6. Aída Moreno, interview, Santiago, July 3–4, 2002.

7. Hugo Verdugo H. and Fernando Tapia A., "La empleada de casa particular: realidad y perspectivas," *Mensaje* 175 (December 1968): 638.

8. Verdugo and Tapia, "La empleada de casa particular," 639.

9. ANECAP, Hugo Verdugo H., "Documentos-Reflexiones," *ANECAP Boletín* 2 (July 1972): 2.

10. AAS, Box 156, Folder 12, "Proyecto Pastoral para las Empleadas de Casa Particular de la Iglesia de Santiago de Chile," mimeo [1969], 1.

11. AAS, "Proyecto Pastoral," 6.

12. ANECAP, "Proyecto Pastoral Santiago," mimeo [1969], 12.

13. ANECAP, "Proyecto Pastoral Santiago," 9.

14. AAS, Box 156, Folder 12, "Resumen de la reflexión de las dirigentes y asesores del 7 de Junio de 1971," mimeo, 2.

15. ANECAP, "Proyecto Pastoral Concepción," mimeo [1969], 12.

16. ANECAP, "Proyecto Pastoral Concepción," 7.

17. AAS, "Resumen de la reflexión," 1.

18. Cecilia Guiraldes C., María del Pilar Ibieta G., and Patricia Dávila L., "La empleada de casa particular: Realidades y perspectivas" (social work thesis, Catholic University of Chile, 1971), 41–42.

19. Piñera, interview, August 29, 2004.

20. Guiraldes et al., "La empleada de casa particular," 43.

21. Guiraldes et al., "La empleada de casa particular," 41–42.

22. Guiraldes et al., "La empleada de casa particular," 42–43.

23. SINTRACAP, Moreno, "Cuadernillo de antecedentes," 9.

24. ANECAP, *ANECAP Boletín* 2 (July 1972): 1. This short-lived, mimeographed bulletin—managed by an ANECAP editorial team that included Hugo Verdugo—is significant because it focused exclusively on union (as opposed to religious) issues, and

included the secular union SINTRACAP in regular news updates.The *Boletín* also provided summaries of recent talks by Verdugo and Tapia, editorials encouraging greater militancy among empleadas (such as Ivania Silva's exhortation to "decide whether we are, or are not, workers like all the rest of them"), and instructions on how to calculate empleadas' and employers' respective social security contributions.

25. ANECAP, "La mujer en Chile hoy," *ANECAP Boletín* 1 (April 1972): 2–3. See also the proposal to organize domestic service as an industrial cleaning service (empresa), which both Guiraldes et al. and feminist economists from CEM discussed with domestic worker activists in 1971 and 1982: Guiraldes et al., "La empleada de casa particular," 69–72. Aída Moreno and other long-time activists founded a cleaning business, Quillay, which in the 1980s and '90s employed domestic workers in crews to do contract cleaning and maintenance for NGOs in Santiago.

26. ANECAP, Ivania Silva, "Afiliación a la CUT," *ANECAP Boletín* 1 (April 1972): 5–6.

27. Some of the points treated in the 1970 proposal had been outlined in a brief letter sent to the Ministry of Labor and Social Welfare two years earlier, apparently without success. SINTRACAP, "Proyecto para las Empleadas Domésticas," SINTRACAP to Minister of Labor, April 4, 1968.

28. SINTRACAP, "A los Partídos de la Unidad Popular. Ref: Solicita estudio derogación Art. No. 62 del Código del Trabajo," SINTRACAP to Unidad Popular, March 1970, 1.

29. SINTRACAP, "A los Partidos," 3.

30. SINTRACAP, Moreno, "Cuadernillo de antecedentes," 8. Evidence of union members' contact with FEGRECH goes back to July 1963, when Aída Moreno and Isabel Sota represented their union at a FEGRECH congress. The union officially joined ASICh in the same year, and began efforts to sponsor a bill for domestic workers (hours, minimum wage, working conditions, statutes, and labor contract) in congress. Actas, July 14, 1963, November 27, 1963, April 1 and 26, 1964.

31. SINTRACAP, Moreno, "Cuadernillo de antecedentes," 8.

32. Guiraldes et al., "La empleada de casa particular," 44; and ANECAP, "Proyecto de ley redactado por ANECAP en base a las observaciones y modificaciones hechas por sus miembros," in Guiraldes et al., 58–62.

33. Guiraldes et al., "La empleada de casa particular," 60.

34. Guiraldes et al., "La empleada de casa particular," 59.

35. Piñera, interview, August 29, 2004.

36. AAS, Box 156, Folder 12, Raúl Cardenal Silva Henríquez, Ismael Errázuriz Gandarillas, and Rafael Maroto Pérez, "Carta pastoral del Sr. Cardenal y de los Vicarios Episcopales de las zonas Centro y Oriente de la Arquidiócesis de Santiago a las empleadas de casa particular y a los dueños de casa," mimeo, September 6, 1971, 1.

37. AAS, Silva Henríquez et al., "Carta pastoral," 5.

38. AAS, Silva Henríquez et al., "Carta pastoral," 6–7.

39. AAS, Silva Henríquez et al., "Carta pastoral," 8.

40. AAS, Silva Henríquez et al., "Carta pastoral," 9.

41. ANECAP, "Agenda: Los sindicatos de Santiago se entrevistan," *Boletín informativo de los Sindicatos de Empleadas* 1 (April 1972): 7.

42. ANECAP, "Agenda: De nuevo el proyecto de ley," *Boletín informativo de los Sindicatos de Empeladas* 2 (July 1972): 9.

43. For the name change enacted by Law No. 17,795, see Humberto Bravo Navarette, "Régimen jurídico Laboral de las Trabajadores de Casa Particular" (law thesis, University of Concepción, 1976), 14.

44. Moreno, interview, July 3-4, 2002.

45. SINTRACAP, Moreno, "Cuadernillo de antecedentes," 8.

46. Bravo, interview, August 27, 2004.

Chapter 5

1. Peter Winn, "The Pinochet Era," in *Victims of the Chilean Miracle: Workers and Neoliberalism in the Pinochet Era, 1873–2002*, ed. Peter Winn (Durham, NC: Duke University Press, 2004), 14–70.

2. Brian H. Smith, *The Church and Politics in Chile: Challenges to Modern Catholicism* (Princeton, NJ: Princeton University Press, 1982); Patricio Orellana and Elizabeth Quay Hutchison, *El movimiento de derechos humanos en Chile, 1973–1990* (Santiago: CEPLA, 1991).

3. Marguerite Guzmán Bouvard, *Revolutionizing Motherhood: The Mothers of the Plaza de Mayo* (Wilmington, DE: Scholarly Resources, 1994); María Teresa Tula, *Hear My Testimony: María Teresa Tula, Human Rights Activist of El Salvador*, ed. and trans. Lynn Stephen (Boston: South End Press, 1994). On the relevance of frameworks for women's strategic protest, see Lisa Baldez, *Why Women Protest: Women's Movements in Chile* (Cambridge: Cambridge University Press, 2002).

4. Steve J. Stern, *Battling for Hearts and Minds: Memory Struggles in Pinochet's Chile, 1973–1988* (Durham, NC: Duke University Press, 2006); Manuel Antonio Garretón, *The Chilean Political Process* (Boulder, CO: Westview Press, 1989); Paul W. Drake and Iván Jaksić, eds., *The Struggle for Democracy in Chile, 1982–1990* (Lincoln: University of Nebraska Press, 1991).

5. Alison J. Bruey, *Bread, Justice, and Liberty: Grassroots Activism and Human Rights in Pinochet's Chile* (Madison: University of Wisconsin Press, 2018); Cathy Schneider, *Shantytown Protest in Pinochet's Chile* (Philadelphia: Temple University Press, 1995).

6. Aída Moreno, "Autobiografía" (unpublished manuscript, July 7, 2007) electronic file, 45.

7. Although police were required to supervise the meetings, the women of the union got on well with them, and eventually were allowed to meet in private while the policeman waited outside. Aída Moreno Valenzuela, *Evidencias de una líder: Memorias de una trabajadora de casa particular* (Santiago: LOM Ediciones, 2012), 66.

8. Moreno, *Evidencias*, 68.

9. Although the ANECAP board that was in place prior to the coup remained legal, officers could be asked to resign and vacancies could be filled by decree of the district's military quartermaster (intendente). ANECAP, letters from ANECAP to Intendente, 1973–1987.

10. The surviving institutional archives of the association illustrate the extreme care with which ANECAP leadership guarded the association's legitimacy in the months following the coup; minutes of meetings held by the General Assembly and Directorate had been sparsely kept in the years prior to the coup, but were meticulously recorded from February 1974 through seventeen years of dictatorship. ANECAP, National Assembly Minutes, January 15, 1974, 1.

11. ANECAP, Junta de Gobierno to ANECAP, June 4, 1974. The cultural celebration included various musical and spoken performances, including Anita González, la Desideria. ANECAP, National Board Minutes, October 3, 1974, 5.

12. ANECAP, National Board Minutes, September 5, 1974, 4.

13. In 1977, ANECAP signed an agreement with the Vicariate of Solidarity that granted ANECAP the right to legal defense and other "activities in solidarity with the workers." ANECAP, "Agreement," signed by Aída Moreno and Christian Precht, mimeo, April 18, 1977.

14. ANECAP, National Board Minutes, April 3, 1975, 8.

15. Humberto Bravo Navarette, "Régimen jurídico laboral de trabajadores de casa particular," 13–14. The meeting with government officials was "cordial": ANECAP, National Board Minutes, July 3, 1975, 9.

16. ANECAP, "El Proyecto de Estatuto Legal de la Trabajadora de Casa Particular," mimeo, September 1975, 3. Not surprisingly, the appended short history of ANECAP virtually excised the history of union activism of 1967–1973, focusing instead on the technical, pastoral, and associational activities of the group since 1949.

17. ANECAP, "El Proyecto de Estatuto Legal," 3.

18. ANECAP, "El Proyecto de Estatuto Legal," 3.

19. The regime's slow and halting commitment to the free market economic policies for which the regime's "economic miracle" would later be known is documented in Winn, "The Pinochet Era," in *Victims of the Chilean Miracle*, 4–70.

20. This formulation of "women's rights" may have been related to board meetings in early 1976 that addressed "Women's Rights" and "Women's Role in Society." ANECAP, National Board Minutes, April 8, 1976, 14. See also DEPAL workshops offered October 17, 1976, "Estatuto de Capacitación y empleo" and "Women's rights." ANECAP, National Board Minutes, September 24, 1976, 21.

21. ANECAP, "Memorias de actividades 1976 'ANECAP' Asociación Nacional de Empleadas de Casa Particular," [1977], mimeo, 2.

22. For an excellent analysis of the discourse of Catholic solidarity as it impacted religious and nongovernmental organizations operating under military rule, see Alison Bruey, "Transnational Concepts, Local Contexts: Solidarity at the Grassroots in Pinochet's Chile," in *Human Rights and Transnational Solidarity in Cold War Latin America*, ed. Jessica Stites-Mor (Madison: University of Wisconsin Press, 2013), 120–142.

23. ANECAP, Minutes of National Board, September 24, 1976, 21.

24. ANECAP, Minutes of National Assembly, April 3, 1975.

25. ANECAP, Minutes of National Assembly, May 8, 1975.

26. SINTRACAP, Moreno, "Cuadernillo de antecedentes," 10; Moreno, *Evidencias*, 69.

27. Correspondence with Santiago Intendencia, February 16, 1977, designating Aída Moreno president, Francisca Chaihueque, secretary, and Paulina Venegas, treasurer. ANECAP, National Board Minutes, March 9, 1977, 24.

28. National Congressional Archive, Santiago, Contraloría General de la República, "Title XIII: Special Contracts," *Recopilación de Decretos Leyes* 73, no. 7 (1978): 203–203.

29. Winn, "The Pinochet Era," 32–38.

30. Bravo Navarette, "Régimen Jurídico Laboral," 14–15.

31. ANECAP, National Board Minutes, April 4, 1978, 35.

32. ANECAP, National Board Minutes, April 25, 1978, 46.

33. ANECAP, National Board Minutes, August 25, 1978.

34. ANECAP, National Board Minutes, September 12, 1979, 50.

35. SINTRACAP, Moreno, "Cuadernillo de antecedentes," 10.

36. ANECAP, "Reglamento de la Comisión de Coordinación de las Organizaciones del Gremio de T.C.P.," n.d., 1.

37. ANECAP, "Acta de la primera reunión de las Comisión de Coordinación de las Organizaciones del Gremio," n.d., 1.

38. ARNAD, Fondo Organizaciones Sociales, *Caminando* (1983-n.d.), nos. 3, 5, 7, 9, 10, and 12.

39. ANECAP, Comité Ejectutivo Nacional de Anecap, "Historia del movimiento de la trabajadora de casa particular de Chile, 1926–1983," mimeo, June 1983.

40. ANECAP, "Pastoral Santiago," mimeo, 1979.

41. SINTRACAP, "Petitorio del Sindicato Interempresa de Trabajadoras de Casa Particular del Area Metropolitana," mimeo, June 1981.

42. ARNAD, Fondo Organizaciones Sociales, *SINTRACAP Boletín* 0 (August 1982): 8, 17.

43. ARNAD, Fondo Organizaciones Sociales, *Amistad y Esperanza* 9 (May 1984): 7. Emphasis by author. Thirty issues of the twelve-page bulletin, the official organ of the National Association of Household Employees (ANECAP), were published between 1982 and 1990.

44. ARNAD, Fondo Organizaciones Sociales, *Amistad y Esperanza* 9 (May 1984): 3. Editors of the newsletter had modified the Nobel Laureate's poem, inserting "setting the table" in the list of "small tasks" and omitting Mistral's final stanzas praising service to God through prayer.

45. ARNAD, Fondo Organizaciones Sociales, *Amistad y Esperanza* 5 (March-April 1983): 4; *Amistad y Esperanza* 6 (May-June 1983): 3; *Amistad y Esperanza* 7 (July-August 1983): 2; *Amistad y Esperanza* 19 (September 1987): 3

46. ARNAD, Fondo Organizaciones Sociales, "Actualidad," *Amistad y Esperanza* 9 (May-June 1983): 3.

47. ANECAP, "Te invitamos a conocer nuestros derechos laborales," [1984].

48. One of the best accounts of Latin American feminisms in this period remains Nancy Saporta Sternbach, Marysa Navarro-Aranguren, Patricia Chuchryk, and Sonia E. Alvarez. "Feminisms in Latin America: From Bogota to San Bernardo," *Signs* 17, no. 2 (Winter 1992): 393–434. On feminists' attention to domestic service relations, see Hildete Pereira de Melo, "Feminists and Domestic Workers in Rio de Janeiro," in *Muchachas No More: Household Workers in Latin America and the Caribbean,* ed. Elsa M. Chaney and Mary Garcia Castro (Philadelphia: Temple University Press, 1989), 245–270; Ana Lau, "El nuevo movimiento feminista mexicano a fines del milenio," in *Feminismo en México, ayer y hoy,* ed. Eli Bartra, Anna M. Fernández Poncela, and Ana Lau (Mexico: Universidad Autónoma Metropolitana, 2000).

49. Asunción Lavrin, *Women, Feminism, and Social Change in Argentina, Chile, and Uruguay, 1890–1940* (Lincoln: University of Nebraska Press, 1995); Elizabeth Quay Hutchison, *Labors Appropriate to Their Sex: Gender, Labor, and Politics in Urban Chile, 1900–1930* (Durham, NC: Duke University Press, 2001), chap. 4.

50. Rosemblatt, *Gendered Compromises*; Corinne Antezana-Pernet, *Movilización femenina en la época del Frente Popular: Feminismo, clases sociales y política en el Movimiento Pro Emancipación de las Mujeres Chilenas, 1935–1950* (Santiago: Sur, CEDEM, 1997).

51. Lisa Baldez, *Why Women Protest: Women's Movements in Chile* (Cambridge: Cambridge University Press, 2001).

52. Alicia Frohmann and Teresa Valdés, *Democracy in the Country and in the Home: The Women's Movement in Chile* (Santiago: FLACSO, 1983); Jadwiga Pieper Mooney, *The Politics of Motherhood: Maternity and Women's Rights in Twentieth-Century Chile* (Pittsburgh: University of Pittsburgh Press, 2009), 134–162; Marcela Ríos Tobar, Lorena Godoy, Elizabeth Guerrero, *¿Un nuevo silencio feminista?: la transformación de un movimiento social en el Chile posdictadura* (Santiago: CEM/Cuarto Propio, 2003).

53. Jadwiga Pieper Mooney, "Feminist Activism and Women's Rights Mobilization in the Chilean *Círculo de Estudios de la Mujer*: Beyond Maternalist Mobilization" (Ann Arbor: Center for the Education of Women [CEW], University of Michigan, March 2009), http://www.cew.umich.edu/PDFs/PieperMooney3-09.pdf.

54. Thelma Gálvez, email message to author, May 23, 2007.

55. ANECAP, Thelma Gálvez and Rosalba Todaro, "Proyecto de asesoría al Sindicato de Trabajadoras de Casa Particular (SINTRACAP) y Asociación Nacional de Empleadas de Casa Particular (ANECAP)," mimeo, November 1981.

56. Thelma Gálvez and Rosalba Todaro, *Trabajadoras de casa particular: Tábita, Clementina, Lidia* (Santiago, CEM, 1984); Rosabla Todaro and Thelma Gálvez, *Trabajo doméstico remunerado: Conceptos, hechos, datos* (Santiago: CEM, 1987); Thelma Gálvez and Rosalba Todaro, *Yo trabajo así, en casa particular* (Santiago: CEM, 1985).

57. ARNAD, Fondo Organizaciones Sociales, Rosalba Todaro, "El trabajo doméstico: tarea de mujeres?" *Boletín No. 7,* Círculo de Estudios de la Mujer (December 1981): 3.

58. ARNAD, Fondo Organizaciones Sociales, "Trabajo doméstico: un encuentro con las trabajadoras" *Boletín No. 7,* Círculo de Estudios de la Mujer (December 1981): 12.

59. Thelma Gálvez, email message to author, May 23, 2007.

60. ARNAD, "Trabajo doméstico," 12.

61. ARNAD, Fondo Organizaciones Sociales, "Los problemas vistos por el gremio," *Boletín No. 7*, Círculo de Estudios de la Mujer (December 1981): 3.

62. ANECAP, Thelma Gálvez and Rosalba Todaro, "Guía para aprender en Grupo. Trabajadoras de Casa Particular. Nuestros Derechos Legales," mimeo, Centro de Estudios de la Mujer, Proyecto Trabajo Doméstico, Santiago, 1985.

63. Political cooperation between empleadas and feminist patronas also facilitated the long research and political cooperation between Aída Moreno and Elsa Chaney, who over the next twenty years coauthored presentations to multiple international audiences of domestic service scholars and activists. Chaney and Castro, *Muchachas No More*.

64. ARNAD, Fondo Organizaciones Sociales, Patricia Crispi, "Auto-pregunta," *Boletín No. 7*, Círculo de Estudios de la Mujer (December 1981): 8–9.

65. Thelma Gálvez, email message to author, May 23, 2007.

66. ARNAD, Fondo Organizaciones Sociales, "Protestamos," *Amistad y Esperanza* 22 (1988): 17.

67. SINTRACAP, "Petitorio de las trabajadoras de casa particular," mimeo, [November 14, 1988].

68. "Legislación más justa piden asesoras del hogar," *Fortín Mapocho*, November 16, 1988; "Asesoras del hogar piden jornada laboral de 8 horas," *La Tercera*, November 16, 1988; "Limpieza en sus derechos," *La Cuarta*, November 16, 1988; "Asesoras quieren jubilar," *El País*, November 16, 1988.

69. SINTRACAP, SINTRACAP to Guillermo Hartur, Minister of Labor and Social Security, March 27, 1989, in Moreno, "Cuadernillo de antecedentes," 32–34.

70. SINTRACAP, "Press release," March 30, 1989, in Moreno, "Cuadernillos de Antecedentes," 29–30.

71. Despite the activists' persistence, at least one news story reporting favorably on their actions also took advantage of puns and colloquial expressions to make light of the workers' political participation and labor demands. "Trabajadoras de casa particular pidieron asear problemillas," *La Cuarta*, April 4, 1989, 9. In *La Epoca*, by contrast, the same press release was treated with solemnity: "Trabajadroas del hogar reclamaron por falta de respuesta de Arthur," *La Epoca*, March 31, 1989.

72. ANECAP, "Circular No. 2," March 22, 1989.

73. SINTRACAP, "Declaración pública," Valparaíso, August 8, 1990; ARNAD, Fondo Organizaciones Sociales, "Proyecto de Ley: Normas legales para la mujer trabajadora de casa particular," August 8, 1990.

74. ANECAP, Fernando Ariztia Ruíz, "Carta pastoral a las Trabajadoras de Casa Particular," [1989].

75. ANECAP, "Jornada de asesores de Anecap, January 19–20, 1990," 7.

76. SINTRACAP, Moreno, "Cuadernillo de antecedentes," 12.

Conclusion

1. Carlos Pérez and Rosario Mendía, "Cuál es el future del trabajo doméstico? El empleo más gopeado por la crisis," *La Tercera,* July 31, 2020. https://www.latercera.com /tendencias/noticia/cual-es-el-futuro-del-trabajo-domestico-el-empleo-mas-golpeado -por-la-crisis/J5XZXWZFBFEDHOV7JLEH6DALL4/.

2. International Labour Organization, "Livelihoods of more than 55 million domestic workers at risk due to COVID-19," June 16, 2020. https://www.ilo.org/global/about -the-ilo/newsroom/news/WCMS_748093/lang—en/index.htm.

3. This has been one effect, for example, of Elizabeth Kuznesof's influential 1989 essay on domestic service in Spanish America, which attributed women's subordination through domestic service to the Spanish colonial state, a situation gradually remedied through liberal state-building and women's emancipation in the modern period: "A History of Domestic Service in Spanish America, 1492–1980," in *Muchachas No More*, ed. Chaney and Castro, 17–36.

4. Scholars who also employ this longer historical view of domestic service include Boris and Fish, "Decent Work for Domestics" in *Towards a Global History*, ed. Hoerder et al.; Shireen Ally, *From Servants to Workers: South African Domestic Workers and the Democratic State* (Ithaca, NY: ILR/Cornell University Press, 2009); Premilla Nadasen, *Household Workers Unite: The Untold Story of African American Women Who Built a Movement* (Boston: Beacon Press, 2016); Nara Milanich, "From Domestic Servant to Working-Class Housewife: Women, Labor, and Family in Chile," E.I.A.L. 16, no. 1 (2005); Ann S. Blum, "Cleaning the Revolutionary Household," *Journal of Women's History* 15, no. 4 (Winter 2004): 67–90; Pérez et al., *Senderos que se bifurcan*; Hoerder et al., eds., *Towards a Global History*; Rebekah Pite, "Entertaining Inequalities: Doña Petrona, Juanita Bordoy, and Domestic Work in Mid-Twentieth-Century Argentina," *Hispanic American Historical Review* 91, no. 1 (2011): 97–128; Cecilia Allemandi, *Sirvientes, Criados y Nodrizas: Una historia del servicio doméstico en la ciudad de Buenos Aires (fines del siglo XIX y principios del XX)* (Buenos Aires: Teseo and Universidad de San Andrés, 2018); Victoria K. Haskins and Claire Lowrie, eds., *Colonization and Domestic Service: Historical and Contemporary Perspectives* (New York: Routledge, 2015); Sara Hidalgo, "The Making of a 'Simple Domestic': Domestic Workers, the Supreme Court, and the Law in Postrevolutionary Mexico," *International Labor and Working-Class History* 94 (Fall 2018): 55–97.

5. Inés Pérez and Santiago Canevaro, "Languages of Affection and Rationality: Household Workers' Strategies before the Tribunal of Domestic Work, Buenos Aires, 1956–2013," *International Labor and Working-Class History* 88 (2015): 130–149; Hidalgo, "The Making of a 'Simple Domestic.'"

6. Jennifer Fish, *Domestic Workers of the World Unite! A Global Movement for Dignity and Human Rights* (New York: New York University Press, 2017).

7. Elizabeth Quay Hutchison, *Labors Appropriate to Their Sex: Gender and the Politics of Labor in Urban Chile, 1900–1930* (Durham, NC: Duke University Press, 2001), chap. 7.

8. Karin Rosemblatt, *Gendered Compromises: Political Cultures and the State in Chile, 1920–1950* (Chapel Hill: University of North Carolina Press, 2000).

9. This so-called "NGOization" of Chile's diverse and powerful women's movements, for example, led to increased conflict over political strategy, issue priorities, and generational feminisms after the transition. Marcela Ríos Tobar, Lorena Godoy, and Elizabeth Guerrero, *¿Un nuevo silencio feminista?: la transformación de un movimiento social en el Chile posdictadura* (Santiago: CEM/Cuarto Propio, 2003). See also Winn, ed., *Victims of the Chilean Miracle*; Lessie Jo Frazier, *Salt in the Sand: Memory, Violence, and the Nation-State in Chile, 1890 to the Present* (Durham, NC: Duke University Press, 2007); Steve J. Stern, *Reckoning with Pinochet: The Memory Question in Democratic Chile, 1989–2006* (Durham, NC: Duke University Press, 2010); Paul Drake and Ivan Jaksic, eds., *El modelo chileno: Democracia y Desarrollo en los noventa* (Santiago: Ediciones LOM, 1999); Thomas Miller Klubock, *La Frontera: Forests and Ecological Conflict in Chile's Frontier Territory* (Durham, NC: Duke University Press, 2014); Florencia E. Mallon, *Courage Tastes of Blood: The Mapuche Community of Nicolás Ailío and the Chilean State, 1906–2001* (Durham, NC: Duke University Press, 2005); Edward Murphy, *For a Proper Home: Housing Rights in the Margins of Urban Chile, 1960–2010* (Pittsburgh: University of Pittsburgh Press, 2015); Brian Loveman and Elizabeth Lira, *Las ardientes cenizas del olvido: Vía chilena de Reconciliación Política 1932–1994* (Santiago: Ediciones LOM, 2000); Patricia Richards, *Race and the Chilean Miracle: Neoliberalism, Democracy, and Indigenous Rights* (Pittsburgh: University of Pittsburgh Press, 2013).

10. https://www.bcn.cl/leychile/navegar?idNorma=1068531. Nicolas Ratto, "Las estrategias sindicales de las trabajadoras de casa particular en Chile en su lucha contra la precariedad (2010–2014)," *Izquierdas* 49 (2020): 1155–1176.

11. Carolina Stefoni and Rosario Fernández, "Mujeres inmigrantes en el trabajo doméstico: Entre el servilismo y los derechos," in *Mujeres inmigrantes en Chile: Mano de obra o trabajadoras con derechos?*, ed. Stefoni (Santiago: Ediciones Universidad Alberto Hurtado, 2011; Soledad Ortega, "In Search of the Chilean Paradise: Peruvians in Chile Forge a Community," *NACLA Report on the Americas* 35, no. 2 (September/October 2001), 18–23.

12. Sandra Leiva, Miguel Ángel Mansilla, and Andrea Comelin, "Condiciones laborales de migrantes bolivianos que realizan trabajo de cuidado en Iquique," in *Si Somos Americanos. Revista de Estudios Fronterizos* 17, no. 2 (2017): 11–37.

13. Silke Staab and Kristen Hill Maher, "The Dual Discourse about Peruvian Domestic Workers in Santiago de Chile: Class, Race, and a Nationalist Project," *Latin American Politics and Society* 48, no. 1 (Spring 2006): 87–116.

14. Karina Elizabeth Vázquez, "Corre Muchacha, Corre: Estructura de clases y trabajo doméstico en La nana (2009), de Sebastián Silva," *Chasqui* 43, no. 2 (November 2014):161–178. 8. http://worldscholar.tu.galegroup.com/tinyurl/4kpca2.

15. Felipe Saleh, "Caso nanas de Chicureo: el escándalo de la semana," *El Mostrador*, January 19, 2012).

16. "Carta a socios desenmascara discriminación a 'nanas' en el Club de Golf Las Brisas de Chicureo," *El Mostrador*, December 23, 2011.

17. Evelyn Matthei, quoted in Saleh, "Caso nanas de Chicureo."

18. These efforts can be traced on the SINTRACAP website at http://sintracapchile .cl/. See also Andrea Del Campo and Soledad Ruiz, "Empoderamiento de Trabajadoras de Casa Particular Sindicalizadas," *PSYKHE* 22, no. 1 (2013): 17–18.

19. ANECAP, SINDUCAP, and SINTRACAP, Petition submitted to the Ministerio de Trabajo y Previsión Social, August 2018. http://sintracapchile.cl/wp-content/uploads/2018/09/Carta-de-SINTRACAP-SINDUCAP-y-ANECAP-para -MINTRAB.pdf.

20. Muriel Solano, "Estudiantes y académicas junto al Archivo Nacional buscan relevar memoria de mujeres trabajadoras del hogar," Universidad de Chile, June 3, 2019. https://www.uchile.cl/noticias/154347/estudiantes-y-academicas-relevan-archivos -de-mujeres-trabajadoras.

Archives

Santiago, Archivo Nacional de la Administración (ARNAD). Fondo Organizaciones Sociales, 1926–1988.

Santiago, Archivo Nacional de la Administración (ARNAD). Fondo Dirección del Trabajo, 1906–1985.

Santiago, Archivo de la Asociación Nacional de Empleadas de Casa Particular (ANECAP), 1968–2003.

Santiago, Archivo del Sindicato de Trabajadoras de Casa Particular (SINTRACAP), 1926–1990.

Santiago, Archivo del Arzobispado de Santiago (AAS), 1939–1965.

Government Documents

República de Chile. Congreso Nacional. Cámara de Diputados y Senadores. *Boletín de Sesiones Ordinarias* and *Extraordinarias*. Santiago: Imprenta Nacional, 1926–1973.

República de Chile. Congreso Nacional. Dirección de Estadística. *Censos de población*, 1907–1992.

República de Chile. Congreso Nacional. Ministerio de Bienestar Social. *Boletín de Médico-Social de la Caja de Seguro Obligatorio*, 1930–1973.

República de Chile. Congreso Nacional. Ministerio de Interior. *Recopilación de Decretos con Fuerza de Ley. Ano 1931. Dictados en virtud de las facultades otorgadas al Ejecutivo por la Ley numero 4945 de 6 de febrero de 1931*. Santiago: Talleres Gráficos "La Nación," 1933.

República de Chile. Congreso Nacional. Oficina del Trabajo. *Boletín de la Oficina del Trabajo*, 1905–1985.

Interviews by Author

Beltrán, Zelma and María Elisa Pacheco. Concepción, September 3, 2004.

Bravo, Elba. Santiago. July 4, 2002; August 27, 2004; September 8, 2004.

Bravo, Sonia. Concepción, September 3, 2004.

Hourton, Mariano. Santiago, June 28, 2005.

Moreno, Aída. Santiago, July 3–4, 2002; August 31, 2004; June 18, 2005.

Prado, Elena (pseud.). Santiago, June 19, 2005.

Piñera, Bernardino. Santiago, July 5, 2002; August 29, 2004; June 20, 2005.

Urzúa, Rudy. Santiago, June 25, 2005.

Journals

Mensaje, 1951–1988

La mujer nueva, 1935–1941

Revista de Trabajo, 1931–1945

Surge, 1959–1962

La Voz, 1953–1959

Published Primary Sources

Aliaga Rojas, Fernando. *Itinerario histórico de los círculos de estudios a las comunidades juveniles de base.* Santiago: Equipo de Servidios de la Juventud, 1977.

Arancibia Muñoz, Jorge. *El contrato de trabajo de los empleados domésticos.* Dirección general de prisiones, Santiago: 1939.

Aróstica Fernández, Pamela. "Sindicato de Empleadas de Casa Particular (1930–1960)." Undergraduate thesis, Universidad de Chile, 1997.

Bravo Navarette, Humberto. "Régimen jurídico Laboral de las Trabajadores de Casa Particular." Law thesis, University of Concepción, 1976.

Concha, Juana. *La Empleada Doméstica y sus problemas.* Social Work thesis, Escuela de Servicio Social "Elvira Matte de Cruchaga," 1940.

Debesa, Fernando. *Mama Rosa.* Santiago: Editorial Universitaria, 1995.

Gálvez, Thelma and Rosalba Todaro. *Trabajadoras de casa particular: Tábita, Clementina, Lidia.* Santiago, CEM, 1984.

Gálvez, Thelma and Rosalba Todaro. *Yo trabajo así, en casa particular.* Santiago: CEM, 1985.

Gentilini, Bernardo. *El libro del doméstico (o empleado) y el del artesano (u obrero).* Santiago: Apostolado de la Prensa, 1935.

Guiraldes C., Cecilia, María del Pilar Ibieta G., and Patricia Dávila L. "La empleada de casa particular: Realidades y perspectivas." Social Work thesis, Catholic University of Chile, 1971.

Libreta recibo de la dueña de casa. Cumplimiento y resguardo con los Empleados domésticos de acuerdo con la ley. Santiago: Talleres Graficos Artuffo, 1941.

Moreno Valenzuela, Aída. *Evidencias de una líder: Memorias de una trabajadora de casa particular.* Santiago: LOM Ediciones, 2012.

Paez Boggioni, Violeta. "Empleada doméstica y maternidad." Social Work thesis, University of Chile, Valparaíso, 1948.

Pérez Monardes, Gladys. "La empleada doméstica de casa particular." Social Work thesis, School of Social Work, University of Chile, 1954.

Verdugo H., Hugo, and Fernando Tapia A. "La empleada de casa particular: realidad y perspectivas." *Mensaje* 175 (December 1968): 636–638.

Vío Valdivieso, Francisco. *Prostitución, empleadas domésticas, constitución de la familia.* Santiago: Impresa Aurora de Chile, 1942.

Vizcarra C., Dr. J. "Servicio Domestico." *Boletín Medico-Social de la Caja de Seguridad Obligatorio* 9, nos. 98–99 (August-September 1942): 446–455.

Secondary Sources

Abrantes, Manuel. "A Matter of Decency? Persistent Tensions in the Regulation of Domestic Service." *Revista de Estudios Sociales* (Colombia) (January-April 2013): 110–122.

Acciari, Louisa. "Paradoxes of Subaltern Politics: Brazilian Domestic Workers' Mobilisations to Become Workers and Decolonise Labor." PhD diss., London School of Economics, 2018.

Acha, Omar. "La organización sindical de las trabajadoras domésticas durante el primer peronismo." *Revista de Estudios Marítimos y Sociales* 5/6 (2012–2013): 27–39.

Allemandi, Cecilia. "El servicio doméstico en el marco de las transformaciones de la ciudad de Buenos Aires, 1869–1914." *Diálogos* 16, no. 2 (2012): 385–415.

Allemandi, Cecilia. *Sirvientes, Criados y Nodrizas: Una historia del servicio doméstico en la ciudad de Buenos Aires (fines del siglo XIX y principios del XX).* Buenos Aires: Teseo and Universidad de San Andrés, 2018.

Ally, Shireen A. *From Servants to Workers: South African Domestic Workers and the Democratic State.* Ithaca, NY: ILR Press/Cornell University Press, 2009.

Antezana-Pernet, Corinne. "Mobilizing Women in the Popular Front Era: Feminism, Class, and Politics in the Movimiento Pro-Emancipación de la Mujer Chilena (MEMCH), 1935–1950." PhD diss., UC Irvine, 1996.

Baldez, Lisa. *Why Women Protest: Women's Movements in Chile.* Cambridge: Cambridge University Press, 2001.

Banerjee, Swapna M. *Women, Men, and Domestics: Articulating Middle-class Identity in Colonial Bengal.* New Delhi: Oxford University Press, 2014.

Bergot, Solène. "caracterización y mapeo del servicio doméstico en Santiago de Chile. Una radiografía en 1895 a través del diario "El Chileno." *Historia* 396:1 (2017): 11–41.

Blofield, Merike. *Care Work and Class: Domestic Workers' Struggle for Equal Rights in Latin America.* University Park: Pennsylvania State University Press, 2012.

Blofield, Merike and Merita Jokela. "Paid domestic work and the struggles of care workers in Latin America." *Current Sociology Monograph* (2018): 1–16.

Blum, Ann. "Cleaning the Revolutionary Household: Domestic Servants and Public Welfare in Mexico City, 1900–1935." *Journal of Women's History* 15, no. 4 (2004): 67–90.

Boris, Eileen, and Jennifer N. Fish, "Decent Work for Domestics: Feminist Organizing, Worker Empowerment, and the ILO." In *Towards a Global History*, edited by Hoerder et al., 530–552.

Boris, Eileen and Jennifer Klein. *Caring for America: Home Health Workers in the Shadow of the Welfare State*. New York, NY: Oxford University Press, 2012.

Bruey, Alison. "Transnational Concepts, Local Contexts: Solidarity at the Grassroots in Pinochet's Chile." In Human Rights and Transnational Solidarity in Cold War Latin America, edited by Jessica Stites-Mor, 120–142. Madison: University of Wisconsin Press, 2013.

Del Campo, Andrea, and Soledad Ruiz. "Empoderamiento de Trabajadoras de Casa Particular Sindicalizadas." *PSYKHE* 22, no. 1 (2013): 15–28.

Canevaro, Santiago. *Como de la familia. Afecto y desigualdad en el trabajo doméstico*. Buenos Aires: Editorial Prometeo, 2020.

De Casanova, Erynn Masi. *Dust and Dignity: Domestic Employment in Contemporary Ecuador*. Ithaca, NY: ILR Press/Cornell University Press, 2019.

Chaney, Elsa, and Mary García Castro, eds. *Muchachas No More: Household Workers in Latin America and the Caribbean*. Philadelphia: Temple University Press, 1988.

Correa Pereira, Verónica. "Más allá de la racionalidad económica: una nueva aproximación para la comprensión de la emigrante latinoamericana que llega a Santiago de Chile." *Revista de Estudios Sociales* 49 (May 2014): 176–189.

Fernández, Rosario. "Mujeres de elite y trabajo doméstico remunerado en Chile: ¿crisis de cuidados o de la familia?" *La manzana de la Discordia* 12, no. 1 (2017): 33–47.

Fish, Jennifer. *Domestic Workers of the World Unite! A Global Movement for Dignity and Human Rights*. New York: New York University Press, 2017.

Frohmann, Alicia, and Teresa Valdés. *Democracy in the Country and in the Home: The Women's Movement in Chile*. Santiago: FLACSO, 1983.

Gálvez, Thelma, and Rosalba Todaro. *Trabajo doméstico remunerado. Conceptos, hechos, datos*. Santiago: CEM, 1987.

Gill, Lesley. *Precarious Dependencies: Gender, Class, and Domestic Service in Bolivia*. New York: Columbia University Press, 1994.

Gutiérrez Rodríguez, Encarnación. Migration, Domestic Work and Affect. New York: Routledge, 2010.

Haskins, Victoria K., and Claire Lowrie, eds. *Colonization and Domestic Service: Historical and Contemporary Perspectives*. New York: Routledge, 2015.

Hidalgo, Sara. "The Making of a 'Simple Domestic': Domestic Workers, the Supreme Court, and the Law in Postrevolutionary Mexico." *International Labor and Working-Class History* 94 (Fall 2018): 55–97.

Hoerder, Dirk, Elise Van Nederveen Meerkerk, and Silke Neunsinger, eds. *Towards a Global History of Domestic Workers and Caregiving Workers*. Leiden: Brill, 2015.

Hutchison, Elizabeth Quay. *Labors Appropriate to Their Sex: Gender, Labor, and Politics in Urban Chile, 1900–1930.* Durham, NC: Duke University Press, 2001.

Hutchison, Elizabeth Quay. "Many *Zitas*: The Young Catholic Worker and Household Workers in Postwar Chile." Special Issue on Workers, the Nation-State, and Beyond: The Newberry Conference, *Labor: Studies in the Working-Class History of the Americas,* 6, no. 4 (Winter 2009): 67–94.

Hutchison, Elizabeth. "Shifting Solidarities: The Politics of Household Workers in Cold War Chile." *Hispanic American Historical Review* 91, no.1 (2011): 129–162.

Jaffe, Tracey. "In the Footsteps of Cristo Obrero: Chile's Young Catholic Workers Movement in the Shantytown, Factory, and Family, 1946–1973." PhD diss., University of Pittsburgh, 2009.

Kuznesof, Elizabeth. "A History of Domestic Service in Spanish America, 1492–1980." In *Muchachas No More*, edited by Chaney and García Castro, 17–36.

Lauderdale Graham, Sandra. *House and Street: The Domestic World of Servants and Masters in Nineteenth-Century Rio de Janeiro.* Cambridge: Cambridge University Press, 1988.

Leiva, Sandra, and César Ross. "Migración circular y trabajo de cuidado: Fragmentación de trayectorias laborales de migrantes bolivianas en Tarapacá." *Psicoperspectivas* 15, no. 3 (2016): 56–66.

Leiva, Sandra, Miguel Ángel Mansilla, and Andrea Comelin. "Condiciones laborales de migrantes bolivianas que realizan trabajo de cuidado en Iquique." *Si Somos Americanos* 17, no. 2 (2017): 11–37.

Macarena Mack, Paulina Matta, and Ximena Valdés. *Los Trabajos de las Mujeres Entre el Campo y la Ciudad, 1920–1982.* Santiago: CEM, 1986.

Maher, Kristen Hill, and Silke Staab. "Nanny Politics. The Dilemmas of Working Women's Empowerment in Santiago, Chile." *International Feminist Journal of Politics* 7, no. 1 (2005): 71–88.

Milanich, Nara. *Children of Fate: Childhood, Class, and the State in Chile, 1850–1830.* Durham, NC: Duke University Press, 2010.

Milanich, Nara. "From Domestic Servant to Working-Class Housewife: Women, Labor, and Family in Chile." *Revista EIAL* 16, no.1 (January-June 2005).

Milanich, Nara, "Women, Children, and the Social Organization of Domestic Labor in Chile," *Hispanic American Historical Review* 91, no. 1 (2011): 29–62.

Nadasen, Premilla. *Household Workers Unite: The Untold Story of African American Women Who Built a Movement.* Boston: Beacon Press, 2015.

Olcott, Jocelyn. "Introduction: Researching and Rethinking the Labors of Love." *Hispanic American Historical Review* 91, no. 1 (2011): 1–27.

Pereyra, Francisca, "El acceso desigual a los derechos laborales en el servicio doméstico argentino: una aproximación desde la óptica de las empleadoras." *Revista de Estudios Sociales* (Colombia) (January-April 2013): 54–66.

Pérez, Inés. Presentación del dossier "Historias del trabajo doméstico (remunerado) en América Latina." *Nuevo Mundo, Mundos Nuevos* (2013): 1–8.

Pérez, Inés, and Santiago Canevaro. "Languages of Affection and Rationality: Household Workers' Strategies before the Tribunal of Domestic Work, Buenos Aires, 1956–2013." *International Labor and Working-Class History* 88 (2015): 130–149.

Pérez, Inés, Romina Cutuli, and Débora Garazi, with Santiago Canevaro. *Senderos que se bifurcan: Servicio Doméstico y derechos laborales en la Argentina del siglo XX.* Mar del Plata, Argentina: EUDEM, 2018.

Pérez, Leda M. "On her shoulders: unpacking domestic work, neo-kinship and social authoritarianism in Peru." *Gender, Place & Culture* 28:1 (2021): 1–21

Pérez Solano, Sergio, and Roicer Flórez Bolívar. "Política y trabajo. Debates sobre las normas jurídicas y las relaciones laborales de servidumbre en el Bolívar Grande (Colombia) en el siglo XIX." *Revista de Estudios Sociales* (Colombia) (January-April 2013): 16–28.

Pieper Mooney, Jadwiga. "Feminist Activism and Women's Rights Mobilization in the Chilean *Círculo de Estudios de la Mujer*: Beyond Maternalist Mobilization." Center for the Education of Women (CEW), University of Michigan, March 2009.

Pieper Mooney, Jadwiga. *The Politics of Motherhood: Maternity and Women's Rights in Twentieth-Century Chile.* Pittsburgh: University of Pittsburgh Press, 2009.

Pite, Rebekah. "Entertaining Inequalities: Doña Petrona, Juanita Bordoy, and Domestic Work in Mid-Twentieth-Century Argentina," *Hispanic American Historical Review* 91, no. 1 (2011): 97–128.

Ratto, Nicolas. "Las estrategias sindicales de las trabajadoras de casa particular en Chile en su lucha contra la precariedad (2010–2014)." *Izquierdas* 49 (2020): 1155–1176.

Remedi, Fernando. "'Esta descompostura general de la servidumbre.' Las trabajadoras del servicio doméstico en la modernización argentina. Córdoba, 1869–1906." *Secuencia* 84 (2012): 41–69.

Rojas Flores, Jorge. *La Dictadura de Ibáñez y los sindicatos (1927–1931).* Santiago: Dirección de Bibliotecas, Archivos y Museos, 1993.

Romero, Mary. *Maid in the U.S.A.* New York: Routledge, 2002.

Rosemblatt, Karin. *Gendered Compromises: Political Cultures and the State in Chile, 1920–1950.* Chapel Hill: University of North Carolina Press, 2000.

Rossi, María Julia, and Lucía Campanella, eds. *Los de abajo: Tres siglos de sirvientes en el arte y la literatura en América Latina.* Rosario, Argentina: UNR Editores, 2019.

Ruiz Vera, María Elisa. *Ana González: Primera Actriz.* Santiago: Edebé, Editorial Don Bosco, 2002.

Salazar Parreñas, Rhacel. *Servants of Globalization: Women, Migration, and Domestic Work.* Stanford CA: Stanford University Press, 2001.

Smith, Brian H. *The Church and Politics in Chile: Challenges to Modern Catholicism.* Princeton, NJ: Princeton University Press, 1982.

Staab, Silke, and Kristen Hill Maher. "The Dual Discourse about Peruvian Domestic Workers in Santiago de Chile: Class, Race, and a Nationalist Project." *Latin American Politics and Society* 48, no. 1 (Spring 2006): 87–116.

Stefoni, Carolina, ed. *Mujeres inmigrantes en Chile ¿Mano de obra o trabajadoras con derechos?* Santiago: Ediciones Universidad Alberto Hurtado, 2011.

Stefoni, Carlina, and Fernanda Stang, "La construcción del campo de estudio de las migraciones en Chile: notas de un ejercicio reflexivo y autocrítico." *Íconos* 58 (2017): 109–129.

Stewart-Gambino, Hannah W. *The Church and Politics in the Chilean Countryside.* Boulder, CO: Westview Press, 1992.

Tinsman, Heidi Elizabeth. "The Indispensable Services of Sisters: Considering Domestic Service in United States and Latin American Studies." *Journal of Women's History* 4, no. 1 (1992): 37–59.

Tizziani, Ania. "El Estatuto del Servicio Doméstico y sus antecedentes: debates en torno a la regulación del trabajo doméstico remunerado en la Argentina." *Nuevo mundo, mundos nuevos* (2013): 1–16.

Todaro, Rosalba, and Thelma Gálvez. *Trabajo doméstico remunerado: Conceptos, hechos, datos.* Santiago: CEM, 1987.

Valenzuela, María Elena, and Claudia Mora, eds. *Mujeres peruanas en Chile. Trabajo doméstico: un largo camino hacia el trabajo decente.* Santiago: OIT, 2009.

Vázquez, Karina Elizabeth. "Corre Muchacha, Corre: Estructura de clases y trabajo doméstico en La nana (2009), de Sebastián Silva." *Chasqui* 43, no. 2 (November 2014):161–178. http://worldscholar.tu.galegroup.com/tinyurl/4kpca2.

Zárate Campos, María Soledad, and Elizabeth Quay Hutchison. "Clases medias en Chile: Estado, género y practicas políticas, 1920–1970." In *Historia Política de Chile 1810–2010*, edited by Iván Jakšić, Juan Luis Ossa, Susana Gazmuri, Francisca Rengifo and Andrés Estefane, 271–300. México: Fondo de Cultura Económica, 2017.

Zurita, Carlos. *Trabajo, servidumbre y situaciones de género. Algunas acotaciones sobre el servicio doméstico en Santiago del Estero, Argentina.* Santiago del Estero: Universidad Nacional de Santiago del Estero, 1997.

INDEX

Abortion, and domestic service, 41, 63
Asociación Nacional de Empleadas de
    Casa Particular (ANECAP), 1, 82–83,
    99, 104–12, 128–30, 132–36, 138–39,
    141–43, 146–48; Cold War expansion
    of, 112–17, 137; pastoral campaigns by,
    109–11. *See also* Hogar de la Empleada
    and Bernardino Piñera

Caja de Seguro Obligatorio (CSO),
    41–43, 53–54. *See also* Social Security
    Law of 1924
Cardijn, Father Joseph, 71, 88
Catholic Action, 71, 99

Employment agencies, 31–32, 50–51

Federación de las Empleadas, 3, 69,
    71–88, 93, 159. *See also* Juventud
    Obrera Católica (JOC)
Feminist movements, 24, 161; and
    domestic service, 143–51

Hogar de la Empleada, 2, 65, 69, 75–79,
    82–83. *See also* Asociación Nacional
    de Empleadas de Casa Particular
    (ANECAP); Federación de las
    Empleadas; Juventud Obrera Católica
    (JOC); Piñera, Bernardino

Housing cooperatives for domestic
    workers, 97–98, 135
Hurtado, Father Alberto, 74

Industrial education, and domestic
    service, 29–31, 85–86, 148–49
International Labour Organization
    (ILO), 7; and Convention 189, 5, 155,
    157; and domestic service, 43

Juventud Obrera Católica (JOC), 68;
    and labor movements, 87–88. *See also*
    Cardijn, Father Joseph; Federación de
    las Empleadas

La Desideria, 36–37, 42, 163. *See also*
    Social Security Law of 1924
Labor movement and domestic workers,
    25–26, 32–35, 48–49, 61–65, 100,
    119, 124–25
Lazo, Carmen, 103–4, 119–24, 126
Liberation theology, 104–12, 122–24, 160

Male domestic workers, 17, 33,
    44, 61–62, 81
Movimiento Pro-Emancipación de la
    Mujer Chilena (MEMCH), 62–63, 159
Migration of domestic workers, 8–11,
    78–80, 162–63
Moreno Valenzuela, Aída, 3–4, 8, 72–73,
    80, 106, 114–15, 117, 119, 124–25, 131–
    32, 135, 139, 154, 156–57

National day of the empleada, 90–92

Patronas, 12–13, 23, 57–58
Piñera, Bernardino, 2–3, 69, 71–75, 93